Researching Global Religious Landscapes

The Study of Religion in a Global Context

Series editors

Satoko Fujiwara
Executive Editor
University of Tokyo

Katja Triplett
Series Editor
Leipzig University

Alexandra Grieser
Managing Editor
Trinity College Dublin

The series, published in collaboration with the International Association for the History of Religions, encourages work that is innovative in the study of religions, whether of an empirical, theoretical or methodological nature. This includes multi- or inter-disciplinary studies involving anthropology, philosophy, psychology, sociology and political studies. Volumes will examine the continuing influence of postcolonial, decolonial and intercultural dynamics, as well as contemporary responses from intersectional studies. They will also address the relevance and application of more recent approaches such as cognitivist, as well as ones concerned with aesthetic culture – art, architecture, media, performance and sound.

Published

Global Phenomenologies of Religion
An Oral History in Interviews
Edited by Satoko Fujiwara, David Thurfjel and Steven Engler

Philosophy and the End of Sacrifice
Disengaging Ritual in Ancient India, Greece and Beyond
Edited by Peter Jackson and Anna-Pya Sjödin

Power and Agency in the Lives of Contemporary Tibetan Nuns
An Intersectional Study
Mitra Härkönen

Religion as Relation
Studying Religion in Context
Edited by Peter Berger, Marjo Buitelaar and Kim Knibbe

The Relational Dynamics of Enchantment and Sacralization
Changing the Terms of the Religion Versus Secularity Debate
Edited by Peik Ingman, Terhi Utriainen, Tuija Hovi and Måns Broo

Translocal Lives and Religion
Connections between Asia and Europe in the Late Modern World
Edited by Philippe Bornet

Forthcoming

Embodied Reception
South Asian Spiritualities in Contemporary Contexts
Edited by Henriette Hanky, Knut. A. Jacobsen and István Keul

Researching Global Religious Landscapes
A Methodology between Universalism and Particularism

Edited by
Peter Nynäs, Ruth Illman, Nurit Novis-Deutsch
and Rafael Fernández Hart

SHEFFIELD UK   BRISTOL CT

Published by Equinox Publishing Ltd.

UK: Office 415, The Workstation, 15 Paternoster Row, Sheffield, South Yorkshire S1 2BX

USA: ISD, 70 Enterprise Drive, Bristol, CT 06010

www.equinoxpub.com

First published 2024

© Peter Nynäs, Ruth Illman, Nurit Novis-Deutsch, Rafael Fernández Hart and contributors 2024

All rights reserved. No part of this publication may be reproduced or transmitted in any form or by any means, electronic or mechanical, including photocopying, recording or any information storage or retrieval system, without prior permission in writing from the publishers.

British Library Cataloguing-in-Publication Data
A catalogue record for this book is available from the British Library.

Library of Congress Cataloging-in-Publication Data
Names: Nynäs, Peter, editor.
Title: Researching global religious landscapes : a methodology between universalism and particularism / edited by Peter Nynäs, Ruth Illman, Nurit Novis-Deutsch, and Rafael Fernández-Hart.
Description: Sheffield, South Yorkshire ; Bristol, CT : Equinox Publishing, Ltd, 2024. | Series: The study of religion in a global context | Includes bibliographical references and index. | Summary: "This volume explores current challenges pertinent to cross-cultural research on religion in today's world. It reflects important aspects of global cultural and religious diversity. All articles stem from the international research project "Young Adults and Religion in a Global Perspective". The project implemented a mixed methods study in twelve different countries across the world"—Provided by publisher.
Identifiers: LCCN 2023042091 (print) | LCCN 2023042092 (ebook) | ISBN 9781800503908 (hardback) | ISBN 9781800503915 (paperback) | ISBN 9781800503922 (epdf)
Subjects: LCSH: Religion and culture. | Religion and sociology.
Classification: LCC BL65.C8 .R468 2024 (print) | LCC BL65.C8 (ebook) | DDC 306.6--dc23/eng/20240125
LC record available at https://lccn.loc.gov/2023042091
LC ebook record available at https://lccn.loc.gov/2023042092

ISBN-13   978 1 80050 390 8   (hardback)
          978 1 80050 391 5   (paperback)
          978 1 80050 392 2   (ePDF)

Typeset by JS Typesetting Ltd, Porthcawl, Mid Glamorgan

To Professor Nils G. Holm
for his contribution to the study of religions
and for the directions for future research that he laid the foundation for

Contents

List of Figures and Tables	ix
List of Online Appendices	xi
Foreword by Alana Vincent	xii
Editorial Preface by Peter Nynäs and Ruth Illman	xvii

1 Contesting the Dichotomy of Universalism and Particularism: A Mixed-Methods Approach to the Study of Religions from a Global Perspective
Peter Nynäs, Ruth Illman and Nurit Novis-Deutsch — 1

2 Translation and Major Categories in the Study of Religions: The Case of "Religion" and "Spirituality" in West Bengal
Måns Broo, Marcus Moberg, Peter Nynäs, Mallarika Sarkar Das and Sohini Ray — 25

3 The Cognitive Study of Religiosity and Contemporary Lived Religion: Complementarity as a Methodological Approach
Sławomir Sztajer, Rafael Fernández Hart, Ben-Willie Kwaku Golo and Sidney Castillo — 55

4 Heteronormative Religion? Attitudes to Abortion and Same-Sex Relationships on a Global Scale
Peter Nynäs, Ariela Keysar, Clara Marlijn Meijer and Sofia Sjö — 79

5 The Multiplicity of Chinese and Indian Religions: A Critical Reappraisal of the Notion of "Eastern Religion"
Måns Broo and Ruby Sain — 113

6 Conceptualisations of the "Sacred Individual": A Comparative Study of Russian and Finnish Young Adults
Polina Vrublevskaya, Marcus Moberg and Karoliina Dahl — 141

7 Secular Identities in Context: Emerging Prototypes among Non-religious Young Adults
Janne Kontala, Ariela Keysar and Sawsan Kheir — 167

8 Multiple Identifications: Growing Diversity and Complexity in Religious and Secular Worldviews
   Ruth Illman, Peter Nynäs and Nurit Novis-Deutsch 197

9 Towards a New Methodological Perspective: Concluding Reflections on Cross-cultural Research in the Study of Religions
   Peter Nynäs, Ruth Illman and Rafael Fernández Hart 225

Index 243

List of Figures and Tables

Figures

1	FQS record sheet and layout	6
2	GDP/per capita and support for abortion and same-sex marriage	89
3	Schwartz 1992 value structure	93
4	CHAID Tree for support for same-sex marriage	98
5	CHAID Tree for support for legal abortion	98
6	Non-religious as share of all YARG students	181
7	Prototype scoring per country	182
8	Religious upbringing and levels of non-religiosity	183
9	Prototype differences for levels of non-religiosity	184
10	Prototype differences for levels of attendance at religious services	185
11	Prototype differences for level of private religious or spiritual practices	185
12	Forms of multiplicity	209

Tables

1	Examples of statements from the Faith Q-set	8
2	Number of prototypes globally and per country	14
3	Measures of religiosity	85
4	Measures of heteronormativity: abortion and marital relationships	86
5	Means and standard deviations on heteronormative values per prototype 1–4	88
6	GDP/capita, support for legal abortion and same-sex marriage and mean values / country	89
7	Mean values for attitudes to same-sex marriage and same-sex adoption for clusters 1–3	91
8	Mean values for attitudes to abortion for clusters 1–3	91
9	FQS statements as sorted in four countries	118

10	Scores for the "sacred individual sub-set" in FQS	150
11	Non-religious prototype summary	179
12	Examples of internal religious multiplicity	210
13	Examples of inter-religious multiplicity	211
14	Examples of religio-secular multiplicity	211
15	Examples of selective multiplicity	212
16	Examples of common humanity	213

List of Online Appendices

The following appendices are freely available at https://www.equinoxpub.com/home/interdisciplinary-studies-sensitizing/

Appendix 1 The YARG Faith Q-set (Version b)
Peter Nynäs, David Wulff, Mika T. Lassander, Ruth Illman, Rafael Fernández Hart, Ariela Keysar, Maria Klingenberg, Ben-Willie Kwaku Golo, Nurit Novis-Deutsch, Ruby Sain, Marat Shterin and Sławomir Sztajer

Appendix 2 The YARG Prototypes: Results from a Cross-Cultural Q-Methodological Study of Religiosity – Short National Descriptions of Faith Q-set Prototypes
Peter Nynäs, Janne Kontala, Mika T. Lassander and Sofia Sjö

Appendix 3 The YARG Survey
Peter Nynäs, Mika T. Lassander and Marcus Moberg

Appendix 4 The YARG Interview Model
Peter Nynäs, Ruth Illman, Marcus Moberg and Sofia Sjö

Foreword

ALANA VINCENT

On the whole, as Werner Cohn wrote in 1962, "[t]he role of religion in society seems to have been rather consistently over or underestimated". Cohn was writing at the vanguard of a trend that has become nearly ubiquitous in Anglo-American scholarship on religion: a deep scepticism concerning whether or not the object of such scholarship actually exists, articulated most concisely in J. Z. Smith's claim that "There is no data for religion" (Smith 1982). This scepticism has been aired at length in debates over the definition of religion (Schilbrack 2022; Smith 2019; Woodhead 2011; Smith 1998; Saler 1987; Southwold 1978; Ferré 1970; Horton 1960), as well as, more recently, a body of scholarship which attempts to trace the history of such definitions (Nongbri 2013; Lincoln 2010; Masuzawa 2005).

The root of the fixation on the coherence of religion as a category of analysis is precisely the tension between the universal and particular which this volume aims to address, moving beyond the primarily Anglo-centric theoretical debate, instead producing a truly global set of data which can underpin a long-overdue attempt to re-theorise the subject. What previous studies have failed to generate is an adequate framework for describing religion as an element within the complex constellations of cultural influence which shape worldviews, values and behaviour. Such a description is essential to studies across a range of disciplines, in which religion is likely to be a key variable, but for which one-dimensional descriptors of group membership, or even two-dimensional descriptors of behaviours which are assumed to map, somehow, to belief – such as the classic Allport–Ross Religious Orientation Scale – are inadequate (Allport and Ross 1967).

This disconnect between theoretical descriptions of what religion is and methodological accounts of how to study it presents a serious limitation for projects which wish to use religion as a variable. I have lost track of the number of times I have sat down with colleagues from other disciplines and attempted to explain the limitations of the ROS and similar scales. On one memorable occasion, I was obliged to point out to a group of colleagues in a lab-science-based discipline that low numbers of people reporting regular attendance at Bible study probably does not actually suggest that Indonesia, with its majority Muslim population, is among the most secularised nations in the world. This turned into a lengthy disciplinary standoff between the scientists, who insisted that the result obtained by the proper use of a standard instrument of measurement must be correct, no matter how absurd, and the scholars of religion, who insisted that a result so absurd on the face of it must be an indication that the instrument itself is wrong.

For the entirety of my academic career, the prevailing assumption about religion and young people has been that no natural link exists between the two. Within religious communities, young people are a problem to be solved – youth recruitment is the much-touted One Simple Trick to solve the problem of declining membership, and young people themselves are often held responsible for such declines when efforts to engage them fail. This framing is the practical outworking of the so-called "secularisation thesis" which dominated sociology of religion from the mid-twentieth century onwards (Bruce 2002; Wilson 1982; Weber 1976; Martin 1969). The secularisation thesis holds that declining religiosity is a hallmark of modernity, and post-war liberal optimism tied the progress of generations together with the progress of society in a manner which made data on the rise in religious non-adherence, particularly in Western Europe, the USA, Canada and Australia, appear inevitable. Taken together with a progressive view of history, a belief in the secularisation thesis gives rise to the commonplace assumption that younger people are naturally inclined to be less religious.

The secularisation thesis did not, however, hold up well to an examination of the actual facts on the ground anywhere outside the societies which gave rise to it. While scholars have attempted to account for its failure with the narrative of "resacralisation" (Berger 1999; Kavolis 1988; Saran 1979; Greeley 1970), the reality is that the theory was constructed with reference to far too limited a pool of data to begin with. Indeed, in a 2010 article, Grace Davie begins by reframing the discourse of resacralisation as the problem of Western scholars (particularly sociologists) "coming to terms with the continuing significance of religion".

What the present volume *Researching Global Religious Landscapes* offers is not so much a coming-to-terms, but a course correction. By neither assuming religion's decline nor young people's instrumental role in it, this study has produced a wealth of data on how religious forms persist, shaping and being shaped by the evolving cultural *milieux* in which they are situated. And by utilising a data-gathering method which prioritises participants' own accounts of their activities as religious or not, it has avoided producing data that have been predetermined by their theoretical framework. This has led to some very useful innovations, such as the introduction of the idea of believers who do not view themselves as religious (FQS28), bringing some much-needed nuance to basic categories currently in use, such as "religious", "secular" and "spiritual", while otherwise affirming the utility of these categories.

This volume will offer to readers interested in empirical approaches to the study of religion a valuable primer on method, which I hope will open up new avenues of research – not the least of which is a better method for accounting for religion as a variable in inter-disciplinary studies. But I urge the reader not to neglect or overlook the importance of its theoretical intervention: a culturally responsive model of religion which is built on the self-perceptions and lived experiences of the people the model describes, rather than one that is imposed on them from the outside.

Dr Alana Vincent is Associate Professor of Religious Studies at Umeå University. She holds a doctoral degree from the Centre for Literature, Theology and the Arts at the University of Glasgow (2010), and has previously been appointed as the Barbro Osher Research Fellow in Memory of Krister Stendahl at the Swedish Theological Institute, Jerusalem, and Professor of Jewish Philosophy, Religion and Imagination at the University of Chester. She works primarily on questions of religious change and interactions across both interreligious and religious-secular boundaries, using arts, literature, and popular culture case studies to develop models these interactions under the conditions of religious pluralism prompted by global modernity. Her most recent research has been tracking religious change in response to COVID-19 restrictions in Europe; she has been the co-investigator on the project British Ritual Innovation Under Covid-19 (UK Arts & Humanities Research Council, 2020-2021) and on Religious Communities in the Virtual Age (Collaboration of Humanities and Social Sciences in Europe, 2022-2024). More information, including recent publications, can be found at www.umu.se/en/staff/alana-vincent.

References

Allport, Gordon W., and J. Michael Ross. 1967. "Personal Religious Orientation and Prejudice". *Journal of Personality and Social Psychology* 5: 432–43.

Berger, Peter. 1999. "The Desecularization of the World: A Global Overview". In *The Desecularization of the World: Resurgent Religion and World Politics*, ed. Peter Berger, 1–18. Grand Rapids, MI: William B. Eerdmans Publishing Co.

Bruce, Steve. 2002. *God is Dead: Secularization in the West*. Oxford: Blackwell.

Cohn, Werner. 1962. "Is Religion Universal? Problems of Definition". *Journal for the Scientific Study of Religion* 2(1): 25–35.

Davie, Grace. 2010. "Resacralization". In *The New Blackwell Companion to the Sociology of Religion*, ed. Bryan S. Turner, 160–77. Malden, MA: Wiley Blackwell.

Ferré, Frederick. 1970. "The Definition of Religion". *Journal of the American Academy of Religion* 38(1): 3–16.

Greeley, Andrew M. 1970. "Superstition, Ecstasy and Tribal Consciousness". *Social Research* 37(2): 203–11.

Horton, Robin. 1960. "A Definition of Religion, and its Uses". *The Journal of the Royal Anthropological Institute of Great Britain and Ireland* 90(2): 201–26.

Kavolis, Vytautas. 1998. "Contemporary Moral Cultures and 'The Return of the Sacred'". *Sociology of Religion* 49(3): 203–16.

Lincoln, Bruce. 2010. *Holy Terrors: Thinking about Religion after September 11*. 2nd edn. Chicago: University of Chicago Press.

Martin, David. 1969. *The Religious and the Secular*. London: Routledge.

Masuzawa, Tomoko. 2005. *The Invention of World Religions: Or how European universalism was preserved in the language of pluralism*. Chicago: University of Chicago Press.

Nongbri, Brent. 2013. *Before Religion: A History of a Modern Concept*. New Haven: Yale University Press.

Saler, Benson. 1987. "*Religio* and the Definition of Religion". *Cultural Anthropology* 2(3): 395–9.

Saran, A. K. 1979. "The Meaning and Forms of Secularism: A Note". *Religious Traditions: A New Journal in the Study of Religion* 2(1): 38–51.

Schilbrack, Kevin. 2022. "The Concept of Religion". In *The Stanford Encyclopedia of Philosophy*, ed. Edward N. Zalta. https://plato.stanford.edu/archives/sum2022/entries/concept-religion/

Smith, Jonathan Z. 1982. *Imagining Religion: From Babylon to Jonestown*. Chicago: University of Chicago Press.

Smith, Jonathan. Z. 1998. "Religion, Religions, Religious". In *Critical Terms for Religious Studies*, ed. Mark C. Taylor, 269–84. Chicago: University of Chicago Press.

Smith, Leslie D. ed. 2019. *Constructing "Data" in Religious Studies: Examining the Architecture of the Academy*. London: Equinox.

Southwold, Martin. 1978. "Buddhism and the Definition of Religion". *Man* 13(3): 362–79.

Weber, Max. 1976. *The Protestant Ethic and the Spirit of Capitalism*. London: George Allen & Unwin

Wilson, Bryan. 1982. *Religion in Sociological Perspective*. Oxford: Oxford University Press.

Woodhead, Linda. 2011. "Five Concepts of Religion". *International Review of Sociology* 21(1): 121–43.

Editorial Preface

PETER NYNÄS AND RUTH ILLMAN

As director and vice-director of the research project "Young Adults and Religion in a Global Perspective: A Cross-cultural, Comparative and Mixed-methods Study of Religious Subjectivities and Values in their Context" (YARG) we want to say a few words about the background of this volume entitled *Researching Global Religious Landscapes: A Methodology between Universalism and Particularism* and make some acknowledgements. This volume is one of several publications that stem from YARG, and it is therefore a result of a learning process in which many individuals and organisations have shared and invested time, resources and competence.

YARG was selected as a Centre of Excellence in Research Project 2015–19 by Åbo Akademi University, a form of research funding financed by the Åbo Akademi University Foundation. In addition, we were granted funding by the Academy of Finland 2015–19 (no. 288730). The extensive international scale of the project was rendered possible only through the combination of funding from these two sources, and we are deeply thankful for this. Together, Åbo Akademi University, Åbo Akademi University Foundation and the Academy of Finland made it possible to accomplish what in our eyes is a unique project. We gathered data from thirteen countries – Canada, China, Finland, Ghana, India, Israel, Japan, Sweden, Peru, Poland, Russia, Turkey, and the USA. Japan, however, participated only in one part of our study, namely the survey.

We were very fortunate that internationally renowned researchers accepted our invitation to be part of our scientific committee. Abby Day, Michele Dillon, Shalom Schwartz, Paul Stenner, Linda Woodhead, David Wulff and Fenggang Yang provided invaluable support right from the planning stage and throughout the different stages; they have contributed decisively with their expertise. In particular, we want to mention the contribution of Prof. David Wulff. All this started with his innovative research and design of the Faith Q-sort (FQS). His dedication to research and his willingness to assist us in so many ways with implementing and developing the FQS has been of fundamental importance to the project and the original incentive for YARG. We therefore dedicated our other main volume to him: *The Diversity of Worldviews among Young Adults: Contemporary (Non)Religiosity and Spirituality through the Lens of an International Mixed Method Study*. This was edited by Peter Nynäs, Ariela Keysar, Janne Kontala, Ben-Willie Kwaku Golo, Mika T. Lassander, Marat Shterin, Sofia Sjö and Paul Stenner, and published by Springer (2022).

Additionally, our co-investigators across the world have been vital to the project. They facilitated the collection of data in thirteen different countries, and their expertise in local cultures and religions was critical to the cross-cultural realisation of the project. Several of them are co-authors or editors of this volume or of other publications that stem from the YARG project. Our warmest words of thanks go to:

Dr Benjamin Beit-Hallahmi	Dr Mia Lövheim
Dr Satoko Fujiwara	Dr Nurit Novis-Deutsch
Dr Rafael Fernández Hart	Dr Ruby Sain
Dr Sivane Hirsch	Dr Marat Shterin
Dr Ariela Keysar	Dr Slawomir Sztajer
Dr Ben-Willie Kwaku Golo	Dr Zhejun Yu

Thousands of anonymous young adults have given their time and provided input for the project. Their views were collected by the research assistants in their respective countries. The assistants had a challenging task in following our strict instructions and deadlines, but they performed far beyond our expectations. Thanks to you, we were able to gather all data according to plan in all countries:

Seta Astourian	Sawsan Kheir
Francis Benyah	Avivit Mussel
Sidney Castillo	Thea Piltzecker
Juan Chao	Sohini Ray
Karoliina Dahl	Mallarika Sarkar
Habibe Erdiş Gökce	Mauricio Villacrez
Tang Junchao	Polina Vrublevskaya

Dr Kimmo Ketola and Prof. Mia Lövheim formed, together with us, the steering group of the project and contributed to keeping YARG on the right track.

YARG has meant a lot also to the core research team at Åbo Akademi University: Måns Broo, Karoliina Dahl, Maria Klingenberg, Janne Kontala, Martin Lagerström, Mika Lassander, Marlijn Meijer, Marcus Moberg and Sofia Sjö. They have had to stretch beyond regular working hours and needed to step outside their comfort zones. We are grateful for their commitment.

We also extend our thanks to the artist Mirjam Lillhannus, a young adult herself, who has created the cover image for this volume. The play between the background and the foreground, the grey, bare brick wall, and beautiful panels in a multitude of colours and textures, can be seen as an allusion to the complexity of identities as described in the volume: some aspects come to the fore and seem attractive to others while others may be unknown, even to ourselves, and pushed to the back. Some aspects seem robust and "given" by tradition, upbringing, society, like a brick wall that is hard to move and for others to "unsee". Other aspects are dynamic, like movable frames that we arrange in different ways, add and remove, bringing out different patterns and reflections depending on how we combine them, what light we see them in and so on. For us, this reflects the multiple identifications and the balancing between universal and particular aspects of values, identifications and worldviews described in the book. We also thank Islam Abdalaziz for his meticulous and dedicated work with compiling the index of this book.

Finally, YARG has been dependent on the continued collaboration of close to fifty researchers form many countries. Now, when we look back, we are struck by our experience of this. Generosity in sharing knowledge, experience and support has been characteristic of YARG, and we have learnt that this is a building block in research. For our part, as director and co-director, we also trace this attitude to research back to our professor, supervisor and mentor, Nils G. Holm from Åbo Akademi University. Already at an early stage of our studies and research Prof. Holm directed our attention to the importance of continuously extending our horizon both culturally and methodologically and to the importance of avoiding reductionism. This is all well reflected in the current volume and we therefore dedicate it to him.

Turku, 6 February 2023

Peter Nynäs Dr Theol. is Professor of the Study of Religions at Åbo Akademi University (ÅAU), Finland and Dean of the Faculty of Arts, Psychology and Theology. He is the director and PI of the Åbo Akademi University Centre of Excellence in Research Young Adults and Religion in a Global Perspective Project (2015–19) and earlier the Centre of Excellence in Research Post-secular Culture and a Changing Religious Landscape in Finland Project (2010–14). Among the books he has edited are *On the Outskirts of "the Church": Diversities, Fluidities, and New Spaces of Religion in Finland* (with R. Illman and T. Martikainen, LIT-Verlag, 2015), *Religion, Gender, and Sexuality in Everyday Life* (with A. Yip, Ashgate, 2012), and *The Diversity of Worldviews among Young Adults: Contemporary (Non)Religiosity and Spirituality through the Lens of an International Mixed Method Study* (with A. Keysar, J. Kontala, B.-W. Kwaku Golo, M. Lassander, M. Shterin, S. Sjö and P. Stenner; Springer, 2021). See https://research.abo.fi/en/persons/peter-nynäs.

Dr Ruth Illman is the director of the Donner Institute for Research in Religion and Culture in Turku, Finland. She holds the title of docent in the study or religions at Åbo Akademi University (ÅAU) and in the history of religions at Uppsala University, as well as doctoral degrees in the study of religions (2004) and Jewish studies (2018). Her main research interests include cultural encounters and diversity, contemporary Judaism, religion and the arts (especially music) and ethnographic research, primarily by developing the analytical approach of vernacular religion. Illman acted as Co-PI for the Centre of Excellence Young Adults and Religion in a Global Perspective at ÅAU (2015–19). Currently, she leads the research project Boundaries of Jewish Identities in Contemporary Finland and acts as editor-in-chief of the open-access peer-review journal *Nordisk judaistik / Scandinavian Jewish Studies* with Svante Lundgren. Recent publications are found at https://research.abo.fi/en/persons/ruth-illman

Contesting the Dichotomy of Universalism and Particularism

A Mixed-Methods Approach to the Study of Religions from a Global Perspective

PETER NYNÄS, RUTH ILLMAN AND
NURIT NOVIS-DEUTSCH

In this chapter we will introduce and discuss the research project behind this volume, namely the Centre of Excellence in Research project "Young Adults and Religion in a Global Perspective" (YARG). This project implemented a cross-cultural, comparative and mixed-methods study of religious subjectivities and values in their context. In addition to providing a background to the volume, it is essential to the volume as a whole to describe the conceptual and methodological underpinnings of YARG, including the mixed methods, the research process and the data we have collected. In addition to clarifying the epistemological claims of the research project, we also bring up some elementary observations stemming from the Faith Q-study in the project and provide a framework for understanding the separate chapters.

Introduction

In a fast-changing and increasingly interconnected world, changes and transformations in the field of religion need to be studied and approached in close connection with currently ongoing general global processes of social and cultural change. This volume seeks to contribute one complementary perspective to the study of contemporary religion in a cross-cultural or global perspective. We believe that the debate on universalism versus particularism is of direct relevance for the growing interest in religion from a global perspective. Such discussions can simply not be put aside, but as scholars of religion, we need to reflect seriously on the implications of this dichotomy, both for the current study of religions in general and for our own research endeavours in particular.

Jakob de Roover claims that "the contemporary study of religion has a unique opportunity to settle the debate on the cultural universality of religion" (de Roover 2014, 7). What does this mean? In this study, we have taken this to signify the need to explore a third option beyond the dichotomous academic positions on universality vs. particularism. Hence, we argue, we need to be cautious with regard to essentialist, limited, generic understandings of religion which are based on theistic, doctrinal, institutionally based faith (Beckford 2003; Day 2010, 2011). Many of the perspectives in the study of religions (including questions, concepts, assumptions and empirical data) are limited in terms of the tension between universalistic and particularistic claims. Within the research field, religion has often been perceived one-sidedly as a trans-historical essence, while religion as a concept has often in practice been provincial (e.g. Asad 1993, 2003; Chakrabarty 2000; Masuzawa 2005; Balagangadhara 2005; Winzeler 2008). Despite a growing awareness of these problems, scholars often presuppose a conceptual correspondence between religions across time and local contexts that may be illusory. For example, as Balagangadhara (2014) states concerning the application of "Western" understandings of religion on the study of religion in India, scholars tend to assume "that religion is a cultural universal and that the difference between Indian and western culture (among other things) lies in the difference between their 'religions'". In short, we delve into and explore a set of questions relating to this. To what extent can, and should, we rely on universal categories in the study of religions, or do we need to accept a radical notion of cultural differences and particularism in our research? Are there epistemological options beyond the dominant dichotomy between universal and particular? Can the study of religions widen its perspective in light of the growing relevance of diversity, including ranges of secular positions?

In this volume, we argue that a critical view of universality is needed in order to address the problem of cross-cultural incommensurability, albeit acknowledging that such an approach simultaneously implicitly risks becoming the victim of an opposite methodological and conceptual trap, which is equally problematic and challenging. The assumption of the *totally* different Western culture in relation to a *totally* different Asian or African culture easily becomes dependent on the process of essentialising cultural differences and historicities. In order to form an alternative to a universal paradigm, the radical nature of difference and the fundamentally other character of different cultures is often underscored, and by doing so an explicit or implicit idea of cultural or other boundaries is promoted (cf. Illman and Nynäs 2017). In this volume, we look for signs that help us contest such infusion of categorical cultural and religious boundaries. We strive to strike a balance between the equally problematic extremes of the debate, offering novel methodological strategies for addressing global religion from a nuanced, in-depth perspective. We strive to find a dialogical and dialectical perspective between diverging academic positions; a pragmatic way that, following Lambek (2014), could be described as upholding a "moving balance between distinct epistemological positions". This explains the choice of title for the volume: *Researching Global Religious Landscapes: A Methodology between Universalism and Particularism*.

In other publications originating from the same project, we have dealt with additional themes related to the overall rationale of YARG, especially in the volume *The Diversity of Worldviews among Young Adults: Contemporary (Non)Religiosity and Spirituality through the Lens of an International Mixed Method Study* (Nynäs et al 2022), which summarises the main findings of the entire project. A special issue on religion and socialisation was published by the journal *Religion* (Klingenberg and Sjö 2019) and a volume on religion and media, *Digital Media, Young Adults and Religion: An International Perspective* (Moberg and Sjö, 2020), by Routledge. In addition, a chapter on the new method we have developed in the project (Nynäs *et al.* 2021) has been published in the book *Assessing Spirituality in a Diverse World* (Paloutzian *et al.* 2021). In light of these publications, the current volume focuses on exploring a specific theme prevalent in the large body of data generated by the research project through a selection of studies pertaining particularly to issues around universalism and particularism. A summary of the chapters and their relation to the overall theme are presented at the end of the chapter. In the concluding chapter, we pull the threads together and present conclusions.

A Global Study with a Mixed-Methods Approach

The YARG project was defined by a general interest in exploring the characteristics of the religious subjectivities and values among young adults globally, investigating how these are shaped by institutional, social, cultural and other related influences. Furthermore, the project sought to examine what methodological and theoretical implications for how contemporary religion is conceived would follow from the observations and findings established by the project. In order to be able to meet these aims, a mixed-methods approach was developed, combining both quantitative and qualitative research instruments in the form of both a survey and interviews. Of specific relevance was the implementation and development of a third method, namely the Faith Q-sort (FQS), originally introduced by David Wulff (2019).

We gathered data from thirteen countries – Canada, China, Finland, Ghana, India, Israel, Japan, Sweden, Peru, Poland, Russia, Turkey and USA. In Japan, however, we only implemented one part of our study, namely the survey. On the one hand, the "global" research horizon of YARG is broad and complex: it includes many culturally, linguistically, politically and historically different contexts that in themselves would require more thorough research efforts than the YARG study was aiming to encompass. On the other hand, we can also critically ask if our multi-national or cross-cultural approach is comprehensive enough with only twelve countries (thirteen when including Japan). In some respects, YARG has much too limited a focus to fully justify the ambitious questions posed above. This relates to many different aspects, ranging from the cross-cultural design of the project and issues relating to sampling, to representativeness, to potential ways of analysing the data and to the dissemination of results. Nevertheless, the connotations of terms such as international, multi-national, cross-cultural and global need to be critically reflected upon in light of the ambition in this volume to sensitise the idea of cultural difference in the study of religions.

The survey used in the YARG project was extensive. It included six item blocks assessing the participants' current life situation, social life, sources for news and information, views and convictions, well-being and happiness, as well as personal details (Appendix 3). It also included the Portrait Value Questionnaire (PVQ) (Schwartz 1992, 2012; Schwartz *et al.* 2012). The survey provided essential demographic data but also provided data for independent analyses, for example on religiosity from a multi-dimensional perspective and various correlations and quantitative patterns across items. Schwartz's PVQ on values has also been an important independent inclusion. From the perspective of sociology (e.g. Inglehart and Welzel 2005; Maio 2017), one can assume that individuals' values are not necessarily influenced by their (religious) worldviews as much as, for example, by the socio-economic context they grow up in (see also Lassander 2014). Maybe religious institutional affiliation does not translate into particular value profiles? Maybe basic values play a more autonomous role in defining and directing how we self-identify today? These are relevant questions in light of the growing number of non-religious people worldwide, many of whom still maintain complex and meaningful relationships to customs, traditions and institutions originating in religious contexts.

Our ambition to investigate current religiosities without imposing pre-defined criteria of religious, spiritual and secular were met by the FQS. Wulff (2019) designed the FQS in order to overcome some of the shortcomings of earlier approaches to surveys on religiosity and simultaneously to find a nuanced and less biased way to assess religious subjectivities. The principles and method of a FQS study are described below in detail. Here we can mention that it is based on participants sorting a set of cards pertaining to being religious, spiritual and secular. On this basis we can analyse both individual sorts and patterns extracted from how smaller groups sort the statements. The FQS sorting takes place face to face, with the researcher giving the respondents the opportunity to ask questions and comment on the statements and explain why they had ranked certain statements as they did. The FQS develops into an open and semi-structured interview situation where the respondents are encouraged during the interviews to share personal stories, to express their own thoughts freely and, using their own words, to explain the life-views and priorities they had previously expressed through the FQS-sort. For our purposes and a wider comparability across all interviews, each interview followed a structure that was organised around three main themes of interest:

1. The interviewees' experience of the FQS and thoughts around it, as well as her/his own personal engagement with religion/spirituality or similar positions of a secular character.
2. The interviewees' personal history, self-understanding and current life situation.
3. The interviewees' thoughts about the broader social and cultural contexts and communities that they are embedded and involved in.

The mixed-methods approach has in general meant a fixed sequential multi-phase design, where different parts have equal status (Leech and Onwuegbuzie 2009). The approach was clearly defined in the YARG project from the start, but this fixed frame has also allowed for emerging and dynamic elements and designs when it comes to single studies and analyses. As a whole, the YARG study has enabled a variety of research strands, i.e. the basic chain of research from posing a question and choosing data to analysing and interpreting these (see Teddlie and Tashakkori 2009).

Q-methodology and the Faith Q-sort

Q-methodology is rather unknown and usually not discussed in volumes on methodology, with some exceptions (e.g. Newman and Ramlo 2010; Tashakkori and Teddlie 1998). It has been used in a variety of fields, ranging from studies of political opinions and market research to studies of educational settings and personality psychology, including studies that assess worldviews (Block 1978, 2008; Brown 1980; Gabor, 2013; Watts and Stenner 2012; van Exel and de Graaf 2005; McKeown and Thomas 2013; Nilsson 2013). Q-methodology was developed in the 1930s by William Stephenson (1993/1994) for assessing subjective viewpoints on a specific topic. Although McKeown (2001) developed a Q-set for Christian orthodoxy, Q-methodology is relatively new in the study of religions and FQS is currently the only tool for assessment of religiosity based on Q-methodology. The FQS was developed to meet the challenge of how to assess individual religiosity and spirituality, and by using Q-methodology, Wulff (2019) designed an instrument that differs substantially from most other instruments in the field, such as the well-known Allport–Ross Religious Orientation Scale, ROS (Allport 1950; Allport and Ross 1967).

In a study with Q-methodology, respondents rank-order a number of statements in relation to each other (see Figure 1). This allows for

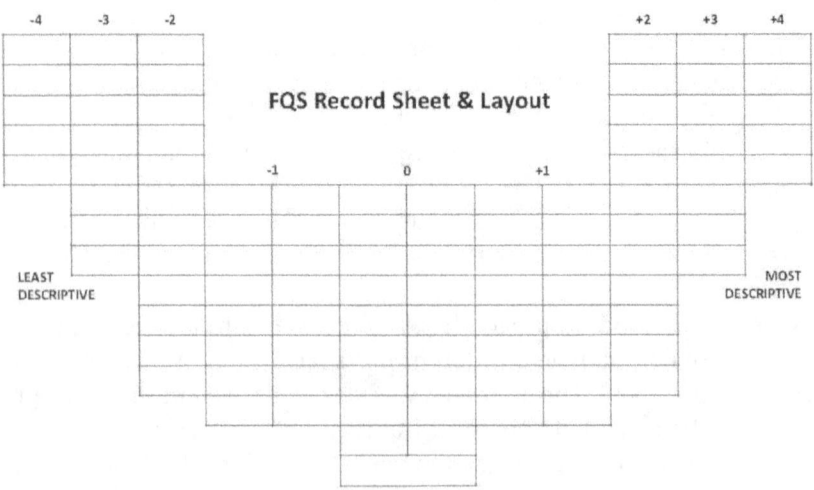

Figure 1. FQS record sheet and layout. The 101 statements of FQS-set are printed on cards and the respondent ranks these statements by placing them in different categories on a layout. The placement should reflect the extent to which the respondent identifies with a certain statement in comparison with other statements in the Q-set of FQS.

individual expression of nuances and complexity, and consequently for a variety of expected and unexpected configurations to emerge. A Q-set needs, therefore, to be broad enough to reflect potential subjectivities and variations. Interviews, observations and popular and academic literature on the topic in question are important sources for generating a specific Q-set, i.e. all sources that reflect relevant discourses (van Exel and de Graaf 2005). There is not, of course, an endless option of significant positions that individuals take in relation to a certain subject, and the assumption behind Q-methodology is that only a limited number of distinct viewpoints exist on any topic (Brown 1980).

FQS is ideally suited to cross-cultural research. The rich item pool and flexibility of FQS promotes methodological attentiveness to the many different ways of living, experiencing and expressing religiosity. Wulff (2019) compiled 101 statements that reflect major religious traditions, including observations from the study of religions and its subfields. He developed his version in a North American context, but it was successfully used also in studies with both religious and non-religious groups (Terho 2013; Pennanen 2013; Lassander and Nynäs 2016; Kontala 2016). For our project, we conducted a thorough evaluation of this version. Teams of scholars from all involved countries proposed revisions of current statements and suggested new ones with regard to the religious and spiritual views and practices in their contexts, also pointing out statements that they found to be problematic for some reason. This evaluation provided us with a significant input for a revision of the FQS during an international seminar with a team of co-investigators from all countries involved in the project. Throughout this process, we strove to be attentive to more local forms of religiosity, non-religiosity and secular positions.

As a result of our revision process, we introduced, for instance, a new statement: "Believes in some way, but does not view him- or herself as religious" (FQS28). This refers to a form of simultaneity and has been identified as central to Scandinavian religiosities (see af Burén 2015; Kalsky and van der Braak 2017). Moreover, this statement proved to be significant to many respondents across the countries involved in the project, and came to contribute to defining religious subjectivities in, for instance, China. Another example of a new statement reflects to what extent "His or her sexuality is strongly guided by a religious or spiritual outlook" (FQS59), tapping into how many issues about morality are topical and form religiosities. The statement "Values his or her own purity and strives to safeguard it" (FQS48) also resonated well with many respondents beyond its contextual background, and came to contribute to forming our results. This exemplifies the importance of stretching beyond

Table 1. Examples of statements from the Faith Q-set.

No.	Statement
12.	Participates in religious activities chiefly on special occasions.
16.	Being religious or spiritual is central to whom he or she is.
29.	Is inclined to embrace elements from various religious and spiritual traditions.
46.	Feels that one should remain loyal to the religion of one's nation.
70.	Rejects religious ideas that conflict with scientific and rational principles.
86.	Is committed to following a spiritual path that is in harmony with the environment.

our own predefined categories in the study of religions. Our revision process resulted in a new version: the FQS-b (Appendix 1). Nonetheless, the ambition to produce an FQS version that has multi-cultural validity requires modesty. To achieve true multi-cultural validity might involve item-by-item international, multi-lingual and cross-cultural validation of all individual items (Wolf *et al.* 2019). Is this at all possible across twelve to thirteen localities simultaneously?

As a research instrument, the FQS constitutes a qualitative procedure that involves and is assisted by quantitative analyses. This makes it an inherently mixed-methods tool (Newman and Ramlo 2010). As we noted earlier, the individual sorts from a FQS study can be used to explore views of single individuals, but it is more common to analyse how individuals jointly form patterns. We call these configurations prototypes, and they represent significant shared patterns that have been extracted through an analysis of correlations among Q-sorts, which are then factor-analysed. In the YARG study, we have used the PQMethod based on the Principal Component Analysis for the statistical part. PQMethod is a widely used software program maintained by Schmolck (2017) and is available online. We also used the online software Ken-Q Analysis (Banasick 2019), which builds on PQMethod.

The definition of prototypes is based on the analysis of factor data. The outcome of the statistical analysis includes tables that describe factors with, for instance, factor scores, item factor scores and distinguishing statements for each of the factors (prototypes). This presents in detail how factors are distinguished by particular characteristics. Based on this, the researcher has to determine both which items *define* a particular prototype, and which items *distinguish* one prototype from the other. To put it simply, behind every prototype we find individual respondents that more or less resemble the general description of a specific prototype is. Sometimes a prototype is constituted by a very small number of participants, but it remains relevant because it is distinct compared to other prototypes and represents a unique point of view (Watts and Stenner 2012). The factor data are complex and requires reflection and judgement on the part of the researchers. The final prototypes are always an informed interpretation and can take the form of longer or shorter narratives and often also include the labelling of prototypes (e.g. Kontala 2016; Watts and Stenner 2012). The data from a FQS study, and the prototypes, can be used and analysed in many ways.

To conclude this short introduction to FQS, an important quality is its capacity to expose new and emerging subjectivities and defining elements within them. These allow, on the one hand, comparisons across samples and, on the other, the possibility of investigating these samples in large-scale surveys. The unique nature of Q-methodology requires us to speak of its quality as a method in contrast to assessing validity and reliability. Q-method has rightly been criticised for lacking the possibility of quantifying generalisations: it is not primarily concerned with what proportion of a larger population is associated with which prototype (see e.g. Thomas and Baas 1992/1993). Therefore, the emerging results will be more like concluding that a certain set of flowers grows in a garden we visited. We do not claim anything about how common they are or that they are limited to only certain colours. Nevertheless, we claim that our mixed-methods approach in general and the Q-sort in particular provide a methodological position that allows us to move between the universal and the particular in a more systematic way. This is reflected throughout the chapters in this volume.

The Research Process

The complex research process was made possible by an international research network. The YARG study as a whole was managed by a core team at Åbo Akademi University, led by a principal investigator and senior researchers. Local implementation in the countries included was administered by co-investigators, and commonly research assistants and/or doctoral students were employed for the collection and handling of data. The YARG study was also supported by a scientific advisory board. Planning and training sessions, as well as seminars, were held on a regular basis at Åbo Akademi University. The YARG data were collected in

2015–16 in Canada, China, Finland, Ghana, India, Israel, Sweden, Peru, Poland, Russia, Turkey and the USA. These countries were chosen to represent a broad variety of national, cultural and linguistic contexts as well as a significant variety with regard to world religions, historical traditions and contemporary religious developments and trends. The selection of countries covers all the main cultural value areas identified through the World Value Survey and "the Global Cultural Map" (Inglehart and Welzel 2005).

As a contrast to this broad approach, our sampling in each country highlights a notable limitation to the project. For our initial survey we recruited university students (aged approximately 18–28; $n \approx 300$ per country). In all countries, we have selected a small number of universities where the data has been collected. Universities with a specifically limited focus or character have not been included. Rather, we have initially tried to ensure diversity among the respondents. The fact that the YARG project is based on convenience sampling evidently means that there is no way to tell if the sample is representative of a larger population, and data from the survey do not allow us to draw conclusions about any specific population or to make valid statistical inferences. Rather, in conformity with the YARG study as a whole, the approach is more exploratory.

Turning to university students was a deliberate choice motivated by our interest in contemporary religiosity and change. In comparison to previous generations, young people born after 1990 are not characterised by having been gradually accustomed to consumer culture and digital media during their lifetime. Instead, these social phenomena have constituted an inherent and unquestioned part of their childhood and youth (cf. Possamai 2009). Palfrey and Gasser (2008) refer to this generation as "the born digital" and the "digital natives". They have been raised during social and cultural conditions that are particularly relevant to a study of religious change. Beyer (2019, 278) draws similar conclusions about the identities of the so-called "millennials" that have grown up with expanding global horizons and contexts that are "better regarded as dynamic and contextual projects, as fluid nodes in networks of relations". Our assumption was that university students generally have relatively extensive capital in this respect, also in comparison with other young adults.

The FQS does not require a large number of respondents, but it is important to find enough respondents representing a variety of viewpoints. Our initial survey enabled a broad selection of participants for FQS ($n \approx 45$ per country) with regard to gender, ethnicity, religious affiliation, language groups and class. These, in combination with other characteristics (e.g. value priorities based on Schwartz's PVQ), guaranteed diversity among the study's participants and their Faith Q-sorts.

The YARG study was conducted in local languages in all countries. All material intended for the use of our respondents, including the presentation of the study, the consent form, the survey and the FQS, was translated from English into target languages: Arabic, Bengali, Mandarin Chinese, Finnish, French, Hebrew, Polish, Russian, Spanish, Swedish and Turkish. We used a double back-translation method to guarantee the highest comparability and reliability across cultures (Brislin 1970, 1980; Geisinger 1994; Hambleton 1993, 1994; Harkness 2003; Lin, Chen and Chiu 2005; Plake and Hoover 1979; van de Vijver and Hambleton 1996). Our experience is that religious vocabulary can often be marked by biases emerging from the fact that religion in one culture or nation is often much more multi-faceted than any translator may be aware of. We often received different proposals from our translators and therefore also relied on local academic expert teams to be able to decide on the most adequate version (see Paloutzian *et al.* 2021). The challenge involved in translating items is central to the theme we explore in this volume, and therefore investigated in depth in a separate chapter (Chapter 2).

Religious and secular views are often considered to be sensitive information, and many ethical concerns were raised as part of the project. The participants were well informed about the nature of the project, that their participation was voluntary, and that they would remain anonymous. We especially emphasised that no teachers or parents would be able to request information about their participation in any form. The participants were informed that the data would be used for academic purposes only and by the YARG research team only, and that it would be securely archived after this. On the consent form that they signed and received a personal copy of, the participants were given contact information in case questions should arise later or in case they wanted to withdraw from the study at any point. These are standard regulatory procedures. Overall, we have followed the national guidelines on the ethical principles of research in the humanities and social and behavioural sciences in Finland (2009), defined by the Finnish National Board on Research Integrity (TENK 2009), as well as the European Code of Conduct for Research Integrity Revised Edition (ALLEA 2017). In October 2015, we received approval for the YARG project as a whole from the Åbo Akademi University Research Ethics Committee and, in addition, all co-investigators have followed corresponding national procedures. These vary a lot between the countries. In some national contexts, personal worldviews are also politically sensitive. We have therefore largely refrained from further descriptions of the universities that are involved in the YARG study and where the data have been collected.

The YARG network is extensive, and it involves a variety of linguistic and academic contexts. In line with ethical guidelines for international projects, we have tried to promote the careers of involved researchers at all levels. Throughout the process, we have also put efforts into being inclusive in our dissemination process in order to recognise the important contribution of all network members. This is also reflected in our document on principles for YARG authors. It defines some guidelines and rules for dissemination of results and emphasises the role of co-authoring. Co-authoring can be a difficult process in international projects for many reasons. Yet we find that it is worth the effort. At its best, it is a dialogical process, where a fusion of horizons materialises in text and in new perspectives. The vast majority of chapters included in this volume have been co-authored by cross-disciplinary and international teams of researchers.

Some Preliminary Observations from the FQS Data

There is a need to de-centre taken-for-granted categories and perspectives in the study of religions today (see Bender *et al.* 2013). A key asset of FQS is that it is anchored in self-reference rather than in preconceived theories or systems of classification. Therefore, it aptly opens up new vistas in light of challenges posed by religious change and religion in a global cross-cultural perspective. We will now turn to some observations on how FQS produces relevant systematic observations that are well grounded empirically. In particular, we would like to draw attention to the main prototypes identified in the project and to some basic questions raised by our findings. On the one hand, we analysed the total sample of individual sorts from all countries together ($n = 562$) and on the other we ran analyses on each country sample separately ($n = 37–90$). The first gave a global snapshot on the main ways of being (non-)religious, the latter mapped the countries one by one.

In a separate study drawing on this project (Nynäs *et al.* 2022a) we presented the main global worldview prototypes identified through the analysis of the total sample ($n = 562$). Based on their characteristics, these prototypes were called the "Secular Humanist", the "Active Confident Believer", the "Non-committed Traditionalist", the "Spiritually Attuned" and the "Disengaged Liberal". Our findings clearly reflect the relevance of the basic categories of secular, religious and spiritual. The narrative descriptions of the five global prototypes are found in Appendix 2. At a closer look, we could also confirm that on an overarching level, the prototypes were structured by the polarising function of the religious–secular divide. Both the factor correlation analysis and our survey measures of religiosity validated this general pattern. Nonetheless, our analyses also confirmed the distinctiveness of all five prototypes and not only a typology based on secular, religious and spiritual accompanied by various interesting interrelations between them. There is a significant positive correlation between the global prototypes 1 ("Secular Humanist") and 4 ("Spiritually Attuned"), as well as between global prototypes 2 ("Active Confident Believer") and 3 ("Non-committed Traditionalist"). In contrast, global prototype 5 ("Disengaged Liberal") can be said to play hard to catch and presents more situational and varying identifications that defy these patterns. In some respects our results reflect a study conducted by the Pew Research Center (2018). This was based solely on a US sample but seven different types of being religious emerged in a cluster analysis.

The prototypes clearly differ in how they rely on and give authority to, for instance, science, individual and independent agency, personal experience, in-group affiliations etc. Interestingly, also levels of openness, trust and well-being play an important role. In contrast to global prototypes 3 and 5, the three global prototypes 1 ("Secular Humanist"), 2 ("Active Confident Believer") and 4 ("Spiritually Attuned") stand out in how their representatives trust other people. A similar pattern emerges from our analyses of differences between global prototypes and basic human values and social moral attitudes. The global prototypes are especially divided along an axis consisting of universalism and self-direction vs. tradition and conformity. There is an apparent close affinity between the value types 2 ("Active Confident Believer") and 3 ("Non-committed Traditionalist"). Similarly, the two prototypes 2 ("Active Confident Believer") and 3 ("Non-committed Traditionalist") form a contrast to the liberal social values cluster that global prototypes 1 ("Secular Humanist") and 4 ("Spiritually Attuned") clearly express, and that the global prototype 5 ("Disengaged Liberal") taps into.

Our results also indicated that both gender and cross-cultural contextual differences influence how different worldview configurations are formed. The prototypes were well distributed across all countries in our study, but one could still see that some prototypes were more strongly anchored among persons from certain countries. It is therefore important to explore how the five worldview prototypes are reflected in our country-specific samples. We dedicated a separate study to this issue, and the results were just as exciting (Nynäs et al. 2021, ch. 4). Table 2 summarises the findings in numbers.

Table 2. Number of prototypes globally and per country.

Case	Prototypes	n	Case	Prototypes	n
Global	5	562			
Canada	5	37	Peru	3	43
China	6	46	Poland	4	45
Finland	3	50	Russia	5	45
Ghana	4	45	Sweden	3	30
India	8	45	Turkey	5	37
Israel	6	90	USA	5	49

When we investigated how ways of being secular, religious and spiritual were reflected in samples from twelve different countries worldwide, we could initially only work with the bird's eye view we had methodologically established when we examined the whole sample. At first glance, there did not seem to be any good way to compare the total number of fifty-seven different prototypes that we identified. In each country, we found three to eight prototypes. Of course, we could easily see that the distinct patterns of being religious, spiritual and non-religious were replicated to some extent in each country. Yet they were all different between themselves, and in most country samples we found yet other prototypes. Only Finland, Peru and Sweden were limited to three prototypes.

Usually, spirituality differentiates itself from religion in a value-laden way, giving centrality to individual outlooks, seekership, openness and holism. It is often associated with an emphasis on practices and means to attain insights, sustaining a connection to progressive liberal values and activism (Woodhead 2013). Comparing some of these prototypes we concluded that, both in the case of religious prototypes and spiritual prototypes, the two categories of prototypes were respectively constituted by several elements that vary in significant ways from one context to another and in different ways reflected the global prototypes. In short, we were able to conclude that being religious was not clearly defined by some specific distinguishing statements that would have been replicated in all country prototypes. Rather, we came across an open-ended multi-dimensional character of what being religious meant to the respondents. There was a play of theme and variations going on, but the variations could sometimes fall into very different genres or orchestrations and thus were not easily recognisable. The same held true in the case of spirituality – with a significant difference: spirituality presented an even broader variation across countries. An interesting observation was, furthermore, the fact that some prototypes were also built on what we tend to see as conflicting or incompatible elements, such as being both religious and secular, or rooting spirituality in nationalism. A specific quality of the FQS is that it has proved to be sensitive to such ambiguities, liquidities and simultaneities in how religious subjectivities are configured, thus challenging previous conceptions of congruence and compatibility when it comes to forming worldviews today.

How, then, can one make sense of these findings, without referring simply to the obvious, namely the impact and relevance of cultural differences? In this case we suggested the term "family resemblance" as a means of capturing and describing this observation (Nynäs et al. 2022b). The term was introduced by Ludwig Wittgenstein as part of his philosophy of language (Wittgenstein 1998; Andersen 2000), and presents a fruitful way to conceptualise the dynamic we found in the data. On the one hand, it accounts for how religion and spirituality are constituted by overlapping shared features, without, on the other hand, any of these necessarily being common to all manifestations. This means that the taxonomies of being religious and spiritual are dynamic, open and subject to change. They are evasive multi-dimensional categories often constituted by simultaneity and ambiguity, confluence but also contradictions. With regard to this, the term "family resemblance" can strike a significant methodological balance between the universal and the particular, including similarity-in-difference in a non-binary conceptualisation of subjective existential positions. As mentioned by way of introduction, we find both analytic and ethical reasons to question the dichotomy and the term "family resemblance" helps us to put this criticism into words.

Why do we summarise these results here? Our main findings from studying ways of being religious, secular and spiritual across twelve countries by using the FQS provide an important background to this volume and they motivate our aims. The results frustrate our taken-for-granted categories and concepts, and encourage us to try to open up new critical outlooks on current religiosity. They point to the importance of de-centring taken-for-granted categories and perspectives in the study of religions (see Bender et al. 2013). They also address the need to move beyond both European and American borders and the focus on Christianity as the implicit yardstick for "religion" in general and the idea of congregations and organisations as the main, even sole, *locus* of religion. The "contextual historical and ideological template that continues to inform" how what we think of as religion emerges in our studies, and this should be taken seriously (Bender et al. 2013, 287). These are wide-reaching ambitions and ideals, but we hope to illustrate at least some aspects of this with the chapters in the volume.

The Outline of the Volume

As mentioned above, all articles in this volume are based on the data collected by the YARG project, addressing the dichotomy of universality vs. particularism in the study of religious diversity, spirituality and non-religion from various vantage points. This introduction is followed by a chapter focusing on the complex epistemological and methodological challenge of translating the research instruments into the various vernacular languages of the countries sampled in the YARG project. In Chapter 2, Måns Broo, Marcus Moberg, Peter Nynäs, Mallarika Sarkar Das and Sohini Ray describe in depth how the research team sought to overcome the challenges of sensitively adapting the questionnaire and the Q-sort to local contexts and languages while maintaining the exactness of wording and intent needed to ensure comparability and methodological validity. Taking the translation of the research tools into Bengali as their example, the authors highlight how the impact of linguistic, conceptual and cultural differences influenced the work, but criticise the ideal that cross-cultural boundaries can be overcome by a technically "perfect" translation. Instead, the authors propose the translingual practice approach as a viable option, focusing on the translation process as a constantly ongoing interpersonal and interpretative process where meaning is sought in dialogue. As a result, the authors emphasise, comprehensibility and understanding emerge through various forms of linguistic contact, interaction and interpretation.

Chapter 3 continues to discuss methodological aspects of the YARG project. In this chapter, Sławomir Sztajer, Rafael Fernández Hart, Ben-Willie Kwaku Golo and Sidney Castillo describe and debate how perspectives deriving from the cognitive study of religion and the lived religion approach can be contrasted in order to find complementary ways of researching contemporary worldviews. By using YARG data primarily from China, Peru and Ghana, the authors seek to identify to what extent and in which ways traditional forms of religiosity come to the fore in the contemporary value profiles formulated in the project. To pinpoint both universal and particular aspects of these prototypes, the authors propose an analytic model that interlaces the study of general cognitive mechanism with sensitivity to cultural and contextual factors, thus creating an integrated and nuanced way of describing the complex nature of contemporary positions to religion, spirituality and secularity.

Chapter 4 contributes to the growing field of research focusing on religious views on sexuality, specifically the role of sexuality in religious communities, beliefs and practices. Starting from a critical elucidation of heteronormativity, Peter Nynäs, Ariela Keysar, Clara Marlijn Meijer and Sofia Sjö explore the association between religion and heteronormativity in the YARG data. Using triangulation as their approach, they present results that are largely consistent with many previous studies confirming the association between religion and heteronormativity, and on the other, they also indicate that for example tradition as a value is also an independent and relevant factor. However, the variations between countries and contexts, as well as within each national sample, are significant, and the authors stress the significance of working with mixed methods and across data sets when trying to understand the relationship between religion, value profiles and attitudes towards abortion and same-sex relationships as explored within the current research project. The results express the relevance of reflectively moving between the universal and the particular.

Chapter 5 deals with the multiplicity of Asian religiosities, as reflected in the YARG data. The authors Måns Broo and Ruby Sain take their starting point in a critical dismantling of the generic divisions between "Eastern" and "Western" religion, which have often functioned as a basic model for structuring the study of religions and religious change in the West. Their analysis of the FQS material gathered for the project in China and India brings out the inherent and neglected diversity of so-called "Eastern" religion and sheds a more nuanced light on the stereotypical assumptions that have often left this diversity unexplored in previous research.

In Chapter 6, Polina Vrublevskaya, Marcus Moberg and Karoliina Dahl analyse the concept of the "sacred" as it appears in the YARG data. Having been designed explicitly so as not to presuppose or maintain the general and mutually exclusive categories of sacred, spiritual and secular, it is intriguing to follow how this concept has been formulated and interpreted in the FQS and interview data of the project. On the basis of an inductive approach, and inspired by the originally Durkheimian conception of the sacred, the authors compare different ways of narratively constructing the concept of the "sacred individual" in the data gathered from the Russian and Finnish subsamples. As a conclusion, the authors point out that respect, tolerance, rights and the well-being of others stand out as key conceptions attached to the idea of the "sacred individual" in both samples.

The following chapter, Chapter 7, turns to secular identities and their contextualisations in the data. As the authors Janne Kontala, Ariela Keysar and Sawsan Kheir point out, non-religious self-identifications are becoming increasingly popular all over the world, especially among young adults. However, there is still meagre research on the varieties of non-religious identities and how such identities are shaped by national context, cultural varieties, gender issues and upbringing as well as the power balance between majority and minority groups in society. On the basis of their detailed analysis of the YARG data, the authors point to the inherent internal diversity within the category of "nones", ranging from active atheists to spiritual seekers.

Yet another aspect of debate on universality vs. particularism is addressed in Chapter 8, dealing with multiple religious identifications in the data. The authors Ruth Illman, Peter Nynäs and Nurit Novis-Deutsch argue that there is a need to critically assess current scholarship on multiple religious identifications in relation both to social structures and to individual worldviews by anchoring the discussion in ethnographic data and to include recent contributions advocating a more open and positive approach to multiple religious belonging. An analysis of the YARG research data shows that multiple identifications are common among young adults worldwide, and to account for the multiplicity of positions displayed in the data five interlinked categories of multiple identifications are proposed: internal religious multiplicity, inter-religious multiplicity, religio-secular multiplicity, selective multiplicity and common humanity.

Finally, Chapter 9 draws together the main findings of the volume and suggests themes and prospects for future research.

Peter Nynäs Dr Theol. is Professor of the Study of Religions at Åbo Akademi University (ÅAU), Finland and Dean of the Faculty of Arts, Psychology and Theology. He is the director and PI of the Åbo Akademi University Centre of Excellence in Research Young Adults and Religion in a Global Perspective Project (2015–19) and earlier the Centre of Excellence in Research Post-secular Culture and a Changing Religious Landscape in Finland Project (2010–14). Among the books he has edited are *On the Outskirts of "the Church": Diversities, Fluidities, and New Spaces of Religion in Finland* (with R. Illman and T. Martikainen, LIT-Verlag, 2015), *Religion, Gender, and Sexuality in Everyday Life* (with A. Yip, Ashgate, 2012), and *The Diversity of Worldviews among Young Adults: Contemporary (Non)Religiosity and Spirituality through the Lens of an International Mixed Method Study* (with A. Keysar, J. Kontala, B.-W. Kwaku Golo, M. Lassander, M. Shterin, S. Sjö and P. Stenner; Springer, 2021).

Dr Ruth Illman is the director of the Donner Institute for Research in Religion and Culture in Turku, Finland. She holds the title of docent in the study or religions at Åbo Akademi University (ÅAU) and in the history of religions at Uppsala University, as well as doctoral degrees in the study of religions (2004) and Jewish studies (2018). Her main research interests include cultural encounters and diversity, contemporary Judaism, religion and the arts (especially music) and ethnographic research, primarily by developing the analytical approach of vernacular religion. Illman acted as Co-PI for the Centre of Excellence Young Adults and Religion in a Global Perspective at ÅAU (2015–19). Currently, she leads the research project Boundaries of Jewish Identities in Contemporary Finland and acts as editor-in-chief of the open-access peer-review journal *Nordisk judaistik/ Scandinavian Jewish Studies* with Svante Lundgren. Recent publications are found at https://research.abo.fi/en/persons/ruth-illman

Dr Nurit Novis-Deutsch is a social psychologist researching values and moral development in the Department of Learning and Instructional Sciences at the University of Haifa in Israel. Her research concerns the ways in which people create and manage contradictory frames of meaning and values and how they organise their identities and relate to others in social contexts. Other aspects of her research apply these topics to the field of education. Recent and current research projects include pluralistic reasoning; outgroup dehumanisation; the challenges of ultra-religious college students; religious meaning-making during the COVID-19 crisis; prejudice and religiosity; the religious subjectivities of young adults globally (the YARG project); interdisciplinary education; and Holocaust education and memory. Dr Novis-Deutsch's research has been published in various psychological and educational journals and books.

References

af Burén, Ann. 2015. *Living Simultaneity: On Religion among Semi-secular Swedes*. Huddinge: Södertörn University.

ALLEA. 2017. *The European Code of Conduct for Research Integrity* (revised edn). Berlin: ALLEA. Retrieved from www.allea.org/wp-content/uploads/2017/05/ALLEA-European-Code-of-Conduct-for-Research-Integrity-2017.pdf. Accessed 15 March 2021.

Allport, Gordon W. 1950. *The Individual and his Religion*. New York: Macmillan.

Allport, Gordon W., and Michael J. Ross. 1967. "Personal Religious Orientation and Prejudice". *Journal of Personality and Social Psychology* 5(4): 432–43.

Andersen, H. 2000. "Kuhn's Account of Family Resemblance: A Solution to the Problem of Wide-open Texture". *Erkenntnis* 52: 313–37.

Asad, Talal. 1993. *Genealogies of Religion: Discipline and Reasons of Power in Christianity and Islam*. Baltimore, MD: Johns Hopkins University Press.

Asad, Talal. 2003. *Formations of the Secular: Christianity, Islam, Modernity*. Stanford, CA: Stanford University Press.

Balagangadhara, S. N. 2005. *The Heathen in his Blindness …: Asia, the West, and the Dynamics of Religion* (2nd edn). Delhi: Manohar Publishers.

Balagangadhara, S. N. 2014. "On the Dark Side of the 'Secular': Is the Religious–Secular Distinction a Binary?" *Numen* 61: 33–52.

Banasick, Shawn. 2019. "KADE: A Desktop Application for Q Methodology". *Journal of Open Source Software* 4(36): 1360. https://doi.org/10.21105/joss.01360

Beckford, James. 2003. *Social Theory and Religion*. Cambridge: Cambridge University Press.

Bender, Courtney, Wendy Cadge, Peggy Levitt and David Smilde, eds. 2013. *Religion on the Edge: De-centering and Re-centering the Sociology of Religion*. Oxford: Oxford University Press.

Beyer, Peter. 2019. "Conclusion: Youth, Religion, and Identity in a Globalizing Context: International Case Studies". In *Youth, Religion, and Identity in a Globalizing Context*, ed. Paul L. Gareau, Spencer C. Bullivant and Peter Beyer, 278–84. Leiden: Brill.

Block, Jack. 1978. *The Q-sort Method in Personality Assessment and Psychiatric Research*. Palo Alto, CA: Consulting Psychologists Press.

Block, Jack. 2008. *The Q-sort in Character Appraisal: Encoding Subjective Impressions of Persons Quantitatively*. Washington, DC: American Psychological Association.

Brislin, Richard W. 1970. "Back Translation for Cross-cultural Research". *Journal of Cross-cultural Psychology* 1(3): 185–216.

Brislin, Richard W. 1980. "Translation and Content Analysis of Oral and Written Materials". In *Handbook of Cross-cultural Psychology*, ed. Harry C. Triandis and J. W. Berry, 389–444. Boston, MA: Allyn & Bacon.

Brown, Steven. 1980. *Political Subjectivity: Applications of Q Methodology in Political Science*. New Haven, CT: Yale University Press.

Chakrabarty, Dipesh. 2000. *Provincializing Europe: Postcolonial Thought and Historical Difference*. Princeton, NJ: University of Princeton Press.

Day, Abby. 2010. "Propositions and Performativity: Relocating Belief to the Social". *Culture and Religion* 11(1): 9–30.

Day, Abby. 2011. *Believing in Belonging: Belief and Social Identity in the Modern World*. Oxford: Oxford University Press.

de Roover, Jacob. 2014 "Incurably Religious? Consensus Gentium and the Cultural Universality of Religion". *Numen* 61(1): 5–32. https://doi.org/10.1163/15685276-12341301

Gabor, Manuela. 2013. "Q-methodology (Q Factor Analysis): Particularities and Theoretical Considerations for Marketing Data". *International Journal of Arts and Commerce* 2(4): 116–26.

Geisinger, Kurt F. 1994. "Cross-cultural Normative Assessment: Translation and Adaptation Issues Influencing the Normative Interpretation of Assessment Instruments". *Psychological Assessment* 6(4): 304–12.

Hambleton, Ronald K. 1993. "Translating Achievement Tests for Use in Cross-National Studies". *European Journal of Psychological Assessment* 9 (1): 57–65.

Hambleton, Ronald K. 1994. "The Rise and Fall of Criterion-Referenced Measurement?" *Educational Measurement: Issues and Practice* 13(4): 21–6. https://doi.org/10.1111/j.1745-3992.1994.tb00567.x

Harkness, Janet A. 2003. "Questionnaire Translation". In *Cross-cultural Survey Methods*, ed. Janet A. Harkness, Fons van de Vijver and Peter Mohler, 35–56. New York: John Wiley & Sons.

Illman, Ruth, and Peter Nynäs. 2017. *Kultur, människa, möte: Ett humanistiskt perspektiv*. Lund: Studentlitteratur.

Inglehart, Ronald, and Christian Welzel. 2005 *Modernization, Cultural Change, and Democracy: The Human Development Sequence*. New York: Cambridge University Press.

Kalsky, Manuela, and André van der Braak. 2017. "Introduction to the Topical Issue 'Multiple Religious Belonging'". *Open Theology* 3: 662–4.

Klingenberg, Maria, and Sofia Sjö. 2019. "Introduction: Theorizing Religious Socialization: A Critical Assessment". *Religion* 49(2): 163–78.

Kontala, Janne. 2016. *Emerging Non-religious Worldview Prototypes: A Faith Q-sort-Study on Finnish Group-Affiliates*. Turku: Åbo Akademi University Press.

Lambek, Michael. 2014. "Recognizing Religion: Disciplinary Traditions, Epistemology, and History". *Numen* 61(2–3): 145–65.

Lassander, Mika. 2014. *Post-Materialist Religion: Pagan Identities and Value Change in Modern Europe*. London: Bloomsbury.

Lassander, Mika, and Peter Nynäs. 2016. "Contemporary Fundamentalist Christianity in Finland: The Variety of Religious Subjectivities and their Association with Values". *Interdisciplinary Journal for Religion and Transformation in Contemporary Society* 2 (3): 154–84.

Leech, Nancy, and Andrew Onwuegbuzie. 2009. "A Typology of Mixed Methods Research Designs". *Quality and Quantity* 43(2): 265–75. https://doi.org/10.1007/s11135-007-9105-3

Lin, Yi-Hsiu, Chen-Yueh Chen and Ping-an Chiu. 2005. "Cross-cultural Research and Back: An Overview on Issues of Cross-cultural Research and Back-Translation". *The Sports Journal* 8(4). Retrieved from www.thesportjournal.org/article/cross-cultural-research-and-back-translation. Accessed 15 March 2021.

Maio, Gregory. 2017. *The Psychology of Human Values*. New York: Routledge.

Masuzawa, Tomoko. 2005. *The Invention of World Religions: Or how European universalism was preserved in the language of pluralism*. Chicago, IL: University of Chicago Press.

McKeown, Bruce. 2001. "Loss of Meaning in Likert Scaling: A Note on the Q Methodological Alternative". *Operant Subjectivity* 24(4): 201–6. dx.doi.org/10.15133/j.os.2001.009

McKeown, Bruce, and Dan Thomas. 2013 *Q Methodology* (2nd edn). London: Sage.

Moberg, Marcus, and Sofia Sjö, eds. 2020. *Digital Media, Young Adults and Religion: An International Perspective*. New York: Routledge.

Newman, Isadore, and Susan Ramlo. 2010. "Using Q Methodology and Q Factor Analysis in Mixed Methods Research". In *Mixed Methods in Social and Behavioral Research* (2nd edn), ed. Abbas Tashakkori and Charles Teddlie, 505–30. Thousand Oaks, CA: Sage.

Nilsson, Artur. 2013 *The Psychology of Worldviews: Toward a Non-reductive Science of Personality*. Lund: Media-Tryck Lund University.

Nynäs Peter, Ariela Keysar, Janne Kontala, Ben-Willie Kwaku Golo, Mika T. Lassander, Marat Shterin, Sofia Sjö and Paul Stenner. 2022. *The Diversity of Worldviews among Young Adults: Contemporary (Non)Religiosity and Spirituality through the Lens of an International Mixed Method Study*. Cham: Springer. https://doi.org/10.1007/978-3-030-94691-3

Nynäs, Peter, Ariela Keysar and Martin Lagerström. 2022a. "Who are they and what do they value? The Five Global Worldviews of Young Adults". In *The Diversity of Worldviews among Young Adults: Contemporary (Non)Religiosity and Spirituality through the Lens of an International Mixed Method Study*, ed. Peter Nynäs, Ariela Keysar, Janne Kontala, Ben-Willie Kwaku Golo, Mika T. Lassander, Marat Shterin, Sofia Sjö and Paul Stenner, 47–71. Cham: Springer. https://doi.org/10.1007/978-3-030-94691-3_3

Nynäs, Peter, Janne Kontala and Mika Lassander. 2021. "The Faith Q-Sort: In-Depth Assessment of Diverse Spirituality and Religiosity in 12 Countries". In *Assessing Spirituality in a Diverse World*, ed. Amy L. Ai, Paul Wink, Raymond F. Paloutzian and Kevin A. Harris, 554–73. Cham: Springer.

Nynäs, Peter, Janne Kontala, Mika Lassander, Nurit Novis-Deutsch, Sofia Sjö and Paul Stenner. 2022b. "Family Resemblance in Variations of Contemporary Religiosity and Spirituality: Findings from a Cross-Cultural Study". In *The Diversity of Worldviews among Young Adults: Contemporary (Non)Religiosity and Spirituality through the Lens of an International Mixed Method Study*, ed. Peter Nynäs, Ariela Keysar, Janne Kontala, Ben-Willie Kwaku Golo, Mika T. Lassander, Marat Shterin, Sofia Sjö and Paul Stenner, 73–92. Cham: Springer. https://doi.org/10.1007/978-3-030-94691-3_4

Palfrey, John, and Urs Gasser. 2008. *Born Digital: Understanding the First Generation of Digital Natives*. New York: Basic Books.

Paloutzian, Raymond F., Zuhâl Agilkaya-Sahin, Kay C. Bruce, Marianne Nilsen Kvande, Klara Malinakova, Luciana Fernandes Marques, Ahmad S. Musa, Marzieh Nojomi, Eyüp Ensar Öztürk, Indah Permata Putri and Suk-Kyung You. 2021. "The Spiritual Well-Being Scale (SWBS): Cross-cultural Assessment Across 5 Continents, 10 Languages, and 300 Studies". In *Assessing Spirituality in a Diverse World*, ed. Amy L. Ai, Paul Wink, Raymond F. Paloutzian and Kevin A. Harris, 413–44. Cham: Springer.

Pennanen, Felix. 2013. *Meningsskapande matvanor: En mixed-methods-studie av värderingar och världsåskådningar hos den svenska LCHF-rörelsen*. Turku: Åbo Akademi University.

Pew Research Center. 2018. "The Religious Typology: A New Way to Categorize Americans by Religion". 29 August. Retrieved from www.pewforum.org/2018/08/29/the-religious-typology. Accessed 27 September 2021.

Plake, Barbara S., and H. D. Hoover. 1979. "An Analytical Method of Identifying Biased Test Items". *Journal of Experimental Education* 48(2): 153–4.

Possamai, Adam. 2009. *Sociology of Religion for Generations X and Y*. London: Equinox Publications.

Schmolck, Peter. 2017. "PQ Method for Mac". Retrieved from http://schmolck.userweb.mwn.de/qmethod/. Accessed 15 March 2021.

Schwartz, Shalom H. 1992. "Universals in the Content and Structure of Values: Theoretical Advances and Empirical Tests in 20 Countries". *Advances in Experimental Social Psychology* 25: 1–65. https://doi.org/10.1016/S0065-2601(08)60281-6

Schwartz, Shalom H. 2012. "An Overview of the Schwartz Theory of Basic Values". *Online Readings in Psychology and Culture* 2(1). Retrieved from https://scholarworks.gvsu.edu/orpc/vol2/iss1/11/. Accessed 15 March 2021.

Schwartz, Shalom H., Jan Cieiuch, Michele Vecchione, Eldad Davidov, Ronald Fischer, Constanze Beierlein, Alice Ramos, Markku Verkasalo, Jan-Erik Lönnqvist, Kursad Demirutku, Ozlem Dirilen-Gumus and Mark Konty. 2012. "Refining the Theory of Basic Individual Values". *Journal of Personality and Social Psychology* 103(4): 663–88.

Stephenson, William. 1993/1994. "Introduction to Q-Methodology". *Operant Subjectivity* 17(1–2): 1–13.

Tashakkori, Abbas, and Charles Teddlie. 1998. *Mixed Methodology: Combining Qualitative and Quantitative Approaches*. Thousand Oaks, CA: Sage.

Teddlie, Charles, and Abbas Tashakkori. 2009. *Foundations of Mixed Methods Research: Integrating Quantitative and Qualitative Approaches in the Social and Behavioral Sciences*. London: Sage.

TENK. 2009. "Advice and Materials". Retrieved from https://tenk.fi/en/advice-and-materials. Accessed 15 March 2021.

Terho, Johan. 2013. *En FQS-studie av världsbilder hos medlemmar i finska Lutherstiftelsen*. Turku: Åbo Akademi University.

Thomas, Dan, and Larry Baas. 1992/1993. "The Issue of Generalization in Q Methodology: 'Reliable Schematics' Revisited". *Operant Subjectivity* 16(1/2): 18–36.

van de Vijver, Fons, and Ronald Hambleton 1996. "Translating Tests: Some Practical Guidelines". *European Psychologist* 1(2): 89–99.

van Exel, Job, and Gjalt de Graaf. 2005. "Q Methodology: A Sneak Preview". Retrieved from www.jobvanexel.nl. Accessed 15 March 2021.

Watts, Simon, and Paul Stenner. 2012. *Doing Q Methodological Research: Theory, Method, and Interpretation*. London: Sage.

Winzeler, Robert L. 2008. *Anthropology and Religion: What we know, think, and question*. Lanham, MD: AltaMira Press.

Wittgenstein, Ludwig. 1998. *The Blue and Brown Books. Preliminary Studies for the "Philosophical Investigations"* (2nd edn). Oxford: Blackwell.

Wolf, Melissa, Elliott Ihm, David Maul and Ann Taves. 2019. "Survey Item Validation". *PsyArXiv*, 23 July. doi:10.31234/osf.io/k27w3.

Woodhead, Linda. 2013. "New Forms of Public Religion: Spirituality in Global Civil Society". In *Religion beyond its Private Role in Modern Society*, ed. Wim Hofstee and Arie van der Kooij, 29–54. Leiden: Brill.

Wulff, David. M. 2019. "Prototypes of Faith: Findings with the Faith Q-Sort". *Journal for the Scientific Study of Religion* 58(3): 643–65.

– 2 –

Translation and Major Categories in the Study of Religions

The Case of "Religion" and "Spirituality" in West Bengal

MÅNS BROO, MARCUS MOBERG, PETER NYNÄS,
MALLARIKA SARKAR DAS AND SOHINI RAY

The translation of research instruments presents a window to the many difficult conceptual problems related to commensurability or incommensurability. We often face them in cross-cultural studies involving different cultures and languages. Hence, a translation process may gain a methodological value in itself and produce significant data. In this chapter we examine the process of translating the Faith Q-set (FQS) into Bengali. This case study reflects many of the issues that we came across in working with translations of the Faith Q-set from English to eleven different target languages. The impact of linguistic, conceptual and cultural differences become evident in this study, and we question the ideal that one can overcome cross-cultural boundaries, and modestly prefer to refer to the quality of a translation process with respect to target groups. Yet, in contrast to the impact of cultural differences, and supported by a translingual-practice approach, we emphasise that comprehensibility and understanding still emerge through different forms of linguistic contact, interaction and interpretation. This happens on a historical and societal level as well as on a micro-level within the interviews.

Introduction

A topical question within the study of religions today concerns how we approach and cross-culturally implement concepts deemed central within the field, such as "ritual", "asceticism" or indeed "religion" itself (see e.g. Satlow 2005). This question also becomes specifically relevant through the study of translations of such terms – that is, both the translation process itself and the use of such translations within multi-lingual and multi-cultural research projects. In the research project Young Adults and Religion in a Cross-cultural Perspective (YARG) we faced several of the challenges involved in translation and cross-cultural adaptation of various survey items used in our mixed-methods approach. The challenges were in particular evident in the translation of the Faith Q-set (FQS). All statements are listed in Appendix 1. The FQS is an instrument for assessing religiosity originally developed by David Wulff (2019). It involves 101 statements, covering ideas, practices, attitudes and so on of significance to different religious, spiritual and secular life-views and traditions. The translation and use of these in an international study raise important questions and concerns with regard to cross-cultural validity.

In this chapter we explore the translation of the FQS with the aim of exploring some relevant issues related to cross-cultural research. The YARG project was implemented in thirteen countries; its background, design and implementation is presented and discussed in Chapter 1 (see also Nynäs *et al.* 2021). An essential part of the implementation was the translation of the FQS from English into Arabic, Bengali, Finnish, French, Hebrew, Mandarin Chinese, Polish, Russian, Spanish, Swedish and Turkish. In this chapter we focus on the translation from English to Bengali, beginning with an examination of the translation of some central concepts within the study of religions. After this, we move on to look at translations at work in the field, that is, how in this case the terms "religion" and "spirituality" were understood and used both in English and Bengali by our West Bengali interviewees. Since many of these individuals were fluent in both English and Bengali, and since Bengalis, while speaking the same language, use different concepts depending on whether they are Hindus or Muslims, this particular case within the rich YARG material proved felicitous.

The Bengali case reflects well the challenges we also met in many other instances in the YARG project. The linguistic aspect of translation requires us to be attentive to a range of differences pertaining not only to religious traditions, but also to nationality, ethnicity and local context. In order to highlight this, we will start out with a more general discussion of the category of "religion", moving on to questions pertaining to the difficulties involved in translating such categories into new linguistic contexts. After this we turn back to our specific context of the YARG project and West Bengal, India. We believe that this chapter addresses the complexity involved in what Lambek (2014, 147) calls a "moving balance between distinct epistemological positions", referring to the dichotomy of universality vs. particularism in cross-cultural research.

Approaching "Religion" from a Linguistic Perspective

Any consideration of the category of "religion" from a linguistic perspective (broadly understood) needs to be based on an open recognition of the ways in which modern understandings of "religion" as a taken-for-granted "global social fact" initially developed as part of Western colonialist and nationalist efforts from the eighteenth century on. From this perspective, the very category of "religion" needs to be approached and understood as a particularly Western construct for which there exist no direct equivalents in other cultures, languages or historical periods (Hermann 2016, 98; Taira 2016, 132; McCutcheon 1997; Fitzgerald 2007). Moreover, as Fitzgerald (2007, 7, emphasis added) points out, it is equally important to recognise that the "construction of modern discourses on generic religion has been made possible and conceivable by *the parallel construction* of a number of overlapping discourses on nonreligious/secular science, politics, the nation state, economics, law, and education".

A properly historicised understanding of the development and evolution of the Western category of "religion" has a range of important bearings on any attempt to provide translations for "religious" concepts and terms between different languages and cultural contexts (Hermann 2016, 98). For example, the problems that inevitably arise in any such endeavours have been dealt with in several studies focusing on constructions of the category of religion in various Asian (e.g. Schalk 2013; Horii 2016) and indigenous contexts (e.g. Wenger 2005). As Hermann (2016, 101) points out, attempts at finding equivalents for the Western category of "religion" in non-Western contexts easily risk getting "caught up in a tautological paradox, first having to define a specific understanding of 'religion', and then searching for equivalents in ancient European or non-Western languages and cultures and subsequently claiming their existence (or non-existence)". In order to move beyond these difficulties, Hermann argues for a wholesale reconceptualisation of such searches for equivalents. As he argues:

> instead of seeing the global spread of "Western" understandings of "religion" as a *problem*, the global establishment of equivalents of "religion" in non-Western languages has to be understood as the *condition of possibility* for the emergence of a "global discourse of religion".
> (Hermann 2016, 103, emphasis in original)

Moreover, and just as importantly, "the unity of the 'global discourse of religion' has to be described in a way that does not presuppose a tautological definition of a 'phenomenon of religion', 'religious semantics', or the reliance on the self-understanding of 'religious actors'" (Hermann 2016, 103).

The Incommensurability of Languages: the Sapir–Whorf Hypothesis

If we are to translate "religious" concepts from one language into another, how exactly are we to proceed? The German Indologist Jürgen Hanneder (2017, 5–13) compares adaptive translations with literal translations. An extreme example of the first is when a medieval German translator of the *aceitunas*, "olives", in Cervantes's *Don Quixote*, a delicacy unknown to German readers of the time, renders them as "Bratwürste". Literal translations can be exemplified by German translations from the Sanskrit of the school of the poet Friedrich Rückert (1788–1866), where one *almost* understands the translation as soon as one understands the original. Most readers, even scholars, would no doubt prefer something in between these extremes. However, both of these methods presuppose that translation is something that can be achieved, as long as one possesses the right linguistic and cultural tools. Not everyone would agree.

The idea of the incommensurability of different languages occupies a central position in the widely debated so-called Sapir–Whorf hypothesis, also known as "Whorfianism" or simply linguistic relativity. Initially developed (separately) by Edward Sapir and Benjamin Lee Whorf, this hypothesis rests on the notion that language, thought and culture are intimately interlinked and, hence, that different languages simultaneously work to both enable and to restrict the abilities of speakers to construe and construct the social world they inhabit as meaningful in particular ways. In the words of Sapir: "No two languages are ever sufficiently similar to be considered as representing the same social reality. The worlds in which different societies live are distinct worlds, not merely the same world with different labels attached" (Sapir, quoted in Taylor 2016, 321). Echoing post-structuralist and social-constructionist approaches to language, this view thus rejects the modernist so-called "picture metaphor" view of language, the view that words and language correspond to and are able to communicate pictures of the world "as it is" (Gergen 1999, 33–5). Language, in this view, is not adequately understood in terms of a "neutral information-carrying vehicle", but rather as something that is always constitutive of social reality, as something that always also "creates what it refers to" (Taylor 2001, 8). But beyond this, the Sapir–Whorf hypothesis also suggests that language plays a crucial role in people's *mental activity*. For as Whorf argues, "each language is not merely a reproducing instrument for voicing ideas but rather is itself a shaper of ideas, the program and guide for the individual's mental activity, for his analysis of impressions, for his synthesis of his mental stock in trade" (Whorf, quoted in Taylor 2016, 321).

Differences in grammar, lexicon, syntax and so on between different languages serve to steer and direct the attention of speakers in different directions and to different things: "The lexico-grammatical properties of a given language may force us to encode certain features in describing a given situation" (Taylor 2016, 323). This becomes particularly evident when we consider linguistic representations of abstract metaphysical or fundamental concepts that relate to such things as time and space and the perceived ultimate sources or foundations of reality (Taylor 2016, 325). Words, terms and concepts that relate to things or entities most commonly associated with the category of "religion" provide apt examples of this. According to the Sapir–Whorf hypothesis, the meaning that people embed in different linguistic contexts as attributes of the particular words, terms, and concepts that they use to refer to perceived "religious" realities or entities will always be crucially dependent on the lexico-grammatical properties of the particular language they are using. But in addition, it is equally important to recognise that the "religious semantics" (von Stuckrad 2010) of a particular society or culture will always stand in a dialectical and mutually affective relationship to a range of other changeable and dynamic modes of linguistic, social and cultural classification. For, as Fitzgerald (2007, 99, emphasis added) observes, "religion" is not adequately understood as "something that simply exists in the world, a 'phenomenon' with a stable and continuous identity but is an ideological category *with shifting semantic content in relation to other unstable and contested categories* like the secular, science, politics, the state, and so on".

The Sapir–Whorf hypothesis has been tested in various ways, most famously by studying the ways in which different languages construct the differences between shades of colour and how this influences how speakers of these different languages react to such colour differences. Most results seem to indicate that the perception of colours is generally governed by physical-biological universals rather than by language, though these results have not gone unchallenged (Lucy 2015, 905). In its "hard form" described above, the Sapir–Whorf hypothesis finds little support from linguists or cognitive scientists today, though many concede that language does affect thought (Seuren 1998; Wolff and Holmes 2011).

Nevertheless, as we have seen, the Sapir–Whorf hypothesis is important in this context, as it connects to the growing awareness of the fact that many established perspectives in the study of religions (including questions, concepts, assumptions and empirical data) are severely limited in terms of the tension between universalistic and particularistic claims. Furthermore, the category of "religion" is not adequately approached as simply possessing some kind of ahistorical or trans-historical "essence", and it has also often been employed in highly provincial ways (e.g. Asad 1993, 2003; Chakrabarty 2000, 2005; Masuzawa 2005; Balagangadhara 2005; Winzeler 2008).

The Translingual-Practice Approach

As stated above, within the YARG project, many Western "religion" and worldview-related terms and concepts were translated into a range of non-Western languages. How are we to understand such an undertaking? Several notable attempts have been made to reorient the search for "'equivalents of religion' in non-Western languages ... towards a historical investigation of the establishment of such equivalents in processes of translingual practice" (Hermann 2016, 103). As developed by Liu (1995), the concept of "translingual practice" does not foreground ideas about radical incommensurability between different languages or the impossibility of translating complex concepts. Nor does it assume the possibility of complete translatability between languages and concepts. Rather, the translingual-practice approach focuses on "translation as a pragmatic practice and on the *production of equivalence* in the context of historical processes of translation" (Hermann 2016, 104, emphasis added). In this approach, translation is thus conceived of and theorised in terms of a "process always already happening" (Hermann 2016, 104). This approach therefore seeks to reconstruct the *historical processes* whereby linguistic and conceptual equivalence are generated, or come closer to being generated (Hermann 2016, 104). Hence, rather than primarily focusing on whether or not equivalents can or cannot be identified or be said to exist, the translingual approach focuses on "their manner of becoming". For as Liu points out, "it is the making of *hypothetical equivalences* that enables the modus operandi of translation and its politics" (Liu 1995, cited in Hermann 2016, 104, emphasis added).

In order to avoid getting bogged down in perhaps unresolvable questions relating to the commensurability or incommensurability of different cultures and languages, or the existence or non-existence of trans-historical and trans-discursive connections between languages, the translingual-practice approach aims to redirect our focus at "the occurrences of historical contact, interaction, translation, and travel of words and ideas between languages" (Liu 1995, cited in Hermann 2016, 105). While remaining keenly aware of the ways in which the Western concept of "religion" originally came to be imposed on non-Western peoples and cultures as part of Western colonialist efforts, any search for supposed non-Western equivalents to "religion" or related terms in other cultures and languages is therefore more adequately understood in terms of a historical process involving the *production* of meaning and equivalence (Hermann 2016, 105). As Liu writes, translatability

> refers to the historical making of hypothetical equivalence between languages. These equivalences tend to be makeshift inventions in the beginning and become more or less fixed through repeated use or come to be supplanted by the preferred hypothetical equivalences of a later generation [...] one does not translate between equivalents; rather *one creates tropes of equivalence in the middle zone of translation between the host and guest languages*. This middle zone of hypothetical equivalence, which is occupied by neologistic imagination, becomes the very ground for change.
> (Liu 1995, cited in Hermann 2016, 105)

In this approach, focus is therefore shifted towards the "historical condition of translation" (Liu 1995, cited in Hermann 2016) and the "process by which new words, meanings, discourses, and modes of representation arise, circulate, and acquire legitimacy within the host language due to, or in spite of, the latter's contact/collision with the guest language" (Liu 1995, cited in Hermann 2016, 105–6). Therefore, "Looking at what happens in the host language in a process of translation allows us to understand the creation of meaning not so much as a 'transformation' of meaning from one language to the other, but rather as an 'invention' of meaning in the host language" (Hermann 2016, 106). And so, rather than being seen as a "neutral" endeavour devoid of ideological and political influence and implications, the process of translation emerges as a central site of ideological and political tensions and struggles (Liu 1995, 26). For, as Liu points out, it is in this process "where the guest language is forced to encounter the host language, where the irreducible differences between them are fought out, authorities invoked or challenged, ambiguities dissolved or created, and so forth, until new meanings emerge in the host language itself" (Liu 1995, cited in Hermann 2016, 106).

The utility of the translingual approach can be illustrated in relation to the gradual emergence of concepts of religion, or "equivalents of religion", in Asian languages and cultures. For example, in the case of China, numerous studies (e.g. Tarocco 2008; Nedostup 2009; Barrett and Tarocco

2011) have explored the ways in which "a variety of cross-cultural translations and processes of cultural adaptation between China, Japan, and the West" (Hermann 2016, 112) throughout the 1800s and early 1900s gradually led to the emergence and establishment of the term *zongjiao* – a Chinese equivalent to "religion". Although the origins of the term *zongjiao* date back much further in history, its status as a Chinese equivalent of religion was cemented partly through Christian missionaries' translations of their own publications into Chinese but more importantly still through the ways in which the term was gradually adopted by the Chinese state. As part of this gradual process of adoption and adaptation, the term *zongjiao* was established as an umbrella term for a large variety of disparate and free-floating beliefs and practices that had previously not been contained under any particular label. In contrast to the previously widely used but more ambiguous term *jiao*, *zongjiao* now also came to incorporate the essentially Western notion that the particular set of beliefs and practices that were to be included under the *zongjiao* label belonged to a "separate" and "independent" sphere of culture and society. In what further reflects a strong Western influence, *zongjiao* at this point was also firmly distinguished from the term *mixin* ("superstition"). The *zongjiao/mixin* distinction subsequently developed into a central element in the construction of the category of "Chinese religion", thus also serving as the principal basis for the Chinese state's initial official recognition of five "religions" (Catholicism, Protestantism, Islam, Buddhism and Taoism) in the early twentieth century. *Zongjiao* therefore also came to connote a certain *type* of "religion" that was differentiated from other sectors in society and characterised by organisational forms reminiscent of Western institutional Christianity.

As this example illustrates, in the translingual-practice approach, questions relating to the supposed "authenticity", "Westernisation" or "Europeanisation" of certain forms of language use are abandoned in favour of an understanding of language as a phenomenon that is "constantly in a state of hybridity as the result of ongoing translations" (Hermann 2016, 106). This approach redirects the focus from a search for equivalence between Western and non-Western terms and concepts towards a focus on their genealogy or "manner of becoming" (Liu 1995, 16).

This shift in focus, by extension, also directly connects to a much broader reconsideration and reconceptualisation of a global history of religion and the emergence of a global discourse of religion that expressly strives to move beyond previous searches for some common or shared *sui generis* "transcendental signified" shared by all phenomena we choose to include under the label "religion" (Hermann 2016, 107).

For this reason, the YARG project was interested in how young people across the world portray and articulate their own subjective worldviews, including those perceived as "religious" or "spiritual", a distinction that of course often proved to play out differently in different cultures and languages.

Translations in the YARG Project

The design and mixed-methods approach of the YARG project is discussed in detail in the introduction to this volume. In this chapter we deal with translation into Bengali of one of the main instruments employed in the project, namely the FQS consisting of 101 statements (Appendix 1). The FQS was based on Q-methodology, meaning that the statements are sorted and ranked by respondents and all sorts are subjected to factor analyses. We were able to conduct this analysis for respondents from each respective country in our study separately but also for all respondents in the YARG study together. Already the very existence of a set of statements, incorporating terms such as "the divine", "salvation", "faith", "beliefs", "scriptures", "sacred", "supernatural", and many others essentially presupposes at least some kind of commensurability between not only individual worldviews but between languages as well. Furthermore, the way Q-methodology works builds on statements being "the same" for each cultural and linguistic context explored. The process of translating these statements into eleven different languages raised a whole host of both interesting and challenging issues. How then were the translations carried out?

Back-translation is perhaps the most widely used technique to detect item bias in surveys, i.e. when some items in a test might function differently for different groups in a study (Brislin 1970, 1980; Geisinger 1994; Harkness 2003; Lin *et al.* 2005; Plake and Hoover 1979). In short, using the back-translation method means that one person first translates the text from the source language to the target language and after this, another person independently back-translates the documents from the target language to their source language (for a definition see Geisinger 1994, 306). This process helps the researchers to compare and check the accuracy and equivalence of the translation based on the discrepancies that are found. Discrepancies and problems that are identified can also be negotiated between the two bilingual translators. In the YARG project, however, we implemented a more rigorous process in the form of the double and back-translation process. This means that one uses two independent and parallel translations and that the researchers have even better opportunities to assess the quality of received translations and select the "best" version (Hambleton 1993, 1994; Harkness 2003; van de Vijver and Hambleton 1996).

In the case of West Bengal, this means that the YARG researchers in Finland commissioned two professional translators in Kolkata ("A" and "B") to translate the 101 FQS statements into Bengali. The two translations that we received were then assessed by an expert team that also negotiated a third version that combined terms, expressions and phrases from the two Bengali versions. The new so-called consensus version produced by the expert team was then independently translated back to English by two translators and a second round of assessment and negotiation was conducted in order to arrive at the final version to be used in the YARG project. The expert team consisted of the Indian co-investigator and partner Professor Ruby Sain, the Indian research assistants Mallarika Sarkar and Sohini Ray, and the project member Måns Broo from Finland. All members had linguistic competence in Bengali, including knowledge of the cultural and religious context, as well as in English. A minor cognitive validation of the final version could be done in the form of test interviews with the Bengali version.

In all translation processes conducted as part of the YARG project we could see that not even the most rigorous translation process provides a highway to a final version. Rather, a well-planned translation process can at its best lay bare problems that are often hidden or subtle. Our experience indicates that translating vocabulary central to the study of religions is often marked by a range of biases related, for instance, to the knowledge, cultural experience, sense of belonging and attitudes of the translators. Despite all the efforts put into translating the FQS-set, this remains a challenging project. The particular expressions still need to be generalised for a variety of different contexts. The double and back-translation process provides a higher degree of sensitivity to subtle ambiguities and potential problems, but the role of expert teams was crucial to our project (see also Paloutzian *et al.* 2021, 433–4).

One of the major issues dealt with by the expert team in the translation process was that of what type of Bengali to use. Generally, it has been pointed out that a back-translation process might result in too literal a translation (Douglas and Craig 2007). This was evident in how one translator in general had used a very technical, Sanskritic Bengali. While the translation in this case was mostly accurate and correct, this type of Bengali made the statements very long and difficult to understand for the regular respondent. Going through the statements one by one, the team therefore often opted for the simpler versions of the other translator. Nevertheless, in many cases, elements from both translations were combined into the consensus translation. The ambition to produce a translation with multi-cultural validity therefore requires modesty even when we look at this from the horizon of one case such as the Bengali translation, which we will do next.

Observations on the Bengali Translation

The research data from India were gathered in the state of West Bengal. Having more than 91 million inhabitants (as of 2011), West Bengal is one of the most populous states of India. While Hindus at 70.54 per cent make up the majority in the state, according to the latest Census of India (Government of India 2011), Muslims comprise 27.01 per cent of the population, making them a large minority. Among the smaller religious minorities, Christians (0.72 per cent) and Buddhists (0.31 per cent) are the most noteworthy. The same census data show the literacy rate of West Bengal to be 77.08 per cent, higher than the national rate of 74.04 per cent.

The capital of West Bengal is Kolkata (Calcutta), often called (particularly by its inhabitants) the cultural capital of India. Nevertheless, West Bengal is predominantly an agricultural economy. To capture this diversity, our local partner Professor Ruby Sain (then of Jadavpur University) arranged for the interviews to be collected among students at three universities in West Bengal: Jadavpur University in metropolitan Kolkata, the semi-urban University of Kalyani in Nadia and Gaur Banga University in rural Malda. While this does not make the material representative of all young university students in West Bengal, let alone India as a whole, it contributes to variation in the data. Most of the metropolitan students interviewed self-identified as Hindus, while many of the rural students held themselves to be Muslims (for more on the Muslim sample, see Broo et al. 2019).

Data from the FQS part of our mixed methods allowed us to identify eight distinct ways of being secular, religious or spiritual in the Indian sample. This number is greater than in any other case in the YARG study and accounts for the significant diversity in India (Nynäs et al. 2021). These subjective worldviews (also called "prototypes") crossed religious boundaries that are taken for granted (see Chapter 5, this volume). This indicates that the Bengali version of the FQS succeeded in what it was intended to do: it allowed the respondents to make sense of and present their worldviews during the interviews and in ways that provided greater depth of information than simply placing them into old classificatory schemes.

Despite the diversity we came across in the study, we will below make extensive use of the dichotomy between Hindu and Muslim. There are two reasons for this. Firstly, while very seldom identifying with any "religious group" or "institution", the interviewees still use the categories of "Hindu" and "Muslim" for themselves in a matter-of-fact way, identifying with one or the other. Secondly, the two groups differed from each other in several important ways. Most of the Muslims in the sample belonged to rural Malda, while most of the Hindus were from metropolitan Kolkata. Muslims also ranked both their own and their parents' religiosity significantly higher than did Hindus. One of the present authors has studied these issues in more depth elsewhere (Broo *et al.* 2019).

For studying issues of translation and conceptual correspondence, West Bengal provided an excellent context, as besides many university students being fluent in both English and Bengali, both the majority Hindus and the minority Muslims speak the same Bengali language. Nevertheless, the two groups use very different words for many of the religious terms of the FQS instrument used within the project. For the word "salvation" (FQS22, FQS38), for example, Hindus might use the Sanskritic *mokṣa* (মোক্ষ, liberation), while Muslims might prefer the Arabic *jānnāt* (জানাত, paradise). Which of these concepts should then be used in the translation?

Both of the FQS translators were Bengali Hindus from Kolkata, who perhaps unreflectingly used the Hindu, Sanskritic terms often taken to be "standard Bengali" in West Bengal. After all, approximately 28 per cent of Bengali words are direct loanwords (তৎসম) from Sanskrit, but when it comes to technical terms of religion and philosophy, the percentage is much higher (Chatterji 2012, 108). In comparison with this, "Musalmānī Bengali", which uses words of Persian and Arabic origin, is for example in Suniti Kumar Chatterji's classic *Origin and Development of the Bengali Language* (2012 [1926]), held to be "rather artificial" (Chatterji 2012, 211) and the around 2000 Bengali words of Persian or Arabic origin are considered a "foreign element" in the language (Chatterji 2012, 208). Both translators therefore proposed *mokṣa* for "salvation", a choice that eventually passed into the consensus translation.

Now, it is doubtful whether *mokṣa* and *jānnāt* according to Hindu and Muslim scholars denote the same idea – but the same applies to the supposedly neutral English "salvation" of the FQS-set, which carries the connotation of being saved by an external agent not found in either the Hindu or the Muslim term. Nevertheless, as with many other Sanskritic terms in the FQS-set, Muslim interviewees (e.g. YINMS001, YINMS032) did not raise any questions around the term *mokṣa* but implicitly translated it into *jānnāt*. The reason for this was of course the familiarity these students had with the Hindu term, a familiarity gleaned from contact with the language of the Hindu majority through university studies, friends, neighbours and so on. This exemplifies on the one hand the important ability of respondents to engage in a process of understanding and trying to make sense of what they encounter. Linguistic and cultural boundaries are not definite. On the other hand, we can see how this everyday process of understanding is formed by minority and majority positions at the same time. This means that power relations in society affect how certain concepts are reinforced.

Another example of a contentious term of the FQS is "the divine", generally intended as a neutral term for "God", "the transcendent" or the like (FQS19, FQS36, FQS39, FQS41, FQS45, FQS49, FQS78, FQS88, FQS53 and FQS85). The English "divine" comes into late Middle English via Old French both from the Latin "divus" and "divinus", something that accounts for the word "divine" also meaning "to foresee the future" or "discover something supernaturally" when used as a verb (Lexico 2019a). In the Bengali FQS translation, this "the divine" was by both translators generally rendered as *īśvara* (ঈশ্বর). The Bengali word is again borrowed from the Sanskrit, where the identical word is usually understood to derive from the verbal root √*īś*, to own, to dispose of, to be master of, to rule, etc. (Monier-Williams 1995, 171). *Īśvara* thus has less of the transcendent, inscrutable sense of the English and more of an active, immanent meaning, as *īśvara* both in Sanskrit and Bengali also can refer to a worldly king.

Even when indicating some kind of superhuman entity, the exact meaning of *īśvara* varies between different Hindu schools of thought, but it is never used as the name of any specific deity (see e.g. Shastri 1935). Today, *īśvara* is therefore routinely used as a "neutral", religiously and denominationally non-specified word for "the divine" in West Bengal, both by Hindus and Christians. The use of the word *īśvara* to translate the English and Christian "God" into Bengali has a colonial history and stems from the efforts of the pioneering Serampore Baptist missionaries, in particular William Carey (1761-1834), who used the term in his Bengali Bible translation (1808 and 1818). The word *īśvara* is used for the Christian God in 34 Indian languages, compared with 15 Indian languages using the similarly Sanskrit-derived *deva* (Richard 2016, 12). While Bengali Muslims might prefer the Persian *khodā* (খোদা) for their God, Muslims have on occasion used *īśvara* for Allah at least from the late sixteenth century (Eaton 1985, 114). We can thus expect the term *īśvara* not to cause much confusion and the interviews bear that out, as none of the interviewees expressed any problems with it.

While both translators generally agreed on the term *īśvara*, the translator with the more Sanskritic style (B) used *param brahma* (পরম ব্রহ্ম,

highest Brahman) for "the divine" in one case (FQS88). For consistency's sake and as this was felt to be too Vedantic and Hindu, *īśvara* became the consensus translation here as well. In another case (FQS19), this translator had chosen *nirguṇ daivaśakti* (নির্গুণ দৈবশক্তি, qualityless divine power), which was rejected on the same grounds. However, here a mistake was made. The statement in question reads in English "Understands and relates to the divine as feminine", something that we had expected to find support for among the famously goddess-worshipping Hindus of West Bengal. As detailed elsewhere (Chapter 5, this volume), it turned out that in the end neither Muslims nor Hindus identified with the statement. This may in part have been occasioned by the word *īśvara*. While Bengali does not have a grammatical gender, the word *īśvara* is masculine in Sanskrit and carries masculine connotations in Bengali as well. This may have led the respondents to read the statement as something like "Sees the Lord as a woman", which is far from what was intended. The potential contradiction in terms at work here might have made it difficult for the respondents to perceive the intent of this statement.

In three FQS statements, "divine" was used as an adjective. One statement speaks about "moments of intense divine, mysterious, or supernatural presence" (FQS10) while statement FQS44 focuses on a "divine or universal luminous element within him- or herself". As the word *īśvara* cannot be used adjectivally, the translators chose in the first case *daivik* (দৈবিক) and *daiva* (দৈব) from the Sanskrit *deva* mentioned above, and in the second case, *atīndriya* (অতীন্দ্রিয়), again a Sanskrit word meaning "beyond the senses".

The last of these three statements, "Deeply identifies with some holy figure, either human or divine" (FQS66) proved difficult. Translator A simplified it into "identifies with *īśvara* or a great person" (ঈশ্বর বা মহা-পুরুষের সঙ্গে একাত্ম বোধ করেন), while translator B rendered it cumbersomely as "deeply identifies with someone of pure mind and behaviour, either human or divine" (পবিত্রচেতা কোনও চরিত্রের সঙ্গে, মনবীয় হোক বা ঈশ্বরীয়), where the adjectival "divine", *īśvarīya*, is derived from the same *īśvara*. Again, in the interest of keeping the translation concise and avoiding burdening it with too many Sanskrit terms, the first version became the consensus translation with the addition of "deeply". This was a clear mistake, as the statement was not supposed to ask about identifying with "the divine" alone but with any "divine" person. This also led to the dropping of the similarly contentious English word "holy" – used in the FQS-set only in this place – which translator B had expanded into "someone of pure mind and behaviour" from the commonly used *pavitra* (পবিত্র, pure, holy) for "holy". Translator A probably justified dropping that term in that both *īśvara* and *mahāpuruṣa* (মহাপুরুষ, great person or saint) are intrinsically holy. Nevertheless, the ensuing translation was not very close to the English version.

In general, the English "the divine" thus became *īśvara* in the Bengali translation, a term consistently back-translated as "God". Do the words "the divine" and *īśvara* really carry the same meaning, then? Interestingly, the FQS-set does use the word "God" once, in the statement "Feels distant from God or the divine" (FQS45). The two terms presented the translators with a dilemma. Is "or" in the English supposed to be taken inclusively or exclusively? In other words, is the person feeling a distance from "God", who is also known as "the divine", or is he or she feeling a distance from either "God" or "the divine"? Translator A took the first road and conflated both terms into *īśvara* while B followed the second in proposing '*īśvara* or the power of *īśvara*' (ঈশ্বর বা ঈশ্বরশক্তি). The consensus here again followed translator A.

Another FQS term close to "the divine" is "the ultimate". As before, the English term stems from a Latin word, *ultimatus*, the past participle of *ultimare*, "to come to an end" (Lexico 2019b). This term is used as a noun only once in the FQS-set (9, "Thinks about the ultimate as a life force or creative energy rather than a supernatural being") probably as an oversight, as "the divine" would have served the same purpose. For "the ultimate", translator A at any rate used *param brahma* (পরম ব্রহ্ম), while translator B used *cūḍānta satya* (চূড়ান্ত সত্য, topmost truth). As the first term was deemed too Vedantic and Hindu and the second too technical, the team chose to stick with *īśvara* for the consensus translation. If "the ultimate" was intended to be something different from "the divine", this was a mistake.

Finally, and importantly, as the interviewees' understandings of these terms will be discussed in more detail below, both translators generally rendered "religion" and "spirituality" with the Sanskritic *dharma* (ধর্ম) and *adhyātmikatā* (অধ্যাত্মিকতা), respectively, keeping to their general tendency of choosing terms from linguistic usage of the majority Hindu population. Translator B used *paramārthika* (পরমার্থিক, relating to a higher truth) for »spiritual« in three cases (FQS86, FQS97, FQS98), perhaps because the term was used adjectivally in these statements (spiritual path, spiritual community and spiritual reason). For the sake of consistency, the consensus translation nevertheless uses *adhyātmika* in these cases as well.

While routinely critiqued (e.g. Bloch *et al.* 2010), using the word *dharma* for the English "religion" in Bengali has a fairly long history. Like *īśvara*, it was first populariesd by the Baptist missionaries at Serampore, who chose it as a key term in their Bible translation project at the end of the eighteenth century. William Halbfass (1990, 340–2) documents some of its history; here it suffices to say that using the term *dharma* for "religion" soon became an essential part of Hindu self-expression and remains so today. Despite scholarly frustration with the term, none of the interviewees, Hindu or Muslim, voiced any critique of it. Still, it might have been better if the corresponding Muslim terms such as the Arabic-origin *dīn* (দীন, judgement, custom or religion) and *rūhāniyāt* (রুহানিয়াত) had been given as alternatives.

Besides showing how heavily dependent the "religious" Bengali language in West Bengal is on Sanskrit terms, all of these examples show the kind of negotiations behind finding terms deemed to correspond in a sufficient degree with the English version. They also show how despite using a time-consuming and costly process of translation, mistakes were made, and some of them passed on into the final translation. Conducting a cognitive validation and testing the translation with a pilot study might have caught some, but such a pilot study has to be extensive enough. Our validation did not raise these issues.

The Bengali terms that were supposed to be "religiously neutral" were in actual fact taken from a Hindu (and, to some extent, Christian) background. Not having a person within the group working out the consensus translation with a sound knowledge of the "religious" terminology of Bengali Muslims was a weakness. Forcing terms from the Hindu majority upon the Muslim minority where they have their own, as in the cases of "salvation" or "the divine" discussed above, could be seen as a kind of linguistic colonialism or domination, as discussed by Gayatri Chakravorty Spivak, Tejaswini Niranjana, Eric Cheyfitz and others (Bassnett 2013, 5). Using different FQS-sets for people from different religious backgrounds might have made sense but this would again have required us to define people in advance and one of the main ideas behind the FQS was to break free from the "world religions" paradigm (Cotter and Robertson 2016; see also Chapter 1, this volume).

Interestingly, this also mirrors the case with the English original, which is influenced by a Judaeo-Christian worldview and cannot itself be said to have been perfect. The difficulty of translating terms such as "the divine" or "the ultimate" into Bengali sheds light on the English terms as well. "The divine" may sound more neutral or inclusive than "God" to a scholar of religious studies, but it is questionable whether "the divine" and "the ultimate" are terms that the university students really would have used themselves. And if they had, what would they have meant by them? The concept "transcendent" can be problematic for similar reasons. Identifying a concept with universal legacy for cross-cultural use is not necessarily always possible, especially if one needs to meet everyday discourses. Yet, we have previously underlined that interpretative activity and how people manage to make sense of the translation constitute relevant aspects of exploring issues of translation and cross-cultural implementation. To find out more about this, let us now move on to see how the English and Bengali terms mentioned above were used and interpreted in the interviews, focusing on the two terms that were found to elicit most comments, that is, "religion" and "spirituality".

Interpreting "Religious" Terminology in the FQS Interviews

As mentioned above, the Muslim interviewees within the West Bengali sample in general had no problems in understanding the Sanskritic, Hindu terminology of the FQS. In this sense the translation can be said to have functioned well. That is not to say that these Muslim students did not also distance themselves from any aspects of Hinduism (Broo *et al.* 2019). They particularly singled out the ideas of female divinities and reincarnation for criticism, sometimes explicitly as Hindu beliefs not applicable to "us". One student (YINMS010) had the following to say about the doctrine of reincarnation (পুনর্জন্ম):

> Yes, Hindu religion maintains this, but our religion, that is, our Muslim religion does not believe in reincarnation and if I believed in it, it would mean that I am a deviant.

Even if the notion of reincarnation is foreign to this student, the word itself is sufficiently intelligible to create a reaction to it.

That the translations generally worked does not, of course, mean that there were no problems; it is helpful to note that in fact there were different kinds of problems. Issues about linguistic nuances may occur when the correspondence between the source language and the target language is strong and it is a matter of choosing between two good wordings. Other problems might be about conceptual correspondence, i.e. problems with finding a proper concept in the target language or the lack of such concepts. The latter can often be related to situations when cultural differences present obstacles. Yet cultural differences can also occur when there is no particular difficulty in the act of translation as such, but a potential translation more or less lacks meaning and proper correspondence in the target culture.

Sometimes, the difference between a majority and minority status made seemingly simple statements ambiguous. For example, a statement about the "religion of one's nation" (FQS46) was understood by many Bengali Muslims (e.g. YINMS004, YINMS032) to refer to one's own "people", so that the religion of the "nation" of these interviewees is Islam, despite Hinduism of course being the majority religion of India. Here, the minority position of Islam in West Bengal and India as a whole makes sticking to the religion of one's community particularly important (see Broo et al. 2019). This is also a good example of how the concept of "religion" in actual practice very often is contextual, that is, to some extent conditioned by other factors supporting or undermining it, such as the minority status here.

Furthermore, even the most careful translation can be misunderstood, poorly explained or simply understood in a way the translators or the research team did not intend. We find several such examples in the Indian YARG material. One Muslim interviewee (YINMS013) understood the statement "holding that the world's religious traditions point to a common truth" to mean that all the world's religions ultimately point to Islam, the only true religion. Another one (YINMS010) understood "views religion as a never-ending quest" (FQS13) as referring to her boundless faith in Allah.

Sometimes such interpretations are unintentional. Another Muslim informant misunderstood the word "infallible" (অভ্রান্ত ... নয়) in the statement "Considers religious scriptures to be of human authorship – inspired, perhaps, but not infallible" (FQS18). When asked why she had strongly agreed with this statement, she replied, "I believe that our religious scripture is created by our Allah, our Moulobi [Master], so it is not infallible" – clearly giving the word its opposite meaning.

Such instances are not strictly speaking examples of translation issues but rather of interpretation. While the subsequent interviews show exactly how these individuals understood these statements, such idiosyncratic interpretations are nevertheless problematic in the context of the prototypes created by the FQS interviewees, as these persons scored high on statements intended to measure something other than what they represented for these persons. The translation was, in other words, theoretically speaking correct, but the particular linguistic style chosen was too high, even considering that the people studied were university students. These cases of misunderstandings highlight one of the weaknesses of the FQS method, that is, that it relies on a very high level of literacy. If the FQS were to be used on less literate people, it would have to be rewritten in more colloquial language – not only in Bengali, but in English and other languages too.

As we saw above, Fitzgerald (2007, 99) and others hold that "religion" is best understood as having a shifting content in relation to other unstable and contested categories. One such category is "spirituality". Let us therefore now move from general comments on the use of the FQS translation in the West Bengal context to these two categories. The distinction between an external "religion" and an internal "spirituality" is often taken for granted in many Western contexts (Gottlieb 2013), but how are they articulated in the FQS interviews in West Bengal?

Most of the urban interviewees at Jadavpur University are perfectly fluent in English, having gone to English-medium schools since their childhood. Many of them preferred to use the English rather than the Bengali FQS-set and also spoke English when afterwards interviewed by one of the two (Bengali) research assistants. Nevertheless, some of those who opted for the Bengali version (YINSR008, YINSR041, YINSR052) still preferred to use the English word "religion". Notably, one interviewee (YINSR052) used the English "God" when speaking of some kind of transcendental being in general, but the Bengali *ṭhākur* (ঠাকুর) for the divinity she worshipped herself.

Also, just as the word "religion" often carries negative connotations in the West, so it may do in West Bengal. After speaking at some length about the worship, recitations and other rituals that she performs, one interviewee (YINMS092) was asked if she considers herself religious (ধার্মিক). She replied, "Religious! I worship God because I like doing it. Not that I am religious or anything".

When we move on to look at the understanding of the term "spirituality" in the YARG interviews, an interesting pattern emerges. Most of the rural informants of the West Bengali sample – particularly the Muslims – found it hard to differentiate between the terms "religion" and "spirituality" (e.g. YINMS058). As one Muslim interviewee said (YINMS031):

> P: A difference between religion and spirituality? There is no such difference.
> I: So, are they the same?
> P: Yes.

For this person, to differentiate between the two terms was not only unnecessary; it was downright wrong. After all, from a Muslim perspective, if "true religion" is "submission to God" (e.g. Sonn 2016, 21), why would the inner self (*adhyātma*) not be part of that? Rather than contrasting "religion" with "spirituality", many of these Muslim respondents connected "religion" with social life. As one person (YINMS010) said:

> We participate in religious activities since we live in a society. It is necessary for us to follow the social norms and regulations; otherwise, we may be identified as irreligious.

It is common that followers of minority religions tend to safeguard their religious identity by laying greater emphasis on their religious practice

(Anthony *et al.* 2007, 116; Broo *et al.* 2019). Many Muslim interviewees expressed a strong sense of commitment to the religion of their community (e.g. YINMS004, YINMS010, YINMS013), but this "religion" was generally articulated in terms of religious practice. One woman (YINMS032) sums up Islamic practice for women in the following way:

> For girls, four things are essential, that is, *salāt* [prayer], *roja* [fasting during Ramadan], *purdah* [wearing the veil outside] and to care for your husband. If a woman performs all these duties, she will definitely go to *jānnāt*.

Many of the interviewees speak about these practices and particularly prayer, some reporting that they perform all five of them daily (YINMS013, YINMS031), others expressing a feeling of guilt for not being able to do so (YINMS001, YINMS010, YINMS013). While clearly identifying as Muslims, two interviewees (YINMS004, YINM032) did not wish to call themselves "religious" since they were not able to keep up the practices they considered required, particularly the daily prayers.

However, when we look at the interviews with the urban students, we find a different situation altogether. Many of these interviewees reflected on the term spirituality, though not always coming to the same conclusions. One woman (YINSR006) had this to say:

> I don't know what to say, actually. We believe in a divine soul, or I don't know, at least I do, I do believe that there is a God and we are spiritually connected to him, and it is this connection which keeps the faith going. I think spirituality has more to do with belief in oneself, in the divine – that's what I believe.

For this woman, "spirituality" seems to be the underlying power of "faith" or "religion", a belief in the divine soul or spirit, and its connection to the divine. What "religion" then means is unfortunately not articulated by this person, but the following informant (YINSR071) does spell out what seems to be the implied idea here as well:

> Religion and spirituality – they're the same thing apart from the fact that religion is more of the practices, and spirituality is more of the belief in that power. There's a slight difference, but if I have to make a difference then this is it. Religion is more of the practices, you are doing it because it is somewhat ingrained in you, more of a tradition, but spirituality is much more personal. Religion I don't think is that much personal. Sometimes you do certain practices because you are being told by your parents or your grandparents, but spirituality is personal where you know why you are doing a particular thing.

In other words, "religion" is connected to socially transmitted practices and traditions, while "spirituality" is the personal, inner belief that underlies those practices. This is probably why this person, while articulating this difference between the two, still seemed to see religion and spirituality as essentially parts of the same continuum.

While some of the Hindu informants (e.g. YINSR052, YINMS092) did connect "religion" to religious practice, as in the Muslim case above, more common here was to connect the term with family, customs and festivities, in particular with the Durga Puja festival so popular in contemporary West Bengal (Fell McDermott 2011). "Religion" thus becomes a kind of cultural heritage. As one person (YINSR052) said:

> For many years in our house, Ma Durga and goddess Kali are being [regularly] worshipped. What are termed everyday rituals are also being followed by us. It is kind of a heritage which has been passed on. I mean, my grandmother, my mother, me and my sister, we all follow this tradition and worship god. It's like family values and tradition. Today, there is Purnima Puja [full moon worship] at my relatives' place. It's like an entire thing actually.

Generally, such "religion" is described in positive terms in the interviews, but not always. The theme of "religion" being external imposition is articulated more forcefully by yet another young urban student (YINSR075):

> I think there is a difference between spirituality and religion because religion is imposed, because after one is born, one is told that "you are Hindu", "you are Muslim" or "you are Christian". But spirituality is something inner, like you can feel peaceful or you can feel bliss while listening to music or doing something creative. That's it.

Here "spirituality" is divorced from "religion" altogether; it is not just the inner justification for religious action, it is an inner feeling not necessarily connected with "religion" at all. One young woman (YINSR056) followed the same lines when she felt spirituality to be "a positive vibe", echoing the "spiritual but not religion" trend so common among young people in the West (e.g. Fuller 2001).

While "spirituality" thus seems to be a broader category than "religion", in some cases, an underlying materialist worldview makes even "spirituality" an unnecessary term. After describing religion in purely social, external terms, one interviewee has this to say about "spirituality" (YINSR062):

> I wouldn't be thinking about spirituality much. I would rather think about the energy that is present in nature, something like quantum physics. So it is not spirituality much. There are certain vibrations in the society, but I would not call them spirituality, rather I would call them science.

What we see here, then, are various approaches to the distinction between "religion" and "spirituality", from the same to some type of difference, or that either or both terms are irrelevant.

The difference between "religion" and "spirituality" is thus an excellent example of the result of the translingual approach described above. While various notions of an inner spirit or self (*ātmā*), different from both body and mind, are very much part of traditional Hinduism (e.g. Bon 1963), the idea of contrasting an inner spirituality from external duty or religion is a contribution traceable back to Unitarian missionaries in colonial Kolkata, but one that is perfectly intelligible to most educated Hindus today in West Bengal (King 1999). Perhaps particularly when the Sanskritic words for these terms are used, this contrast is much less familiar to Muslims of the same West Bengal.

Concluding Discussion

This chapter has exemplified the methodological value that is intrinsic to a translation process. It is not merely instrumental to a study but it can provide significant data for further investigations of relevance to the subject matter, in this case the cross-cultural conceptual comparison in the study of religions. The translation of the Faith Q-set from English to eleven different target languages in the YARG project presented a major challenge. Concepts related to the field of "religion" are formed by cross-cultural differences; they are shifting in content and unstable. This is evident from our examination of the translation process into Bengali. Not even a rigorous double and back translation was enough to produce a definitive translation, and an expert team with strong local knowledge was central to achieving high quality in the process. The expert team contributed with linguistic, conceptual and contextual competence required in the process. Yet, this context formed by different ethnic and religious groups, and historical tradition, show that linguistic equivalence cannot always be achieved.

For instance, interviewees in our FQS study sometimes questioned particular words or concepts. Key terms here were "religion" and "spirituality". The Muslim respondents generally associated "religion" with both personal and social ritual performance, often explicitly linked with maintaining social conformity within their minority group. The Hindus also connected religion with social life, but even more so with ritual behaviour and with maintaining their cultural heritage. Further, while the predominantly rural Muslim interviewees generally saw no clear distinction between "religion" and "spirituality", the urban interviewees usually did, generally associating "religion" with something external and "spirituality" with an internal faith or feeling.

On that note, we can conclude that there is not always a way to overcome cross-cultural differences in a translation process. In contrast to the ideal of achieving correspondence in cross-cultural studies we would rather speak of levels of quality in the translation work and that a translation can be more or less usable within certain circumstances and target groups. A target group can in itself incorporate significant differences. A process that ensures the best quality will be laborious and needs to involve, in addition to several translators, experts and representatives of the target groups and context. However, the need to encompass many variations and nuances in a translation risks pushing the linguistic expressions to a level of sophistication that does not necessarily echo the particular viewpoints and discourse of relevance for the specific target groups. If a translation becomes too distanced from a real-life discourse, it may end up hard to comprehend, inviting participants to play a guessing game heavily affected by cultural contextual aspects or, alternatively, making them lose interest in the process.

On another note, however, we wish to underline the possibility of comprehension across cultural and linguistical boundaries. Our observations indicate that cross-cultural correspondence is not only about something that is there or not and that we need to uncover; rather, cross-cultural correspondence is produced as a part of a historical situation. The fact that "foreign" terminology presented an obstacle that could be negotiated in the interviews points to the relevance of the translingual approach we have relied on in this chapter. It shifts our focus from the dichotomy of commensurability or incommensurability related to contextual or linguistic differences and gives attention to the production of comprehensibility through historical contact and interaction.

Despite apparent cultural differences, the ways in which the terms "religion" and "spirituality" were interpreted in urban West Bengal came close to how the terms are often defined within a Western context. This is, of course, not a coincidence, but a result of translinguistic processes and how "religious" words are shaped, used and understood from a Western point of view. Colonial structures and minority–majority relations affect how cross-cultural comprehension and correspondence emerges. We also observed similar problems on a micro-level when examining how the translation process had been set up, indirectly reinforcing local power structures and an imbalance in representation. Nonetheless, the active, reflective and imaginative interpretation that could arise in the interview situations entailed the possibility of establishing a position where understanding could take place, in contrast to the idea of the incommensurability of different languages.

Dr Måns Broo is lecturer in the study of religions at Åbo Akademi University, Finland, and an associate research fellow at the Oxford Centre for Hindu Studies. His research interests include historical and contemporary forms of yoga, Gaudiya Vaishnavism and globalised Hinduism. His most recent monograph is a Finnish translation of the Shandilya- and Narada-bhakti-sutra (Gaudeamus, 2021).

Dr Marcus Moberg is professor in the study of religions at Åbo Akademi University. His main research interests include the sociology of religion, religion and media, and discourse theory and analysis in the study of religion. He acted as senior researcher in the Centre of Excellence Young Adults and Religion in a Global Perspective at ÅAU (2015–19). Recent publications include *Religion, Discourse, and Society* (Routledge, 2021) and *Digital Media, Young Adults and Religion: An International Perspective* (co-edited with Sofia Sjö; Routledge, 2020).

Dr Peter Nynäs is professor in the study of religions at Åbo Akademi University (ÅAU) and dean of the Faculty of Arts, Psychology and Theology. He is director and PI of the Åbo Akademi University Centre of Excellence in Research Young Adults and Religion in a Global Perspective Project (2015–19) and previously the Centre of Excellence in Research Post-secular Culture and a Changing Religious Landscape in Finland Project (2010–14). Among the books he has edited are *On the Outskirts of "the Church": Diversities, Fluidities, and New Spaces of Religion in Finland* (with R. Illman and T. Martikainen, LIT-Verlag, 2015), *Religion, Gender, and Sexuality in Everyday Life* (with A. Yip, Ashgate, 2012), and *The Diversity of Worldviews among Young Adults: Contemporary (Non)Religiosity and Spirituality through the Lens of an International Mixed Method Study* (with A. Keysar, J. Kontala, B.-W. Kwaku Golo, M. Lassander, M. Shterin, S. Sjö and P. Stenner; Springer, 2021).

Dr Mallarika Sarkar Das is the assistant professor and MPhil coordinator of the Department of Sociology, University of Calcutta. She served as research assistant for the Åbo Akademi University Centre of Excellence Young Adults and Religion in a Global Perspective Project (2015–19) in India. Her area of specialisation is social gerontology, and her main research interests include the sociology of ageing, urban sociology and social exclusion. Dr Sarkar has developed 36 modules (e-content) on religion and healing under the UGC-MHRD e-PG Pathshala project entitled "Comparative Study of Religions", and acted as Co-I in a UGC-UPE Project entitled "Situating Look East: the Cultural Politics of Connected History".

Sohini Ray has been a teaching associate in the Indian Institute of Management, Joka. She has received her MA and MPhil in sociology from Jadavpur University and graduation from St Xavier's College, Kolkata. She served as research assistant for the Åbo Akademi University Centre of Excellence Young Adults and Religion in a Global Perspective Project (2015-19) in India.

References

Anthony, Francis-Vincent, Chris Hermans and Carl Sterkens. 2007. "Religious Practice and Religious Socialization: Comparative Research among Christian, Muslim and Hindu Students in Tamilnadu, India". *Journal of Empirical Theology* 20(1): 100-28.

Asad, Talal. 1993. *Genealogies of Religion: Discipline and Reasons of Power in Christianity and Islam*. Baltimore, MD: Johns Hopkins University Press.

Asad, Talal. 2003. *Formations of the Secular: Christianity, Islam, Modernity*. Stanford, CA: Stanford University Press.

Balagangadhara, S. N. 2005. *The Heathen in his Blindness ... Asia, the West, and the Dynamics of Religion* (2nd edn). Delhi: Manohar Publishers.

Barrett, Tim H. and Franscesca Tarocco. 2011. "Terminology and Religious Identity: Buddhism and the Genealogy of the Term Zongjiao". In *Dynamics in the History of Religions between Asia and Europe: Encounters, Notions, and Comparative Perspectives*, ed. Volkhard Krech and Marion Steinicke, 307-20. Leiden: Brill.

Bassnett, Susan. 2013. *Translation Studies* (4th edn). Abingdon: Routledge.

Bloch, Esther, Marianne Keppens and Rajaram Hegde. 2010. *Rethinking Religion in India. The Colonial Construction of Hinduism*. Abingdon: Routledge.

Bon, Swami B. H. 1963. *Jiva-atma or Finite Self: The Concept of the Individual Finite Self in Twelve Different Systems of Philosophy*. Vrindaban: Institute of Oriental Philosophy.

Brislin, Richard W. 1970. "Back Translation for Cross-cultural Research". *Journal of Cross-cultural Psychology* 1(3): 185-216.

Brislin, Richard W. 1980. "Translation and Content Analysis of Oral and Written Materials". In *Handbook of Cross-cultural Psychology*, ed. Harry C. Triandis and J. W. Berry, 389-444. Boston, MA: Allyn & Bacon.

Broo, Måns, Sawsan Kheir and Mallarika Sarkar. 2019. "Two Cases of Religious Socialization among Minorities". *Religion* 49(2): 221-39.

Chakrabarty, Dipesh. 2000. *Provincializing Europe: Postcolonial Thought and Historical Difference*. Princeton, NJ: University of Princeton Press.

Chakrabarty, Dipesh. 2005. "Legacies of Bandung: Decolonisation and the Politics of Culture". *Economic and Political Weekly* 40(46): 4812-18. Retrieved from www.jstor.org/stable/4417389. Accessed 19 May 2018.

Chatterji, Suniti Kumar. 2012 [1926]. *The Origins and Development of the Bengali Language*. New Delhi: Rupa & Co.

Cotter, Christopher R., and David G. Robertson. 2016. "Preface". In *After World Religions: Reconstructing Religious Studies*, ed. Christopher R. Cotter and David G. Robertson, vii–viii. London: Routledge.

Douglas, Susan P., and Samuel Craig. 2007. "Collaborative and Iterative Translation: An Alternative Approach to Back Translation". *Journal of International Marketing* 15: 30–43.

Eaton, Richard M. 1985. "Approaches to the Study of Conversion to Islam in India". In *Approaches to Islam in Religious Studies*, ed. Richard C. Martin, 106–23. Oxford: Oneworld Publishing.

Fell McDermott, Rachel. 2011. *Revelry, Rivalry, and Longing for the Goddesses of Bengal: The Fortunes of Hindu Festivals*. New York: Columbia University Press.

Fitzgerald, Timothy. 2007. *Discourse on Civility and Barbarity: A Critical History of Religion and Related Categories*. Oxford: Oxford University Press.

Fuller, Robert C. 2001. *Spiritual but Not Religious: Understanding Unchurched America*. New York: Oxford University Press.

Geisinger, Kurt F. 1994. "Cross-cultural Normative Assessment: Translation and Adaptation Issues Influencing the Normative Interpretation of Assessment Instruments". *Psychological Assessment* 6(4): 304–12.

Gergen, Kenneth. 1999. *An Invitation to Social Construction*. London: Sage.

Gottlieb, Roger S. 2013. *Spirituality: What it Is and Why it Matters*. New York: Oxford University Press.

Government of India. 2011. "Census of India". Retrieved from https://censusindia.gov.in. Accessed 20 March 2021.

Halbfass, William. 1990. *India and Europe: An Essay in Philosophical Understanding*. Delhi: Motilal Banarsidass.

Hambleton, Ronald K. 1993. "Translating Achievement Tests for Use in Cross-National Studies". *European Journal of Psychological Assessment* 9(1): 57–65.

Hambleton, Ronald K. 1994. "The Rise and Fall of Criterion-Referenced Measurement?" *Educational Measurement: Issues and Practice* 13(4): 21–6. https://doi.org/10.1111/j.1745-3992.1994.tb00567.x

Hanneder, Jürgen. 2017. *To Edit or Not to Edit. On Textual Criticism of Sanskrit Works*. Pune: Aditya Prakashan.

Harkness, Janet A. 2003. "Questionnaire Translation". In *Cross-cultural Survey Methods*, ed. Janet A. Harkness, Fons van de Vijver and Peter Mohler, 35–56. New York: John Wiley & Sons.

Hermann, Adrian. 2016. "Distinctions of Religion: The Search for Equivalents of 'Religion' and the Challenge of Theorizing a 'Global Discourse of Religion'". In *Making Religion: Theory and Practice in the Discursive Study of Religion*, ed. Frans Wijsen and Kocku von Stuckrad, 97–124. Leiden: Brill.

Horii, Mitsutoshi. 2016. "Critical Reflections on the Religious-Secular Dichotomy in Japan". In *Making Religion: Theory and Practice in the Discursive Study of Religion*, ed. Frans Wijsen and Kocku von Stuckrad, 260–86. Leiden: Brill.

King, Richard. 1999. *Orientalism and Religion: Post-Colonial Theory, India and "The Mystic East"*. Abingdon: Routledge.

Lambek, Michael 2014. "Recognizing Religion: Disciplinary Traditions, Epistemology, and History". *Numen* 61(2–3): 145–65.

Lexico. 2019a. "Divine". Retrieved from www.lexico.com/en/definition/divine. Accessed 11 November 2019.

Lexico. 2019b. "Ultimate". Retrieved from www.lexico.com/en/definition/ultimate. Accessed 12 November 2019.

Lin, Yi-Hsiu., Chen-Yueh Chen and Ping-Kun Chiu. 2005. "Cross-cultural Research and Back: An Overview on Issues of Cross-cultural Research and Back-Translation". *The Sports Journal* 8(4). Retrieved from https://thesportjournal.org/article/cross-cultural-research-and-back-translation/. Accessed 20 March 2021.

Liu, Lydia H. 1995. "Translingual Practice: Literature, National Culture, and Translated Modernity; China, 1900–37". Stanford, CA: Stanford University Press.

Lucy, J. A. 2015. "Sapir–Whorff Hypothesis". In *International Encyclopedia of the Social and Behavioral Sciences* (2nd edn), ed. James D. Wright, 903–6. Amsterdam: Elsevier.

Masuzawa, Tomoko. 2005. *The Invention of World Religions: Or how European universalism was preserved in the language of pluralism*. Chicago, IL: The University of Chicago Press.

McCutcheon, Russell T. 1997. *Manufacturing Religion: The Discourse on Sui Generis Religion and the Politics of Nostalgia*. Oxford: Oxford University Press.

Monier-Williams, Monier. 1995 [1899]. *A Sanskrit-English Dictionary*. Delhi: Motilal Banarsidass.

Nedostup, Rebecca. 2009. *Superstitious Regimes: Religion and the Politics of Chinese Modernity*. Cambridge, MA: Harvard University Asia Center.

Nynäs, Peter, Janne Kontala and Mika Lassander. 2021. "The Faith Q-Sort: In-Depth Assessment of Diverse Spirituality and Religiosity in 12 Countries". In *Assessing Spirituality in a Diverse World*, ed. Amy L. Ai, Paul Wink, Raymond F. Paloutzian and Kevin A. Harris, 554–73. Cham: Springer.

Paloutzian, Raymond F., Zuhâl Agilkaya-Sahin, Kay C. Bruce, Marianne Nilsen Kvande, Klara Malinakova, Luciana Fernandes Marques, Ahmad S. Musa, Marzieh Nojomi, Eyüp Ensar Öztürk, Indah Permata Putri and Suk-Kyung You. 2021. "The Spiritual Well-Being Scale (SWBS): Cross-cultural Assessment Across 5 Continents, 10 Languages, and 300 Studies". In *Assessing Spirituality in a Diverse World*, ed. Amy L. Ai, Paul Wink, Raymond F. Paloutzian and Kevin A. Harris, 413–44. Cham: Springer.

Plake, Barbara S., and H. D. Hoover. 1979. "An Analytical Method of Identifying Biased Test Items". *Journal of Experimental Education* 48(2): 153–4.

Richard, H. L. 2016. "Speaking of God in Sanskrit-Derived Vocabularies". *International Journal of Frontier Missiology* 33(1): 11–15.

Satlow, Michael L. 2005. "Disappearing Categories: Using Categories in the Study of Religion". *Method and Theory in the Study of Religion* 17: 287–98.

Schalk, Peter, ed. 2013. *Religion in Asien? Studien zur Anwendbarkeit des Religionsbegriffs*. Uppsala: Uppsala Universitet.

Seuren, Pieter A. M. 1998. *Western Linguistics: An Historical Introduction*. Hoboken, NJ: Wiley-Blackwell.

Shastri, M. D. 1935. "History of the Word 'Ishwara' and Its Meaning". In *Proceedings and Transactions of the All-India Conference* 7: 487–503.

Sonn, Tamara. 2016. *Islam: History, Religion, and Politics*. Chichester: Wiley Blackwell.

Taira, Teemu. 2016. "Discourse on 'Religion' in Organizing Social Practices: Theoretical and Practical Considerations". In *Making Religion: Theory and Practice in the Discursive Study of Religion*, ed. Frans Wijsen and Kocku von Stuckrad, 125–46. Leiden: Brill.

Tarocco, Francesca. 2008. "The Making of 'Religion' in Modern China". In *Religion, Language, and Power*, ed. Nile Green and Mary Searle-Chatterjee, 42–56. London: Routledge.

Taylor, Charles. 2016. *The Language Animal: The Full Shape of the Human Linguistic Capacity*. Cambridge, MA: The Belknap Press of Harvard University Press.

Taylor, Stephanie. 2001. "Locating and Conducting Discourse Analytic Research". In *Discourse as Data: A Guide for Analysis*, ed. Margaret Wetherell, Stephanie Taylor and Simeon T. Yates, 5–48. London: Sage.

van de Vijver, Fons, and Ronald K. Hambleton. 1996. "Translating Tests: Some Practical Guidelines". *European Psychologist* 1: 89–99.

von Stuckrad, Kocku. 2010. *Locations of Knowledge in Medieval and Early Modern Europe: Esoteric Discourse and Western Identities*. Leiden: Brill.

Wenger, Tisa. 2005. "'We Are Guaranteed Freedom': Pueblo Indians and the Category of Religion in the 1920s". *History of Religions* 45(2): 89–113.

Winzeler, Robert L. 2008. *Anthropology and Religion: What We Know, Think, and Question.* Lanham, MD: AltaMira Press.

Wolff, Philipp, and Kevin J. Holmes. 2011. "Linguistic Relativity". *Wiley Interdisciplinary Reviews: Cognitive Science* 2: 253–65.

Wulff, David M. 2019. "Prototypes of Faith: Findings with the Faith Q-Sort". *Journal for the Scientific Study of Religion* 58(3): 643–65.

– 3 –

The Cognitive Study of Religiosity and Contemporary Lived Religion

Complementarity as a Methodological Approach

SŁAWOMIR SZTAJER, RAFAEL FERNÁNDEZ HART,
BEN-WILLIE KWAKU GOLO AND SIDNEY CASTILLO

Within the cognitive science of religion, a strong case has been made for the idea that religion can be explained from a perspective of human evolution and cognition. This often relies on observations of universals across time and space, and linguistic and cultural boundaries. In this chapter, we focus on lived religion in Peru, Ghana and China; countries with a distinct history of traditional forms of religion that furthermore are present in various and complex ways. In these cultures, traditional forms of religiosity may still be present and surface in the form of emerging new or revitalised aspects of religiosities within the framework of more recent religious or secular positions. In light of such complex forms of lived religion it becomes relevant to explore the relevance of a cognitive approach to religion. To what extent can it be applied within a framework of the complexity of lived religion? This chapter on the one hand sheds light on the extent and way traditional forms of religion surface in contemporary religiosities and, on the other hand, moves on to explore the extent to which such complex configurations allow for the adaptation of observations from a cognitive study of religion. We propose a model of interpretative complementarity that differentiates between two key ways of understanding current concepts, beliefs and practices. The first points to universal cognitive mechanisms and the second to cultural and contextual factors in light of contemporary forms of lived religion.

Introduction

While the cognitive approach has been successfully applied to the study of various dimensions of religious thought and behaviour, there have been few attempts to use it in the study of lived religion. Since the cognitive science of religion focuses on the structures of religious cognition and as a result is relatively insensitive to the cultural variety of religious phenomena, it seems not to be predisposed to the study of lived religion. Particular manifestations of religiosity are explained by cognitive scientists in terms of universal cognitive mechanisms which are the product of human evolution. Similar observations can be made about neuroscience, the neurological study of religion or what is sometimes called neurotheology. However, there are several points of convergence between the study of lived religion and the cognitive sciences of religion (Sztajer and Drozdowicz 2018). One of them is the criticism of the abstract concept of religion, which was manufactured in the West, but has been widely used in cross-cultural comparisons. The other is an emphasis on actual religious thought and behaviour in contrast to normative images produced by religious traditions.

Is it possible to study lived religion within the methodological framework of the cognitive science of religion? Are there any theoretical assumptions common to the cognitive science of religion and the study of lived religion? Are the two approaches to contemporary religion mutually exclusive or can they be used as complementary? In this chapter, we attempt to answer these questions by analysing data from research on the religiosity of young adults. First, we focus on selected theoretical achievements in the cognitive science of religion. Then, we carry out a critical assessment of the cognitive approach, pointing out its limitation in the study of actual beliefs of individuals within a specific socio-cultural context. An important part of the chapter is devoted to the manifestations of lived religion taken from different cultural contexts. We conclude that despite the methodological differences between the cognitive science of religion and the study of lived religion, the former can provide valuable insights for the latter.

The cognitive science of religion is a multi-disciplinary approach to religious phenomena. Cognitive theories of religion began to evolve from cognitive science in the 1990s. However, the first article dedicated to the cognitive theory of religion was published by Stewart Guthrie in 1980 (Guthrie 1980) and then elaborated in his book *Faces in the Cloud* (Guthrie 1993). Guthrie defined religion as a kind of anthropomorphism. Religious thought is based on attributing human features to the non-human world. Anthropomorphism is by no means limited to religion. But what differentiates religious thought from other kinds of anthropomorphism is its higher complexity and systematicity. The general assumption of the cognitive science of religion is that religious representations do not substantially differ from other types of representations and result from normal operations of the human mind. For instance, religious ideas are built in the same way as all other ideas, though they may have a partly specific structure and content. Thus, religious representations can be studied in the same way as all other mental and cultural representations. Religion is a natural phenomenon (Boyer 1994; Dennett 2006), and as such, it can be studied using scientific methods. The cognitive approach rejects the claim that religion is *sui generis* and that religious cognition is considerably different from ordinary cognition.

According to E. Thomas Lawson (McCauley and Lawson 2002), the cognitive science of religion is mainly focused on the following issues: the representation of religious ideas in human minds, the acquisition of these ideas, and the types of activities that these ideas lead to. In more recent research, these three general issues have been complemented by more detailed issues concerning religious experience (Taves 2009) and the social dimension of religion, including the role of religion in in-group cooperation (Norenzayan 2013; Sosis 2000), magic (Sørensen 2005, 2007), religious narrative (Geertz and Jensen 2011), early Christianity (Czáchesz 2017), religious cognition in children (Kelemen 2004; Barrett 2012), etc.

Looking for cognitive mechanisms that underpin religious thought, cognitive scientists focus on the intuitive theory of mind, the tendency to dualistic thinking in terms of body and mind, teleological thought and cognitive mechanisms regulating social interactions. The theory of mind mechanism is an ability to read other people's minds, i.e. attribute intentional states to other persons (Tremlin 2006).

Many cognitive scientists attempt to explain religion in evolutionary terms (e.g Whitehouse 2000, 2004). Since the psychological mechanisms underlying religious cognition have some evolutionary history, it is assumed that the knowledge of the evolution of the human mind may shed light on why the mind operates in the way it does. There is, however, no agreement on what theoretical framework best explains the evolutionary basis of religious phenomena. Three theoretical views are usually proposed for explaining religious phenomena: adaptationism, the by-product view and the cultural-evolution view (Wilson 2008). Adaptationists claim that religion is a biological adaptation that enhances the fitness of either individuals or social groups. Individual-level adaptation takes place when religion benefits individuals, compared to other individuals in a given group, while group-level adaptation takes place when a social group is benefited relative to other social groups.

According to Harris and McNamara (2008), to be a bio-cultural adaptation a human trait has to be culturally universal, effortlessly acquired and associated with physiological systems. The authors claim that religious behaviour fulfils these three criteria. This is, however, a controversial claim (Schloss and Murray 2009).

The dominant view on the evolutionary foundation of religion is a by-product theory. By-product theorists maintain that though religious belief and behaviour are not adaptive, they are evolutionary by-products of adaptive psychological mechanisms. The latter have evolved during millions of years of the evolution of the human mind. Not all mechanisms are adaptive in modern times, but all of them were adaptive in the past. For instance, alertness to predators and mechanisms responsible for the detection of predators were adaptive in the evolutionary past when people lived in a hostile world full of dangerous animals, but the same mechanisms can be maladaptive in the urban environment, where they increase stress.

Cultural evolution is another possibility discussed by scientists who think of religion in terms of evolution. In this case, the unit of selection is a cultural trait that enhances its own "fitness" through many cycles of cultural transmission. Memetics (Dawkins 1976) and epidemiology of culture (Sperber 1996) are examples of such an approach. Models of cultural transmission based on the idea of cultural evolution help to explain the distribution of religious ideas in a given population. Pascal Boyer's model of transmission of religious ideas emphasises the role of cognitive constraints (Boyer 1994).

Cognitive Science of Religion and Lived Religion

By lived religion we mean here religion as it manifests itself in the circumstances of everyday life. According to Robert Orsi (2010), the study of lived religion is focused on the dynamic relation between religious practice and imagination and the structures of everyday life. It situates religious activity within culture and understands religion first of all as lived experience. As embedded in everyday life, religious activities have meaning only in relation to other cultural activities. For Meredith McGuire, the concept of lived religion "is useful for distinguishing the actual experience of religious persons from the prescribed religion of institutionally defined beliefs and practices" (McGuire 2008, 12). She argues, however, that lived religion cannot be seen as a purely subjective phenomenon because the maintenance of subjective reality requires social support.

Lived religion is often understood as everyday religion, i.e. religion that pervades everyday life. This notion is used, among others, by Nancy Ammerman (2007), who understands it as a religious activity of ordinary people carried out outside religious institutions and organised religious events. Everyday religion is not limited to a repertoire of beliefs and practices officially acknowledged within a given religious tradition. Rather, it involves beliefs and practices that go far beyond shared and institutionally sanctioned doctrines, even if a religious person does not express it in an explicit way (Ammerman 2007; McGuire 2008, 6). This shift of perspective is partly made possible by the reconsideration of the concept of religion. It involves moving from the conceptualisation of religion as an abstract category based on Western theistic ideas to a concept emerging from everyday uses of the term "religion" (Nynäs 2017, 10).

An individual's beliefs constitute a dynamic set of beliefs which not only change over time under the influence of cultural factors but are also situational, in that particular beliefs are activated depending on the situational context in which the interpretation of daily experience takes place. The set of personal religious beliefs is not always a belief system, since it may involve beliefs that, though a person holds them, are contradictory. There are several psychological strategies that allow a religious person to have two contradictory beliefs at the same time. This is why theological correctness, defined and recommended by official religious doctrines, can be easily supplemented by a multitude of incorrect beliefs, which for some reason are useful for religious understanding of the world.

Thinking about religious beliefs in terms of a belief system is typical for world religions and hardly known in most traditional religions. According to Pascal Boyer, "most 'religion' has no doctrine, no set catalog of beliefs that most members should adhere to, no overall and integrated statements about supernatural agents" (Boyer 2011, 13). A set of religious beliefs held by an individual is dynamic, and the temporary changes in a set of beliefs do not necessarily impact other beliefs in the set.

Religious Doctrines vs. Theological Incorrectness

Both researchers of lived religion and cognitive scientists of religion emphasise the importance of actual beliefs and practices in contrast to official religious doctrines and prescriptions. Lived religion can diverge from normative religion, i.e. a form of religion prescribed by religious institutions. It can also combine beliefs and practices coming from different traditions. As such it is not always logically coherent. What counts in lived religion is rather practical than logical coherence, i.e. the degree to which religion makes sense in everyday life (McGuire 2008, 15). The cognitive science of religion provides a convincing explanation of these phenomena.

The cognitive approach to religion does not limit research on religion to official doctrine, nor declared beliefs. Religious thought is much more varied than is presented in most books on the history of religion. Most classical approaches to the study of religion focus on doctrinal teachings and marginalise the actual beliefs of religious persons. A notable exception is the anthropology of religion, which uses research methods and techniques allowing a deeper investigation of systems of religious beliefs, and the study of lived religion. Indeed, it is not easy to get access to actual beliefs because not all beliefs are reflective beliefs. Surveys in which people are asked about their religious beliefs do not provide a very reliable answer to the question about the actual beliefs. When being asked what they believe, religious people tend to answer in terms of the doctrinal tradition to which they belong. However, when they face problems that require a quick and spontaneous response, religious people use non-reflective beliefs. In literature, this phenomenon is known as "theological correctness": generally, people think about supernatural beings in a theologically incorrect way, but if they are asked what they believe (e.g. in a survey), they tend to use "correct" knowledge acquired during religious instruction. How do we know that people hold religious beliefs different from what is correct, i.e. sanctioned by tradition? Justin L. Barrett and Frank C. Keil (1996) conducted experimental research on the two different modes of processing of religious concepts and beliefs. The results of the experiments suggest that in real-time problem-solving, people have difficulty in using abstract theological ideas. They prefer anthropomorphic concepts of supernatural beings, which are much more in agreement with intuitive expectations. The reason for this is that the processing of reflective concepts and beliefs is more difficult and requires more time than the processing of non-reflective beliefs. For, instance, in situations requiring fast processing, a Christian who (reflectively) believes that God is omnipotent, omni-present and all-knowing will tend to think about God in a theologically incorrect, anthropomorphic way. The omni-present God will be represented as a concrete person having human features and unable to be in many places at once.

The phenomenon of theological correctness is based on the ability of the human cognitive system to process information in two different ways. Dual-processing models of cognition explain human cognition in terms of two separate systems or types of processing – one reflective, analytical, explicit and conscious, the other reflexive, intuitive, implicit and unconscious. While the first type is responsible for the processing of reflective beliefs, the second type allows the processing of non-reflective (intuitive) beliefs. In the case of religions having well-developed, rationalised doctrinal systems, theological beliefs take the form of reflective beliefs. However, as empirical evidence shows, it would be a simplification to think that religious people interpret the world only in terms of reflective beliefs. Theological beliefs are secondary to non-reflective beliefs because the former are based on the latter. As Barrett argues (Barrett 2004, 12–13), non-reflective beliefs are not only defaults for reflective beliefs, but they also make reflective beliefs more plausible. Moreover, by making use of non-reflective concepts, which are comprehensible and intuitive, theological concepts become more understandable and are linked to everyday experiences. Religious symbols and metaphors are well-known cognitive devices that bridge the gap between abstract theological concepts and embodied experience. Even if theologically correct representations of supernatural beings are abstract, in situations requiring fast information processing, people tend to think about these beings in an anthropomorphic way. This is a general tendency that can be also observed in the data gathered in the research on the religiosity of young adults.

The Structure of Religious Representations

Although lived religion cannot be reduced to representations and beliefs, mental representations constitute an important part of actual religious thought. The cognitive science of religion provides an explanatory framework that enhances the understanding of mental aspects of lived religion. According to this approach, religious representations are counter-intuitive in the sense that they violate intuitive assumptions. The idea of counter-intuition is based on a theory of intuitive knowledge, called intuitive ontology, that is, domain-specific knowledge that evolved as a solution to adaptive problems. Intuitive ontology involves not only the knowledge of different categories of objects but also principles applied to those categories and rules of learning. This knowledge is intuitive in that it is a non-reflective, automatic and usually unconscious result of the functioning of inferential mechanisms. There are three areas of intuitive knowledge that are important for explaining religious representations: intuitive physics, intuitive biology and intuitive psychology. Intuitive physics is a common-sense knowledge of physical objects in the world. It determines the way people perceive and reason about physical objects. An example of such knowledge is a tacit assumption that humans, as bodily beings, cannot go through a wall. Intuitive biology is responsible for the perception and categorisation of living beings. Intuitive biological thinking is based on the principle of psychological essentialism according to which hidden features of living beings determine their membership of a specific category (Medin and Ortony 1989). The intuitive assumptions typical of this biology include a belief that living beings can eat, breathe and give birth to other beings belonging to the same specific category. The third domain of knowledge, intuitive psychology, involves the theory of mind, that is, the ability to attribute mental states to other persons. This ability to read others' minds, when extended beyond the category of person, can explain a great variety of religious representations. We do not have to claim that intuitive knowledge is innate. Suffice it to say that it appears in the early stages of ontogenetic development and requires no instruction to develop properly. Research on young children shows that intuitive knowledge develops early in life (Kelemen 1999, 2004).

Counter-intuitive representations arise as a result of a violation of intuitive assumptions in the three domains of intuitive ontology mentioned above. According to Pascal Boyer (2001), several ontological categories provide points of departure for building counter-intuitive concepts. These categories include person, animal, plant, artefact and natural object. Each category is based on specific sets of intuitive assumptions. For instance, it is assumed that artefacts and natural objects cannot perceive and think, but they are certainly subject to the laws of physics. On the other hand, persons have thoughts, perceptions and emotions and their behaviour can be explained by reference to hidden intentions. The violation of intuitive assumptions, by the attribution of intentions to artefacts, results in creating a counter-intuitive concept.

What is interesting about the minimally counter-intuitive concepts is that they have a higher likelihood of activation and higher transmission potential than purely intuitive and maximally counter-intuitive concepts. This means that they easily activate mental systems and are easily remembered, which increases the likelihood of their cultural transmission. Research on the recall of supernatural concepts shows that minimally counter-intuitive concepts are better remembered than intuitive and massively counter-intuitive concepts (Barrett 1999; Atran 2002). However, counter-intuitive religious ideas and narratives do not owe their cultural success only to the specific features of the human mind such as the functioning of memory systems; several other factors enhance their transmission. Some of them are related to how human minds operate, others are related to the environment in which the transmission takes place. As for the mind, minimally counter-intuitive ideas probably trigger a large number of mental systems and thus become inferentially rich (Boyer 2003; Porubanova-Norquist *et al.* 2014). High inferential potential makes them exceptionally useful in the interpretation of everyday experience. As for the environmental factors, it has been claimed that the context in which counter-intuitive ideas are embedded plays a significant role in the recall of these ideas. As a result of these factors, religious ideas are readily spread across a population and are easily transmitted to future generations. They become relatively stable sets of cultural representations.

Between Cognition and Culture: Limitations of the Cognitive Approach

There are several limitations in the cognitive approach to religious phenomena. First, the cognitive approach has substantial difficulties in explaining why a particular content (representation, belief, experience) comes into being in a given religious tradition. Religions are very diverse in terms of content. The cognitive approach points to recurrent patterns of religious ideas and ritual behaviours but does not explain the diversity of religious phenomena. Second, the cognitive approach marginalises the role of objectified products of religious behaviour which reflexively impact religious thought. All these products are perceived by religious actors as objects independent of their consciousness. The third limitation is that the cognitive science of religion is interested most of all in unconscious cognitive processes: religious people are not conscious of cognitive factors that determine their ideas and beliefs. Thus, the subjective dimension of religion is marginalised or even eliminated from the study of religious phenomena. However, as John Searle argues, the cognitive system can be studied at least on three planes: brain, cognitive processes and consciousness (Searle 1992). For most cognitive scientists, the main research object is cognitive processes, as well as their neuronal correlates. But religious intentionality is an irreducible dimension of religion and cannot be completely set aside in the study of religious phenomena. Ultimately, whether a given phenomenon is considered religious or not depends on the intentional actions of human beings, who attribute meaning to the world. The very definition of religious phenomena requires references to human consciousness. This is why the study of religion should always consider the perspective of the insider.

The cognitive science of religion is based on several methodological assumptions, which differ fundamentally from the assumptions made by most classical approaches to the study of religion. First of all, it challenges the claim, accepted by some phenomenologists and philosophers, that religion is a special phenomenon and thus its study requires specific methods. According to the view criticised, religion differs from other cultural phenomena because it involves specific experiences, beliefs and categories such as the sacred. As reality *sui generis* it should be studied on its own plane and cannot be reduced to social, psychological, economic and other phenomena. Contrary to this view, cognitive scientists perceive religion as a natural phenomenon that can be studied not only with the methods of human sciences but also with the methods of natural sciences. Since religion is a by-product of ordinary cognition and there is no special mental machinery underlying religious thought, it can be studied in the same way as any other aspect of human reality.

The second methodological assumption challenged by cognitive scientists is related to the role of interpretation and explanation in the study of religion. Many representatives of classical approaches claim that interpretative methods constitute a cornerstone of the study of religion. This view can be traced back to the tradition according to which methods of the humanities differ essentially from the methods of natural sciences. Whereas the latter are based on explanation, the former use interpretation. The methodological exclusivism is criticised by E. T. Lawson and R. N. McCauley (1990), who propose a complementarity of explanation and interpretation and look for a balance between them. It seems, however, that this balance remains a postulate since cognitivists focus on explanation, neglecting at the same time the interpretative endeavour (see e.g. Boyer 1993, 6).

What is important for the comparative study of religion is the search for universal or at least recurrent features of religious phenomena. Although religion is claimed to be culturally universal, i.e. it is present in all known cultures, particular religious beliefs and practices are not universal. All known cultures have some kind of religious ideas, but these ideas differ greatly across cultures. The existence of religious universals, be it some core experiences, beliefs or practices, is highly disputable. There are, however, recurrent patterns of religious thought and behaviour. It seems that this claim is consistent with the assumptions made in the study of lived religion and its tendency to focus on religious activities embedded in cultural context.

According to some phenomenological approaches, the human mind is equipped with an inborn ability to perceive some phenomena as sacred. For Rudolf Otto, the sacred was an *a priori* category (Otto 1978), while for Mircea Eliade (1969) the sacred was part of the structure of human consciousness. None of these approaches have succeeded in explaining the origin of this mysterious mental equipment. Cognitive scientists question the possibility that there is a religious instinct or, using the terminology of evolutionary psychology, an evolved mental module specifically designed for religious purposes. Instead of talking about universal features of religious thought and behaviour, cognitive scientists talk about recurrent features such as certain types of supernatural ideas or ritual structures.

The very notion of religion poses considerable difficulties when we attempt to use it in cross-cultural comparisons. As many recent scholars have pointed out, "religion" is a Western category (Asad 1993), and it well describes so-called world religions. Its application in the study of non-Western cultures might raise many doubts because the category is ideologically loaded. Nonetheless, it is extensively used in non-Western cultural contexts. The problem is that using the Western concept of "religion" for understanding the religious thought of traditional cultures may lead to imposing an ideology related to this concept. It is then easy to attribute "religion" to beliefs and behaviours which are not religious in the Western sense of the word. To avoid such an imposition, Pascal Boyer proposes distinguishing between three different kinds of phenomena: (1) religious thoughts and behaviours, (2) religions, and (3) "religion" (Boyer 2011, 15–16). Religious thoughts and behaviours are present in most known cultures. They involve notions of superhuman agents and artefacts, rules governing rituals, norms regulating interactions between people and superhuman beings, etc. Religions in the second sense are "sets of norms and concepts offered by religious institutions" (Boyer 2011, 15) of various kinds, be it churches, sects or other organised groups. Such religions are not culturally universal; they do not exist in all societies and are a relatively late historical invention. "Religion" in the last sense is an ideologically loaded concept. It is based on a particular ideology that is used to identify religions in the second sense all over the world, in all human groups. The concept of "religion" suggests that there is a special domain of thought that can be subsumed under one term and understood as homogeneous reality. Using this concept, scholars of religion usually impose ideological meanings on cultural phenomena found in various cultures. According to Boyer, we can very well study religious phenomena without this concept. Moreover, the term "religion" is misleading because it takes a local invention as a model for understanding very diverse phenomena.

The conclusion that can be drawn from the above distinction is that the study of religious thought and behaviour in traditional cultures should not use the concept of "religion" uncritically. The point of departure should be particular thoughts and behaviours concerning supernatural beings, irrespective of whether these thoughts and behaviours constitute part of a system or set of religious beliefs. Such an endeavour essentially differs from most classical approaches in so far as it does not primarily focus on what used to be defined culturally or in scholarly terms as "religion" and aims to dismantle "religions" into parts more available for scientific research. Indeed, it proposes a bottom-up approach to religious phenomena, starting from mental processes, and sometimes even from their neural or evolutionary determinants, and seeks to explain higher-level phenomena in terms of lower-level cognitive processes. The problem is that higher-level phenomena such as culture or religion are usually treated as epiphenomena that have no causal influence on the mental/neural processes.

For more culturally oriented students of religion, such epiphenomenalism is unacceptable since it results in cultural eliminativism. As Jeppe Sinding Jensen points out:

> the epiphenomenalist position holds that socio-cultural products such as religion, ideology and various uses of symbolism are created by physical brain processes, but the socio-cultural products cannot have a reciprocal influence on those more basic processes. Religious beliefs, for example, do not have any causal or scientifically verifiable (or falsifiable) influence on our cognitive processes. This frequently results in the opinion that even if religion, culture, economy and other social facts can be discussed in nominal or heuristic terms as abstractions or conceptual generalizations, then they cannot have causal effects on anything: an abstraction, such as "religion" or "culture", cannot be a cause and is thus of no scientific interest to most cognitivists.
>
> (Jensen 2013, 242–3)

If culture is nothing more than individual cognitive processes plus the processes of communication and cultural transmission, then culture, including religion, is only a by-product which can be fully explained without reference to methods specific to cultural studies. The most characteristic example of this strategy is the cognitivist view of interpretation. As we have already seen, although some cognitivists call for the methodological balance between interpretation and explanation in the study of religion, others, such as Dan Sperber (1996), criticise interpretation as merely an extension of interpretative activities of studied individuals. Thus, when interpreting a religious symbol, one develops symbolic meaning and builds new symbolic structures. This activity has little to do with explanation; it is rather part of religious thought.

Cultural eliminativism ignores objectified products of human activity. These products not only interact with the cognitive system but, in many situations, can also be seen as a part of cognitive machinery. Widely discussed ideas of extended and embedded cognition provide a new possibility for explaining causal interconnections between mind and culture (Clark 2008; Hutchins 1995). Causal relations between mind and culture, including material culture, are of central importance for understanding religious thought and behaviour (Keane 2008).

Lived religion and young adults in Ghana, Peru and China

In order to show the complexities of lived religion we focused on interviews from the YARG project conducted in three non-Western countries: Ghana, Peru and China (for more information, see Chapter 1 and Appendix 4 concerning the interview model). The reason why we chose these three countries is the complexity of their religious environment and the presence of traditional forms of religion. The close coexistence of different religious and secular worldviews, including those informed by traditional forms of religion, constitute the environment in which complex religious identities emerge. It is not only the case that the discussed religious landscapes are pluralistic. More to the point, a form of pluralism is present at the individual level since subjective religiosities are often made up of beliefs and practices coming from different traditions. It is doubtful that we can get a comprehensive knowledge of those subjective religiosities on the basis of quantitative sociological data (McGuire 2008, 5). The limited value of standard research tools such as survey results is shown in that they reveal mainly superficial religious declarations which tend to be consistent with a certain normatively understood religious tradition. Moreover, they make use of interpretative concepts that have been worked out within Western culture and assume that religion is a trans-historical and immutable phenomenon (Asad 1993).

As we have seen in the presentation above, the cognitive science of religion predicts the possibility that there are religiosities not only divergent from official doctrines but also informed by many official doctrines. However, the cognitive approach is powerless to explain the ways in which lived religion is constructed.

Both Peru and Ghana are mainly Christian, but the religious composition of each country is different. The majority of Peruvians, more than 70 per cent, declare themselves to be Catholic, while Evangelical

Christians constitute about 17 per cent of the population. Religious syncretism, which combines elements of Catholicism and Inca religion, also plays a part in Peruvian religiosity (Benavides 2014). Ghana is much more pluralistic than Peru. Although the number of Christians exceeds 70 per cent, there are many different Christian churches, denominations and movements, including charismatic Christians, Protestants, Roman Catholics and others. Muslims form a significant minority in Ghana, estimated at about 17 per cent of the population. Another minority includes traditional religions.

While Ghana and Peru are predominately Christian, religious practices in China are organised around a set of traditional beliefs usually referred to as Chinese folk religions. World religions such as Christianity and Islam have much less influence. However, the religious situation in China today is dynamic, especially after the relaxation of religious policies. One can observe revitalisation of such religious practices as ancestor worship, divination, spirit mediumism, exorcism, temple festivals and going to church (Chau 2011).

Religious syncretism is fostered by the fact that some individuals were brought up in multi-religious families. Even if they declare affiliation to one religious tradition, they occasionally practise religion of the second parent. For instance, a male from Peru was brought up in a multi-cultural family. He lived in Japan and Peru. Both of his parents are Catholics, but his father also worships Butsudan, i.e. the Buddhist family altar that can be found in many Japanese homes. The respondent was brought up as Catholic, then converted to Protestantism, but because of his father's attachment to Japanese tradition he remains under the influence of Japanese thought and describes himself as being "syncretic":

> Well, first of all, I believe in God because I am a Protestant. Oh, and therefore, for example I don't fear death and perhaps can also be syncretic because one part of my family is Japanese, maintains some Japanese traditions.
>
> (YPEMV137P)

A multireligious environment can also provide content for religious experimentation, by which we mean the activity of trying out various religious practices and worldviews. This activity is not limited to spiritual seekers and unaffiliated believers, but can also be found among Christian believers who are not fully satisfied with what is on offer from Christian churches. A male interviewee from Peru, who was brought up in a Christian family, maintains that he practises both Catholicism and Buddhism. He attends religious mass but distances himself from the institutional church:

> I don't trust church as an institution [...] I've just realised that I'm contradicting myself a little bit. Oh, but yes, sometimes I attend mass. Generally, with my family.
>
> (YPEMV050PTT)

The same person is interested in and even practises meditation, which in this case is probably connected to the Buddhist tradition:

> I went to an event which a meditation friend invited me [to] and I had no idea what [it] was about. And when I was there they started to talk about *samsara*, I participated in some rituals.
>
> (YPEMV050PTT)

It might seem that he is just a Christian who, like many other young adults, experiments sporadically with other traditions. But a closer look at his religious attitude reveals a syncretic type of religiosity. Asked in the survey which religious or spiritual practice he feels close to, he pointed to no specific religion but instead emphasised that he accepts only selected "segments" of Christianity and Buddhism. Thus, the religious practice and worldview of the interviewee are built up from different religious traditions.

The study of lived religion, and especially religion which is constructed out of heterogeneous elements, reveals fluidity as well as tensions and contradictions within religious worldviews. These incongruities are usually met with various strategies for ensuring coherence. Some respondents perceive their religiosity as incongruent. This can be seen in the case of the aforementioned person who combines Christianity with Buddhism. The awareness of contradiction in this case is not caused by the coexistence of two different traditions but by the ambivalent attitude towards Catholicism, as quoted above.

What is more, religious worldviews and behaviour are changeable through life and undergo various transformations over short periods of time. This is evident in the case of religious experimenters, who try out different religious options. The cognitive approach has little to say about this changeability and internal incoherence of religious worldviews, especially the particular historical and cultural determinants of personal religious worldviews.

An important dimension of lived religion is the way in which religion is experienced by individuals and how strongly it affects everyday life. In this respect, there is a wide range of religious attitudes: a belief in supernatural beings can be either superficial and limited to religious declarations or strictly connected with ritual actions or, in an extreme case, deeply embedded in everyday activity. In the latter case, religious belief can affect many aspects of everyday perception of reality and most everyday activities in such a way that even daily routine is seen through the religious prism. The study of young adults' religiosity provides many examples of such strong presence of religion in everyday life. A Ghanaian interviewee describes her relationship with God in everyday activity as follows:

> So I don't feel distant from God that one, I will feel His presence with me, day in and day out. Or even when am walking about or even when am about leaving my room, I say God am about going please go with me. I don't know what is ahead of me but I commit the day into hands go with me. If there is any problem at home, they call, I pray and I know God will do it. So I don't feel distance from Him because He's the only one I have. I talk to Him whenever am in trouble because man will not help me. It's He that knows my life, it's He that has promised me that my future is bright so if there's anything why don't I go to Him. He's the manufacture of my life so I go to Him every time, I seek His face in every situation so I don't feel distant from God so that one; it's negative, really negative.
>
> (YGHBG010P)

This person thinks of and talks to God not only in times of hardship, but also during ordinary daily activities such as walking or leaving a room. The Christian God is one who helps to overcome difficulties as well as one who helps to make important life-changing decisions. Asked about how faith and convictions influence decisions made in life, another person responds:

> I: How do they inform your decisions that you've made?
> P: OK – I can give examples.
> I: Yes!
> P: OK, choosing my courses is one of them.
> I: Um.
> P: Yes.
> I: What does your faith tell you in choosing your courses at the university, or your convictions?
> P: OK, my faith tells me that is not about what I want. It's not about what I desire but what he desires for me.
>
> (YGHB023P)

The "he" in this statement refers to Jesus Christ, who is not just the object of religious belief and worship. He is a person who is believed to influence important decisions in life and someone in whose hands one can put one's life. In order to grasp this influence, it is necessary to analyse personal narratives of everyday religiosity. Knowledge about declared beliefs and practices provides little information about the way in which these beliefs and practices affect everyday conduct.

The cognitive study of religious communication also needs to be complemented by research on lived religion. By religious communication we mean here not the communication within a religious community or organisation but a conviction held by individual believers that it is possible to get in touch with supernatural beings. Everyday religion abounds in such convictions and experiences. For instance, a Christian believer reports constant communication with God and angels:

> I feel that I am constantly, "I converse with God", in quotation marks, converse, yes, I speak to him, or I think rather of him or the Divine. [...] By the way, I am relating with God: at any moment. I mean, if I think of something or I want to tell God something, I know, I tell you, right? Now I believe in angels too, so I feel that I can communicate with them at every moment. And that I have angels who walk with me and I can ask them things or I can talk to them (mentally, right?) So that I can make contact with them at any time.
>
> (YPEMV138)

From the point of view of the cognitive approach, one can explain such communication in terms of mental representations and cognitive processes. The study of human cognition can provide an answer to the question of how such communication is possible. What mechanisms and processes are involved in the communication with culturally postulated but intangible supernatural beings in everyday life? But the explanation requires prior understanding of how communication is carried out in particular cases; this can be done by studying culturally specific manifestations of religious communication. Even the simple claim that we have to do with religious communication requires prior interpretation of the phenomena in question.

Religious experience plays an important role in lived religion. It takes many forms from ordinary feelings of the presence of God's hand in everyday events to intensive religious and spiritual experience. What is important here is the relevance of this experience for everyday life – its life-transforming power. The consequences of intensive religious experience can be far-reaching as it was in the case of the Ghanaian female mentioned above who had such experience during a funeral:

> P: Hmm. Okay I have had a personal experience! On the day of the funeral, 28th February 2010. Um, I – that was the day of the funeral, actually, and hm, I heard a divine being sent to me. Yes.
> I: You heard a divine being?
> P: Being sent to me. Something I have never heard before and that was what comforted me and gave me the comfort and the assurance that everything will be fine.
>
> (YGHBG010P)

The study of the cognitive dimension of religious experience, as far as it focuses primarily on cognitive processes involved in religious thought and action and ignores the embeddedness of this thought and action in the world of daily experience, cannot explore particular constellations of lived religion extensively.

Putting aside the academic discussion on religious experience that has been carried out for a long time, it is important to emphasise that the study of religious experience can be a focus either of the nature of the experience or on its consequences for personal religious life. While the cognitive approach can offer some explanations of religious experience, it usually ignores the implications of this experience on personal religious belief and action, i.e. the fact that religious experience can function as an interpretative tool by which other experiences, including non-religious ones, can be understood. It can also affect the perception of everyday events and self-understanding.

Concluding Discussion

The cognitive study of religion is often seen as offering a comprehensive approach to religious phenomena. Although it mainly focuses on cognitive processes underlying religious cognition, it provides the explanation of key dimensions of religious thought and behaviour, including religious belief, ritual and experience, as well as important aspects of social organisation. The cognitive approach provides an explanatory framework for understanding lived religion, but encounters serious limitations as long as it restricts its attention to the universal cognitive processes alone. Admittedly, religious phenomena can be explained in terms of universal human cognition. However, the particular manifestations of these phenomena have their own history as well as a specific cultural and social background. Moreover, there is a broad variety of configurations in which religious ideas and practices are involved. These are not only personal syncretic religious worldviews but also encompass unlimited ways in which religious thought permeates everyday life. All those specific manifestations remain invisible when studied in terms of universal types of religious cognition.

The cognitive study of lived religion benefits from a complementary approach which considers both universal cognitive determinants of religious thought and behaviour and particular historical and cultural entanglements of religious thought in everyday conduct. The point of departure for the complementary approach could be a common assumption underlying both the cognitive approach to religion and the study of lived religion, i.e. the idea that the standard concept of religion is inadequate (McGuire 2008, 4; Boyer 2011). Also, the theory of theological incorrectness could be a useful tool for reconsidering the difference between official religion and actual beliefs, which is too often blurred in the study of religion. The data gathered in three countries – Ghana, Peru and China – confirm one of the main predictions made by cognitive scientists, namely, that religious beliefs of individuals diverge from official doctrines.

The main difference between the two approaches is that cognitive scientists emphasise the explanatory framework while the study of lived religion requires interpretative endeavours. Yet both provide methodological approaches to comprehending how religion acquires meaning. However, these two methodological strategies should not exclude each other: the explanatory approach of cognitive science should be complemented with the more detailed interpretative approach of lived religion studies.

Sławomir Sztajer holds a PhD in philosophy from Adam Mickiewicz University, Poznań, Poland, where he is a university professor at the Center of Religious and Comparative Studies. He has published books and articles on religious language, religious cognition and religious change. Recent publications include *Changing Trajectories of Religion and Popular Culture: Cognitive and Anthropological Dimensions* (co-authored with Jarema Drozdowicz; LIT Verlag, 2018) and *Religion and Religiosity in the Processes of Modernization and Globalization* (co-edited with Zbigniew Drozdowicz; WN UAM, 2016).

Rafael Fernández Hart, PhD, is a professor and director of the Facultad de Filosofía, Educación y Ciencias Humanas, Universidad Antonio Ruiz de Montoya, Lima, Peru. His research focuses on issues related to the philosophy of religion, with a special emphasis on the development of the sacred in contexts of secularisation and the links between philosophy, theology and spirituality. He acted as local investigator for the YARG project in Peru. Recent publications include "Revelación y religion en Levinas" in *Estudios de Filosofía* (vol. 57, 2018) and "The Internet, Social Media, and the Critical Interrogation of Traditional Religion among Young Adults in Peru", with Sidney Castillo Cardenas and Marcus Moberg, in Marcus Moberg and Sofia Sjö (eds), *Digital Media, Young Adults, and Religion: An International Perspective* (Routledge, 2020).

Ben-Willie Kwaku Golo, PhD, is a senior lecturer in the Department for the Study of Religion, University of Ghana, Legon. He teaches in the areas of theological studies, religion and society, and ecological theology/ethics. Some of his recent publications are "Religious Environmental Stewardship, the Sabbath and Sustainable Futures in Africa: Implications for Sustainability Discourse", in *Consensus: A Canadian Journal of Public Theology* (vol. 41, issue 1, article 4, 2020), and

"The Contents and Discontents of Internet and Social Media Use in the Religious Lives of Ghanaian Young Adults", in Marcus Moberg and Sofia Sjo (eds), *Digital Media, Young Adults, and Religion: An International Perspective* (Routledge, 2020). Ben-Willie Kwaku Golo was the local investigator for the international research project Young Adults and Religion in a Global Perspective at Åbo Akademi University (ÅAU), Turku, Finland (2015–19).

Sidney Castillo is a PhD candidate in social and cultural anthropology at the University of Helsinki, Finland. He has a master of arts in sociology and social anthropology from Central European University, Budapest, Hungary (2018); and a bachelor's degree in anthropology from Universidad Nacional Mayor de San Marcos, Lima, Peru (2014). He served as research assistant for the Åbo Akademi University Centre of Excellence Young Adults and Religion in a Global Perspective Project (2015–19). Currently, he is working on his dissertation as a member of the research group "Religion, Self, and the Ethical Life" (2021–3), University of Helsinki, unit of Social and Cultural Anthropology. He focuses on the relationship between ayahuasca rituals and ethical self-making among indigenous contexts in the Peruvian Amazon. He is also an associate editor, writer and interviewer for the Religious Studies Project. His research interests encompass youth and religion, ritual and religion, indigenous religions, new religious movements, western esotericism, religion and conflict, and secular identities.

References

Ammerman, Nancy T., ed. 2007. *Everyday Religion: Observing Modern Religious Lives*. Oxford: Oxford University Press.

Asad, Talal. 1993. *Genealogies of Religion: Discipline and Reasons of Power in Christianity and Islam*. Baltimore, MD: Johns Hopkins University Press.

Atran, Scott. 2002. *In Gods We Trust: The Evolutionary Landscape of Religion*. New York: Oxford University Press.

Barrett, Justin L. 1999. "Theological Correctness: Cognitive Constraint and the Study of Religion". *Method and Theory in the Study of Religion* 11(4): 325–39.

Barrett, Justin L. 2004. *Why Would Anyone Believe in God?* Walnut Creek, CA; Oxford: Altamira Press.

Barrett, Justin L. 2012. *Born Believers: The Science of Children's Religious Belief*. New York: Free Press.

Barrett, Justin L, and Frank C. Keil. 1996. "Conceptualizing a Nonnatural Entity: Anthropomorphism in God Concepts". *Cognitive Psychology* 31(3): 219–47.

Benavides, Gustavo. 2014. "Syncretism and Legitimacy in Latin American Religion". In *Syncretism in Religion*, ed. Anita M. Leopold and Jeppe S. Jensen, 194–216. London: Routledge.

Boyer, Pascal. 1993. "Cognitive Aspects of Religious Symbolism". In *Cognitive Aspects of Religious Symbolism*, ed. Pascal Boyer, 4–47. Cambridge: Cambridge University Press.

Boyer, Pascal. 1994. *The Naturalness of Religious Ideas: A Cognitive Theory of Religion*. Berkeley, CA: University of California Press.

Boyer, Pascal. 2001. *Religion Explained: Evolutionary Origins of Religious Thought*. New York: Basic Books.

Boyer, Pascal. 2003. "Religious Thought and Behavior as By-products of Brain Function". *Trends in Cognitive Science* 7(3): 119–24.

Boyer, Pascal. 2011. *The Fracture of an Illusion: Science and the Dissolution of Religion*, ed. Michael G. Parker and Thomas M. Schmidt. Göttingen: Vandehoeck & Ruprecht.

Chau, Adam Yuet. 2011. *Religion in Contemporary China. Revitalization and Innovation*. New York: Routledge.

Clark, Andy. 2008. *Supersizing the Mind: Embodiment, Action, and Cognitive Extension*. Oxford: Oxford University Press.

Cząchesz, István. 2017. *Cognitive Science and the New Testament: A New Approach to Early Christian Research*. Oxford: Oxford University Press.

Dawkins, Richard. 1976. *The Selfish Gene*. Oxford: Oxford University Press.

Dennett, Daniel C. 2006. *Breaking the Spell: Religion as a Natural Phenomenon*. New York: Penguin.

Eliade, Mircea. 1969. *The Quest: History and Meaning in Religion*. Chicago, IL: University of Chicago Press.

Geertz, Armin W., and Jeppe S. Jensen, eds. 2011. *Religious Narrative, Cognition and Culture: Image and Word in the Mind of Narrative*, Sheffield: Equinox.

Guthrie, Stewart. 1980. "A Cognitive Theory of Religion". *Current Anthropology* 21(2): 181–203.

Guthrie, Stewart. 1993. *Faces in the Clouds: A New Theory of Religion*. Oxford: Oxford University Press.

Harris, Erica, and Patrick McNamara. 2008. "Is Religiousness a Biocultural Adaptation?" In *The Evolution of Religion*, ed. Joseph A. Bulbulia, Richard Sosis, Erica Harris, Russell Genet, Cheryl Genet and Karen Wyman, 79–86. Santa Margarita, CA: Collins Foundation Press.

Hutchins, Edwin. 1995. *Cognition in the Wild*, Cambridge, MA: MIT Press.

Jensen, J. S. 2013. "Cognition and Meaning". In *Origins of Cognition, Religion and Culture*, ed. Aarmin W. Geertz, 241–57. Durham: Acumen.

Keane, Webb. 2008. "The Evidence of the Senses and the Materiality of Religion". *Journal of the Royal Anthropological Institute* 14: 110–27.

Kelemen, Deborah. 1999. "Function, Goals and Intention: Children's Teleological Reasoning About Objects". *Trends in Cognitive Sciences* 3(12): 461–8.

Kelemen, Deborah. 2004. "Are children 'intuitive theists'? Reasoning about Purpose and Design in Nature". *Psychological Science* 15(5): 295–301.

Lawson, E. Thomas, and Robert N. McCauley. 1990. *Rethinking Religion: Connecting Cognition and Culture*. Cambridge: Cambridge University Press.

McCauley, Robert N., and E. Thomas Lawson. 2002. *Bringing Ritual to Mind: Psychological Foundations of Cultural Forms*. Cambridge: Cambridge University Press.

McGuire, Meredith B. 2008. *Lived Religion: Faith and Practice in Everyday Life*. Oxford: Oxford University Press.

Medin, Douglas, and Andrew Ortony. 1989. "Psychological Essentialism". In *Similarity and Analogical Reasoning*, ed. Stella Vosniadou and Andrew Ortony, 179–96. Cambridge: Cambridge University Press.

Norenzayan, Ara. 2013. *Big Gods: How Religion Transformed Cooperation and Conflict*. Princeton, NJ: Princeton University Press.

Nynäs, Peter. 2017. "Making Space for a Dialogical Notion of Religious Subjects: A Critical Discussion from the Perspective of Postsecularity and Religious Change in the West". *Journal of Constructivist Psychology* 31(1): 54–71.

Orsi, Robert A. 2010. *The Madonna of 11th Street: Faith and Community in Italian Hrlem, 1880-1950*. New Haven, CT: Yale University Press.

Otto, Rudolf. 1978. *The Idea of the Holy: An Inquiry into the Non-Rational Factor in the Idea of the Divine and tts Relation to the Rational*. Oxford: Oxford University Press.

Porubanova-Norquist, Michaela, Daniel J. Shaw and Dimitris Xygalatas. 2014. "Minimal Counterintuitiveness Revisited: Effects of Cultural and Ontological Vviolations on Concept Memorability". *Journal for the Cognitive Science of Religion* 1(2): 181–92.

Schloss, Jeffrey, and Michael J. Murray. 2009. *The Believing Primate: Scientific, Philosophical, and Theological Reflections on the Origin of Religion*. Oxford: Oxford University Press.

Searle, John R. 1992. *The Rediscovery of the Mind*. Cambridge, MA: MIT Press.

Sørensen, Jasper. 2005. "Religion in Mind: A Review Article of the Cognitive Science of Religion". *Numen* 52(4): 465–94.

Sørensen, Jasper. 2007. *A Cognitive Theory of Magic*. Lanham, MD: AltaMira.

Sosis, Richard. 2000. "Religion and Intra-Group Cooperation: Preliminary Results of a Comparative Analysis of Utopian Communities". *Cross-cultural Research* 34(1): 70–87.

Sperber, Dan. 1996. *Explaining Culture: A Naturalistic Approach.* Oxford: Blackwell.

Sztajer, Slawomir, and Jarema Drozdowicz. 2018. *Changing Trajectories of Religion and Popular Culture: Cognitive and Anthropological Dimensions.* Vienna: Lit Verlag.

Taves, Ann. 2009. *Religious Experience Reconsidered: A Building-Block Approach to the Study of Religion and Other Special Things.* Princeton, NJ: Princeton University Press.

Tremlin, Todd. 2006. *Minds and Gods: The Cognitive Foundations of Religion.* Oxford: Oxford University Press.

Whitehouse, Harvey. 2000. *Arguments and Icons: Divergent Modes of Religiosity.* Oxford: Oxford University Press.

Whitehouse, Harvey. 2004. *Modes of Religiosity: A Cognitive Theory of Religious Transmission.* Walnut Creek, CA: AltaMira Press.

Wilson, David S. 2008. "Evolution and Religion: The Transformation of the Obvious". In *The Evolution of Religion*, ed. Joseph A. Bulbulia, Richard Sosis, Erica Harris, Russell Genet, Cheryl Genet and Karen Wyman, 23–30. Santa Margarita, CA: Collins Foundation Press.

– 4 –

Heteronormative Religion?

Attitudes to Abortion and Same-Sex Relationships on a Global Scale

PETER NYNÄS, ARIELA KEYSAR,
CLARA MARLIJN MEIJER AND SOFIA SJÖ

In this chapter we explore the association between religion and heteronormativity in data from our mixed-methods study with young adults globally. We present some descriptive quantitative results, results from a cluster analysis and a multi-variate CHAID analysis. In addition, interview data help us to further nuance our understanding. On the one hand, our findings are consistent with many previous studies confirming the association between religion and heteronormativity, and on the other, they also indicate for example that tradition as a value is also an independent and relevant factor. In this there are considerable variations between countries and contexts. How LGBTQI persons living in a heteronormative context themselves reproduce, manage or resist negative attitudes also varies significantly. The explorative approach in this chapter does not necessarily present new or surprising results. Rather, our use of a form of triangulation as an approach to our data underscores the value of systematic reflexivity – viewing things from different perspectives and in different lights. This is especially important when it comes to complex phenomena like religion, gender and sexuality, and in cross-cultural studies.

Introduction

This chapter contributes to the growing field of research focusing on religious views on sexuality, specifically the role of sexuality in religious communities, beliefs and practices (see e.g. Boisvert and Daniel-Hughes

2017; Browne *et al.* 2010; Hunt and Yip 2012; Taylor and Snowdon 2014; Yip 2010; Nynäs and Yip 2012; Page and Shipley 2020; Young and Shipley 2020). The dominant academic discourse in this field of research tends to assume or depict religion as "sex-negative": as constraining and restricting in relation to sexuality (Yip and Page 2016, 2). In this chapter, we investigate whether or not it is accurate to claim that religion is heteronormative. The category of religion cannot of course be discussed and explored as one phenomenon without being oversimplified beyond recognition. We are aware of the initial simplifications of both religion and the field of research used in this study; however, we still start from an assumption of heteronormativity in order, at the end, to contribute more nuances. Several recent studies point to the need to reflect a wider range of diversity (Nynäs and Yip 2012; Yip and Page 2016; Young and Shipley 2020), and the cross-cultural approach applied in this study, we argue, contributes to this.

Previous studies have clearly demonstrated that value systems are associated with religiosity and pointed to associations between religious beliefs and heteronormative attitudes (see e.g. Brooks and Bolzendahl 2004; Krok 2015; Lassander and Nynäs 2016; Moore and Vanneman 2003; Saroglou *et al.* 2004; Schwartz and Huismans 1995; Seguino 2011). Many individuals and communities have consequently also experienced how religious institutions and traditions have devalued and stigmatised non-normative identities and ways of life. Many have often also suffered from how religious institutions have contributed to maintaining national legislation that deprive members of sexual minorities of their human rights and equality. Thanks primarily to the persistent work since the 1960s within different predominantly secular movements pursuing feminist – as well as lesbian and gay – politics, an emancipatory development has emerged and opened up new legal and social possibilities of living non-normatively gendered and sexual lives (e.g. Rahman and Jackson 2010; Trappolin *et al.* 2012; Weeks 2007).

Gradually, such work has also found a visible foothold within religious contexts. Various religious LGBT groups around the world have mobilised in order to be recognised as legitimately "religious". Over recent decades, numerous organisations and networks have addressed the particular interests of religious LGBT people (see e.g. Nynäs and Lassander 2015). For instance, the Lesbian and Gay Christian Movement was established in 1976 to challenge homophobia associated with faith-based organisations and to foster a more inclusive church. In the US, from its founding in New York in 1999 until its dissolution in 2012, the Al-Fatiha Foundation supported LGBTQ Muslims in reconciling their sexual orientation or gender identity with Islam and promoted the Islamic notions of social justice, peace and tolerance, to bring all closer to a world that is free from prejudice, injustice and discrimination. Another example is the establishment, as long ago as 1973, of the LGBTQ synagogue in New York City, the Congregation Beit Simchat Torah (Beit Simchat Torah 2021).

Several Pride parades present visible examples of these movements and their work for inclusion and equal recognition. For example, in Stockholm in 2013 and in London in 2014, people participated explicitly and visibly with banners or signs about their Muslim, Jewish or Christian affiliations. Practitioners of yoga and meditation were also visible, and so were humanists. In concert with the emergence of the US Foundation, Al-Fatiha UK had been founded in 1998 and soon developed into Imaan, and this was the organisation behind the Muslim presence in the Pride parade of 2014. Behind the visibility we find a long work of a trans-national nature. The Pride parade in Seoul in 2018 can also be cited as an example of this as the event park had several stands related to religion or spirituality. More evident in this example, however, was how this Pride parade became an object of hate and aggression from religious groups. The event park was surrounded by religious activists aggressively proclaiming how the parade represented "sin", "sickness" and "decay". The event park was therefore protected by a high fence and a large number of police. Foreseeing this reaction, the time and place of the Pride event was kept a secret as long as possible.

This kind of devaluing attitude and behaviour is not uncommon. Hate speech has lately been on the rise and religious authorities have played an evident role in this (ILGA 2021). To various degrees, similar attitudes can often be witnessed as reactions to Pride parades, and they often surface in public debates. The relation between religion, on the one hand, and sexual and gender minorities, on the other, continues to surface publicly even though opinions in general have become more liberal and legislation has been amended (Nynäs, Kejonen and Vullers 2020). For instance, new research has shown that homophobia is declining amongst certain segments of the young heterosexual male population and that this is a sign of a more general trend in Western society (e.g. McCormark and Anderson 2010; McCormack 2012).

The contradictory trends raise the question of progress and modernisation, and how we should apply it in this context. On the one hand, we often tend to rely on an assumption about an inherent "incompatibility between some features of 'modernity' and religious belief" (Taylor 2007, 543). It is a fact that modern and secular nation-states have become increasingly compelled to take the lead and organise and regulate religion through a plethora of policies. Changing legislation in ways that account for human rights and disregard claims by religious authorities or institutions is an example of progress in this respect. It curtails the power of religious institutions and pushes them to change. As Jakobsen and Pellegrini (2008, 2) argue, "Secularism is central to the [European] Enlightenment narrative in which reason progressively frees itself from the bonds of religion and in so doing liberates humanity". The secularist assumption is that its emancipatory and liberatory powers will permeate all aspects of social life. On the other hand, we can no longer neglect the conflicting trends surrounding us. Despite positive changes in law and norms for social life, it would be a mistake to think that equality is established or that we are part of a linear progress. The growing cultural diversification rooted in trans-national influences has created what according to Connolly (2005) can be called a "paradox of sovereignty". This composes what he describes as "a plurality of forces circulating through and under the positional sovereignty of the official arbitrating body" (Connolly 2005, 145).

In other words, the contradictory trends are a result of the fact that alongside the secular and modern organisation of societies, there is today a cluster of discursive public processes rooted not only in traditional institutions, but also in new forms of social movements and cultural trends that strive to transform their particular positions into legitimate societal values and practices. International networks often support this. For instance, more recent campaigns in Europe have been supported by a strategy called "Restoring the Natural Order: An Agenda for Europe", which seeks to change existing laws or hinder human rights progress related, for example, to sexuality and reproduction and equality for sexual and gender minorities. This is a conservative right-wing international religious network. Networks and movements like these strive to reinforce the so-called heteronormative character of religion in culture and society by influencing both public opinion and debate, and politics. This usually conflates with an anti-abortion agenda. Both are visible in overlapping movements and their propaganda, and these conservative right-wing actors arrange demonstrations and engage in public debates often justifying these antagonisms religiously (see Datta 2018).

Trying to understand why sexuality and gender are so contested brings us back to the notion of heteronormativity. Sexuality and gender are key markers of an individual's identity. We live our gender and sexuality in relation to each other; and others relate to us on the basis of their perceptions of our identities in relation to these, and *vice versa*. Sexuality and gender are therefore not only private but also public; they are about social and public relationships, organisations and structures. The concept of heteronormativity is significant in this respect. It does not necessarily refer to a distinct identifiable body of thought, rules and regulations. Rather it informs and organises – albeit ambiguously, in complex ways, and to varying degrees – different kinds of practices, institutions, conceptual systems and social life by *giving privilege to heterosexuality as a norm* (e.g. Berlant and Warner 1998). Chambers addresses this complexity well in his definition of heteronormativity as "the assemblage of regulatory practices, which produces intelligible genders within a heterosexual matrix that insists upon the coherence of sex/gender/desire" (Chambers 2007, 667).

The need to suppress alternatives on the one hand makes heteronormativity dependent on social control and a division of gender in the form of male sexual dominance and female sexual submission (Kitzinger *et al.* 1992; MacKinnon 1982; Rich 1980; Dennis 2003; McCormack and Anderson 2010; Richardson 2010), while, on the other, heteronormativity also comes with a "compulsory narrative of reproductive futurism", manifest in the idealisation of sexual reproduction (Edelman 2004, 21). For these reasons, some theorists therefore prefer to use the concept "heteropatriarchy". This term emphasises the link between heteronormativity and women's subordination. This means that heteronormativity is also manifested explicitly as regulation of female sexuality and reproduction, often symbolised in the sacrosanct figure of the innocent, always-to-be-protected child threatened by the abortionist, a cultural icon that "marks the fetishistic fixation of heteronormativity", as Edelman (2004, 21) puts it.

From the above we can stress two main and overlapping aspects: the idealisation of heterosexuality and the control of sexual female sexuality and reproduction. We recognise them especially as the opposition to same-sex relations and abortion, but gender and sexuality are continuously subject to normativising processes by cultural and social institutions, where religious institutions and authorities tend to play central roles. This means that anti-abortion and anti-LGBTQI attitudes and agendas often conflate and correlate, but how these are configured in relation to each other and religion also varies across cultures. A more nuanced understanding of heteronormativity and religion requires us to be attentive to both.

Heteronormativity cannot be seen as a relic from history, and it is not a stable phenomenon. In spite of international, national and local trends that attest to undeniable progress such as positive changes in law and norms, these are also accompanied by setbacks and backlashes that indicate ongoing shifts with regard to societal power-structures, as suggested by Connolly (2005) above. The current landscape is, at best, uneven, especially when we account for cross-cultural variations of how religion, spirituality, gender and sexuality are comprehended and configured.

There could, for instance, be a relevant difference between the attitudes to gender justice (i.e. equality between women and men) and sexual justice (i.e. equality between heterosexual and LGBT people). Are these two types of attitudes by necessity strongly correlated? People who support gender equality may continue to oppose equality for same-sex relations since religious and cultural discourses may allow people to support sexual justice less than gender equality (e.g. Yip 2008; 2012; Yip et al. 2011). Finally, some studies among young adults have shifted focus and in contrast highlighted how sexuality – intertwined with religious identities – has allowed them to find agencies that challenge the norms (Yip and Page 2016; Young and Shipley 2020). One relevant finding in this respect is how diverse these challenges and negotiations are in relation to sexuality and religious identities (see also Meijer 2022). This is an additional relevant aspect to account for.

Heteronormativity triangulated

The diverse data from the Young Adults and Religion in a Global Perspective project (see Chapter 1) allow several analyses of how heteronormativity is associated or intertwined with religion among young adults around the world (university students with ages ranging from 18 to 30). The YARG involved studies in 13 countries (Canada, China, Finland, Ghana, India, Israel, Japan, Peru, Poland, Russia, Sweden, Turkey and USA) and the mixed-methods approach built on both quantitative and qualitative research instruments in the form of a survey (n = 4964; $n ≈ 300$ per country) and the Faith Q-sort (FQS), combined with semi-structured interviews (n = 562; $n ≈ 45$ per country). In Japan only the survey was completed. Our sample is not representative, but still helps to broaden perspectives on the issue. We have chosen a form of triangulation of our data as our main approach for this study. As a method, triangulation is understood differently but usually applied in order to increase the validity of research findings (e.g. Nastasi et al. 2010). In general, though, triangulation can be defined as the aim to look at things from different angles in order to check if we see the same thing. In the study presented in this chapter, we aim also to differentiate and nuance our findings with regard to the expected association between religion and heteronormativity. We therefore both analyse different data and apply different methods in order to gain results that together converge and add to our general comprehension of the matter (see Fusch et al. 2018; Greene and Hall 2010; Onwuegbuzie and Combs 2010).

The YARG survey comprised several important items (Appendix 3). Of relevance for this chapter are initially the measures of religiosity B8–B13 (Table 3) and of heteronormativity (Table 4). The need to include an extensive set of measures is evident from a cross-cultural perspective; religion is lived quite differently in different contexts and traditions. For instance, in some contexts belonging is decisive whereas in others we need to account for practice. In addition, an extensive set of measures helps us in this chapter to identify to what extent different ways of expressing religion are more or less associated with heteronormativity.

As we claimed in the theoretical introduction, two separate sets of norms are characteristic of heteronormativity – the idealisation of heterosexuality and the control of sexual reproduction. In this study we have therefore also operationalised them in items that reflect attitudes to both same-sex relations and abortion (Table 4). We do not necessarily

Table 3. Measures of religiosity.

B8	Do you consider yourself as belonging to one or more religious groups, communities, or traditions? – No/Yes, which?
B9	Whether or not you belong to any, are there religious, spiritual, or philosophical communities, traditions, or practices you feel close to or that reflect your views? – No/Yes, please describe
B10	Regardless of whether you consider yourself as belonging or close to a particular religious group, community, or tradition, how religious would you say you are? – 0 Not at all religious … 10 Very religious
B11	How religious would you say the family you grew up in was? – 0 Not at all religious … 10 Very religious
B12	Apart from special occasions such as weddings and funerals, about how often do you take part in religious ceremonies or services these days? – Every day / More than once a week / Once a week / At least once a month / Only on special days or celebrations / Less often / Never / I don't know
B13	Apart from when you are at religious ceremonies or services, how often do you engage in private religious or spiritual practices, such as worship, prayer, or meditation? – Every day / More than once a week / Once a week / At least once a month / Only on special days or celebrations / Less often / Never / I don't know

Table 4. Measures of heteronormativity: abortion and marital relationships.

	To what extent do you agree with the following statements? – 1 Strongly disagree ... Strongly agree 5
D1.1	Same-sex marriage should be treated the same as marriage between a man and a woman.
D1.2	Same-sex couples should have the same rights for adoption as heterosexual couples.
D1.3	If a woman became pregnant as a result of rape she should be able to obtain a legal abortion.
D1.4	When a woman's own health is seriously endangered by a pregnancy she should be able to obtain a legal abortion.
D1.5	A pregnant woman should be able to obtain a legal abortion if the woman wants it for any reason.

expect them to correlate, but we think that together they help nuance the complex issue of how religion and heteronormativity are entangled. The respondents were required to specify their level of agreement between (1) Strongly disagree, to (5) Strongly agree.

The measures of religiosity and heteronormativity enables different independent quantitative analyses, and investigation of how they associate with results from the FQS part. Since we gathered mixed-methods data from twelve countries our research horizon is cross-culturally broad: it includes many culturally, linguistically, politically and historically different contexts. Making sense of the cross-cultural aspect with relation to religion and heteronormativity would require much more in-depth research than the YARG study was capable of. Yet, in this chapter we can at least explore some of the cross-cultural variation. The interviews provide an independent addition and rich layer that reflects parts of the lived reality behind the quantitative findings.

The chapter presents three different analyses based on the YARG data. We start from a bird's eye view and some descriptive results of the quantitative relationship between heteronormative attitudes and religiosity among over 4500 students from thirteen countries, including a cluster analysis. Second, we zoom in and turn to a multi-variate analysis to identify and analyse the more complex relationships and explore the role of some possible contributing variables such as values. Finally, we take another perspective and dive into interviews conducted in Ghana, the most religious country in our study. This case study illustrates how

LGBTQI students (of a different but related sample) hold and manage quite strong religious and heteronormative views. Together, these three parts propose a form of triangulation of the association between heteronormativity and religiosity with the aim of capturing additional relevant nuances and variations.

Heteronormative Religion

In Chapter 1 in this volume we refer to our main findings from the FQS study (see also Nynäs *et al.* 2021), the main global worldview prototypes, based on an analysis of the FQS data (n = 562). These were the "Secular Humanist", the "Active Confident Believer", the "Non-committed Traditionalist", the "Spiritually Attuned" and the "Disengaged Liberal". The narrative descriptions of the five global prototypes are found in Appendix 2. Our analyses confirmed both how these reflect a typology based on secular, religious and spiritual life views, and how they are distinctive from each other also in light of how they are associated with variables from the survey, such as measures of religiosity, what authorities they rely on, and basic human values. Already here we could identify noticeable differences in how the prototypes agreed with our statements that measure heteronormativity as presented in Table 5 for the first four prototypes. The fifth prototype is left out since it is of an ambiguous nature and does not bring much to the analyses.

The descriptive values presented in Table 5 indicate that there is a clear division between the secular (prototype 1) and the religious (prototypes 2 and 3) life views, and that the latter stand out as heteronormative. We can further see that the difference is more exaggerated in reference to the same-sex relations items. The spiritually attuned prototype 4 does not conform to heteronormative attitudes.

Opposition to same sex-marriage and opposition to legal abortion do not go hand in hand in these data. In the USA, Sweden, Canada, China, Japan and to some extent Finland, the respondents' support for legal abortions matches their support of same-sex marriages. Such congruency happens in Peru as well, yet with lower levels of support. Gaps between the attitudes are larger or even more evident in Ghana, Turkey, Russia and Poland. Consistently, support for abortion exceeds the support for same-sex marriage (see Table 6 and Figure 2).

The results from our study show that in general low per capita income is associated with more heteronormativity. In Israel, on the other hand, with relatively higher per capita income, we find lower support of same-sex marriage. Another indicator on a societal level is female

Table 5. Means and standard deviations on heteronormative values per prototype 1–4.

	Strongly disagree (1) and strongly agree (5) M (SD)			
	Prototype			
	1 Secular Humanist	2 Active Confident Believer	3 Non-committed Traditionalist	4 Spiritually Attuned
Same-sex marriage should be treated the same as marriage between a man and a woman.	4.49 (1.09)	1.98 (1.39)	2.73 (1.66)	4.40 (1.18)
Same-sex couples should have the same rights for adoption as heterosexual couples.	4.35 (1.17)	2.00 (1.43)	2.67 (1.64)	4.31 (1.25)
If a woman became pregnant as a result of rape she should be able to obtain a legal abortion.	4.85 (0.65)	3.31 (1.55)	4.30 (1.20)	4.79 (0.52)
When a woman's own health is seriously endangered by a pregnancy she should be able to obtain a legal abortion.	4.83 (0.63)	3.87 (1.35)	4.35 (1.19)	4.83 (0.53)
A pregnant woman should be able to obtain a legal abortion if the woman wants it for any reason.	4.36 (1.07)	2.23 (1.39)	3.38 (1.55)	4.05 (1.33)

Table 6. GDP per capita, support for legal abortion and same-sex marriage and mean values/country. Support for abortion and same-sex marriage are rated on a scale from 1 to 5.

Country	GDP per capita (US$, 2019)	Female 15–64 in labour force	Abortion	Same-sex Marriage
Ghana	2000	65.3	3.1	1.3
India	2000	22.2	4.1	3.5
Peru	6000	73.8	3.4	3.5
Turkey	9000	38.1	4.5	2.9
China	10,000	68.8	4.2	4.1
Russia	11,000	69.3	4.5	3.2
Poland	15,000	63.4	3.4	2.2
Japan	41,000	71.4	4.1	4.1
Israel	43,000	69.5	4.1	2.9
Canada	46,000	75.1	4.5	4.5
Finland	48,000	76.2	4.6	4.2
Sweden	51,000	81.1	4.8	4.7
USA	65,000	67.2	4.5	4.5

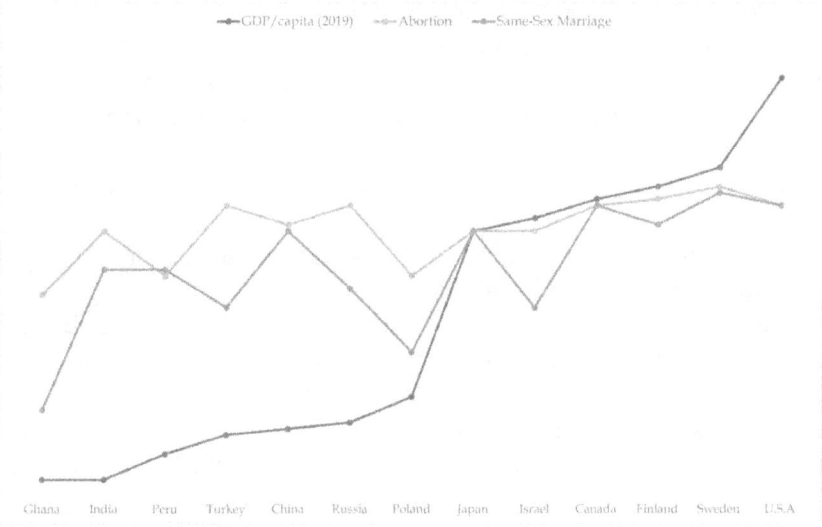

Figure 2. GDP/per capita and support for abortion and same-sex marriage. GDP shown in thousands of US dollars; support for abortion and same-sex marriage rated on a scale from 1 to 5.

labour-force participation. In more progressive societies gender gaps in employment are relatively smaller, and the share of females in the work force is higher. From our understanding of heteronormativity, we expect, in societies with higher gender equality, to also find more support for same-sex marriages and legal abortions. The YARG results only partially support this assumption. Only in some countries with high female labour-force participation (i.e. Sweden, Finland and Canada) do we also find a strong association with support of same-sex marriage and legal abortions (see Table 6).

The incongruity in attitudes is not unique to the YARG sample. In the USA, Michele Dillon (2014) documented the discrepancy in attitudes towards abortion and gay rights. While two-thirds of black Protestants in 2012 favoured the legalisation of abortion in all or most circumstances, only one-third favoured the legalisation of same-sex marriage. Hispanic Catholics, on the other hand, exhibited an inverse pattern. A solid majority, 57 per cent, favoured the legalisation of same-sex marriage while only 43 per cent favoured the legalisation of abortion in all or most circumstances. These attitudes led Dillon (2014, 13) to conclude that "it cannot be taken for granted that someone who opposes same-sex marriage also opposes the legalization of abortion, and vice versa". Dillon challenges as too simplistic the assertion that religion explains the patterns. "Religious affiliation does not stand alone, but inevitably intertwines with ethnoracial divisions, education, social class, region, and other structural variables" (Dillon 2014, 13).

The YARG study provides an international perspective that corroborates Dillon's observations and suggestions that "We need to be more attentive, therefore, to differentiating within religious denominations" (Dillon 2014, 14, see also Perales and Bouma 2019). Other factors can interfere. We address this topic in the multi-variate model that follows this section.

Results similar to the results we received from the FQS analysis above also emerged from our cluster analysis. At this stage it was also evident that we needed to analyse attitudes to same-sex relations and abortion separately since the group sizes did not match. For the cluster analyses we divided the respondents into three clusters, groups 1–3, based on a variable calculated as the sum of the level of agreement for all items in each theme. With regards to same-sex relations this meant the sum of their agreement with both "Same-sex marriage should be treated the same as marriage between a man and a woman" and "Same-sex couples should have the same rights for adoption as heterosexual couples", calculated separately. The descriptive results from this are presented in Table 7 and Table 8. Of these clusters, Group 1 can in both groups be considered to

Table 7. Mean values for attitudes to same-sex marriage and same-sex adoption for clusters 1–3. D1.1: Same-sex marriage should be treated the same as marriage between a man and a woman. D1.2: Same-sex couples should have the same rights for adoption as heterosexual couples). In the right column, "other" includes no response.

(Sum variable)	D1.1: M (SD)	D1.2: M (SD)	N	Male/female/other
Group 1 (2–4)	1.27 (0.53)	1.27 (0.54)	1410	46/52/2%
Group 2 (5–7)	3.08 (0.91)	2.95 (0.94)	862	44/54/2%
Group 3 (8–10)	4.81 (0.45)	4.77 (0.50)	2692	34/65/1%

affirm heteronormative values, whereas this is not the case for Group 3, where we find respondents who clearly agree with the statements. There is a gender difference between the groups in the sense that the majority of members of Group 3 are female. In this study, we exclude Group 2 from further discussions in the chapter since we initially point to descriptive differences associated with heteronormativity.

The corresponding results for abortion items (Table 5) display a similar pattern, also in terms of gender difference, but it is noteworthy and should be kept in mind that the heteronormative cluster is in this case very small ($n = 279$). In some countries, only a few individuals strongly disagreed with these statements. There is, nonetheless, a cross-cultural diversity in this cluster since Ghana ($n = 82$), Peru ($n = 57$), Poland ($n = 37$) and Israel ($n = 34$) are highly represented in this cluster. The rest of the countries contribute with between 2 and 13 respondents each.

Table 8. Mean values for attitudes to abortion for clusters 1–3. D1.3: If a woman became pregnant as a result of rape she should be able to obtain a legal abortion. D1.4: When a woman's own health is seriously endangered by a pregnancy she should be able to obtain a legal abortion. D1.5: A pregnant woman should be able to obtain a legal abortion if the woman wants it for any reason. In the right column, "other" includes no response.

(Sum variable)	D1.3: M (SD)	D1.4: M (SD)	D1.5: M (SD)	N	Male/female/other
Group 1 (3–6)	1.43 (0.70)	1.91 (0.96)	1.30 (0.69)	279	39/56/5%
Group 2 (7–11)	3.63 (1.15)	3.98 (1.02)	1.89 (1.01)	1343	48/50/2%
Group 3 (12–15)	4.94 (0.28)	4.94 (0.24)	4.33 (0.95)	3342	35/63/2%

The cluster analyses confirm the general pattern we are investigating in this chapter, and show that religiosity is associated with heteronormativity. In both groups from both cases, one views one's family background as fairly religious whereas religiosity in terms of belonging (B8) and self-definition (B10) present differences between Group 1 and Group 3, indicating an association between heteronormativity and religiosity. The difference does not seem equally marked when we look at public (B19) and private (B13) religious practices (Table 9). This is consistent with previous research and is in accordance with Perales' and Bouma's (2019, 337–8) findings that "higher levels of religiosity (measured as both importance of religion to one's life and attendance at religious services) were associated with holding more patriarchal attitudes".

Table 9. Measures of religiosity and cluster differences. B8: Do you consider yourself as belonging to one or more religious groups, communities, or traditions? B10: Regardless of whether you consider yourself as belonging or close to a particular religious group, community, or tradition, how religious would you say you are? (0 Not at all religious – 10 Very religious). B11: How religious would you say the family you grew up in was? (0 Not at all religious – 10 Very religious). B12: Apart from special occasions such as weddings and funerals, about how often do you take part in religious ceremonies or services these days? (1 Every day – 7 Never). B13: Apart from when you are at religious ceremonies or services, how often do you engage in private religious or spiritual practices, such as worship, prayer, or meditation? (1 Every day – 7 Never).

	B8 (% yes)	B10 M (SD)	B11 M (SD)	B12	B13
Cluster 1-3 attitudes on same-sex relations					
Group 1	55%	5.73 (2.66)	6.54 (2.57)	M = 4.28 Median = 5	M = 3.24 Median = 2
Group 2	36%	4.37 (2.62)	5.39 (2.63)	M = 5.11 Median = 5	M = 4.48 Median = 5
Group 3	23%	2.85 (2.65)	4.05 (2.87)	M = 5.83 Median = 6	M = 5.47 Median = 6
Cluster 1-3 attitudes on abortion					
Group 1	58%	6.23 (2.73)	6.87 (2.56)	M = 3.95 Median = 4	M = 2.92 Median = 2
Group 2	47%	5.36 (2.66)	6.19 (2.57)	M = 4.50 Median = 5	M = 3.73 Median = 4
Group 3	28%	3.17 (2.73)	4.36 (2.92)	M = 5.68 Median = 6	M = 5.19 Median = 6

Basic Values Interfering with the Pattern

In the previous section we confirmed that our study indicates that religiosity and heteronormativity are associated, in line with what has been shown elsewhere by many other studies. Yet we raised the question of whether other factors are at play. We briefly investigated the impact of background factors such as GDP/capita and female-labour participation. In this section we turn to basic values. Factors that are likely to be associated with attitudes towards both same-sex marriage and legal abortion are the level of religiosity and the extent to which one holds specific values (see e.g. Krok 2015; Nynäs *et al.* 2022; Saroglou *et al.* 2004; Schwartz and Huismans 1995). We included in our survey Schwartz's Portrait Value Questionnaire (Schwartz 1992; Schwartz *et al.* 2012), based on Schwartz's theory of basic human values (Schwartz 1992; see also Maio 2017). In Schwartz's theory, values are seen as motivational goals, i.e. a set of beliefs about what is desirable and what means are appropriate for pursuing the desires. In a later refined theory of basic values (Schwartz *et al.* 2012; Schwartz 2017), a more nuanced categorisation of values and a model based on 19 value types, in contrast to the initial 10, is provided.

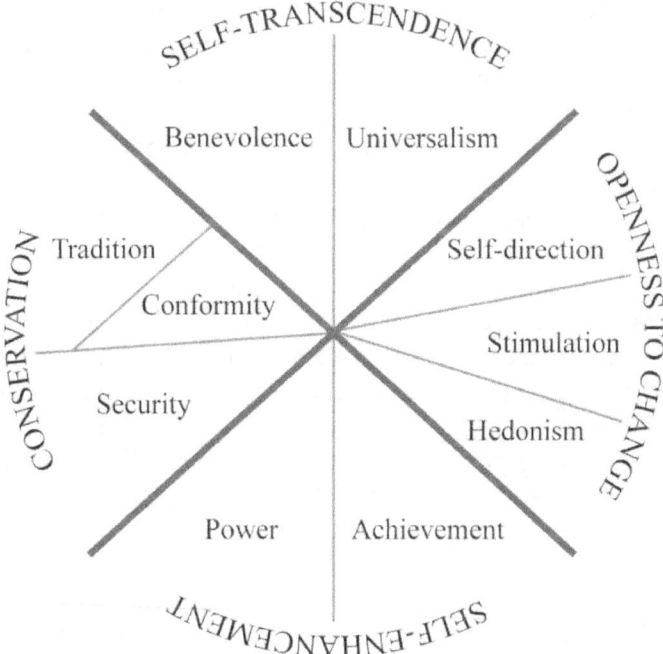

Figure 3. Schwartz 1992 value structure.

In Schwartz's theory of basic values, values are organised along a motivational continuum, forming a circular value structure (Schwartz 2017), as depicted in Figure 3. Values close to each other are complementary or compatible motivational goals, such as conformity and traditional values. Value types opposite to each other are seen as incompatible, such as conformity and self-direction. An important aspect of the theory is that the relative order between the values is stable. Values change from group to group, but due to the associations between values the relationship between them remains more or less stable. Our data confirm the impact of basic values and in particular tradition is negatively correlated to positive attitudes towards legal abortion ($r = -0.43$) and same-sex marriage ($r = -0.47$) – both statistically significant at $p < 0.01$ level. The more traditional the student's values are the less they support abortion and same-sex marriage. Stated differently, traditional students are more likely to exhibit more heteronormative attitudes.

Levels of religiosity and basic values are played out differently in our study samples (Nynäs *et al.* 2021). In order to explore this with respect to heteronormativity we conducted a multi-variate analysis with the chi-square assisted interaction detection (CHAID) method. CHAID is an algorithm for exploring how independent variables explain a dependent, categorical variable. It automatically builds a decision tree. It finds the independent variable that has the strongest explanatory power over the dependent variable and then splits the population into homogeneous groups based on their differing values with respect to that variable. Each homogeneous group is then further split by whatever variable most strongly affects it. These groups are then further split until the process is exhausted.

CHAID is a model-free approach to identify and analyse the complex relationships that may be embedded in higher-order contingency tables. The CHAID method partitions a contingency table produced from cross-tabulation of three or more variables by using a semi-hierarchical, sequential procedure. The procedure is semi-hierarchical in the sense that it determines the smallest number of groupings or splits of the levels of a predictor by means of a process of pair-wise merging (and then separating) of the response levels on each of the predictors. The analysis is sequential in the sense that each of the subgroups of the sample produced by that split is then treated as a new "parent group" (candidate for splitting) and is split in the same fashion until any possible remaining split of a group is not significant, or until the size of the group is too small to provide meaningful probability estimates (Perreault and Barksdale 1980). The rules we imposed for the running of the CHAID procedure force the first variable to be the country of studies, a minimum cell size of 50, and a critical *p*-value of 0.05. Again, we investigate attitudes to abortion and same-sex relations separately.

CHAID Tree for Support for Same-Sex Marriage

Dependent variable: support for same-sex marriage, overall mean = 3.5, see Figure 4.

Independent variables, step 1 – country of studies. Nine distinct nodes (groupings) emerged:

1. Ghana
2. Poland
3. Israel, Turkey
4. Russia
5. Peru, India
6. China, Japan
7. Finland
8. USA, Canada
9. Sweden

Independent variables, step 2 – the relation between values and religion is differently configured in different countries. Unlike with abortion, the level of religiosity, self-defined on the scale from 0 to 10, B10, has emerged as the second-best discriminator only for Israel and Turkey. For the other nodes, holding traditional values is the second-best predictor of support for same-sex marriage.

For node 1 (Ghana) neither factor splits the nodes further. Overall, students in Ghana expressed the lowest support for same-sex marriage (see also Table 6 and Figure 2 above).

Nodes 6 (China and Japan), 5 (Peru and India) and 4 (Russia) are divided into three groups: 1st quartile, i.e. 25 per cent of respondents with the lowest degree of traditional values; 2nd quartile; and 3rd and 4th quartiles of traditional values. Node 2 (Poland) is divided into two groups: 1st and 2nd quartiles; and 3rd and 4th quartiles of traditional values. Node 9 (Sweden) is divided into two groups: 1st quartile; and 2nd, 3rd and 4th quartiles. Nodes 8 (USA and Canada) and 7 (Finland) are divided into four groups: 1st quartile; 2nd quartile; 3rd quartile; and 4th quartile, i.e. 25 per cent of respondents with the highest degree of traditional values.

Interestingly, a few nodes are split further: in node 3 (Israel and Turkey) traditional values split the three lower groups of religiosity – from the non-religious to the somewhat religious. The reverse happens in nodes 5

(Peru and India) and 9 (Sweden), with those holding strong traditional values further split by level of religiosity – the group with a lower level of religiosity expresses stronger support for same-sex marriage.

CHAID Tree for Support for Legal Abortion

Dependent variable: support for legal abortion, overall mean = 4.1, see Figure 5.

Independent variables, step 1 – country of studies. Seven distinct nodes (groupings) emerged:

1. Ghana
2. Poland, Peru
3. Israel, Japan, India
4. China
5. USA, Canada, Russia, Turkey
6. Finland
7. Sweden

Independent variables, step 2 – the CHAID procedure detects two variables associated with religion/tradition as the next-best predictor. In some cases, the self-defined level of religiosity is the next-best predictor in identifying support for abortion, while in others it is the extent of holding traditional values. Initially we recognise the "universal" pattern indicated by our first part of the study, namely the greater the non-religiosity (lower on the religiosity scale), the greater the support for abortion is, and to this we can add that it is accompanied by expressing the least traditional values. However, the branching of the religiosity levels and traditional values varies considerably by country, and contextual variations surface.

Poland and Peru are divided into five religiosity groups: the non-religious 0–1 with abortion support = 4.1; somewhat secular 2–3 with abortion support = 3.8; the middle 4–5 with abortion support = 3.3; somewhat religious 6–7 with abortion support = 3.0; the very religious 8–10 with abortion support = 2.5.

Israel, Japan, India are divided into four quartiles according to degree of traditional values of all YARG respondents: the lower/least tradition quartile – 25 per cent of respondents from all countries – with abortion support = 4.7; second quartile with abortion support = 4.2; third quartile with abortion support = 3.9 and 4; upper quartile – the most traditional – with abortion support = 3.7.

Ghana is divided into two groups: level of religiosity ≤ 6 with abortion support = 3.3; and > 6 with abortion support = 3.0.

China is also divided into two groups but by the extent of traditional values: first and second quartile with abortion support = 4.3; and third and fourth quartile with abortion support = 4.0.

USA, Canada, Russia, Turkey are divided into four groups by the extent of traditional values: the first quartile with abortion support = 4.8; the second quartile with abortion support = 4.5; the third quartile with abortion support = 4.3; and the fourth quartile with abortion support = 4.0.

Finland is divided into three groups: the non-religious 0–2 with abortion support = 4.9; the middle 3–7 with abortion support = 4.6; and the small the religious group, scoring 8–10 with abortion support = 3.8.

Sweden is divided into two groups: the non-religious 0–1 with abortion support = 4.9; and the more religious 2–10 with abortion support = 4.6.

Note that the highest support for abortion among group 2 (4.1 in Poland and Peru) is lower than that of the lowest support among group 7 (4.6 in Sweden).

The flowcharts of the CHAID results are a graphic mapping of the apparent lines of interaction between the various categories of the independent variables and their relative likelihood of supporting same-sex marriage and legal abortion. For simplicity, we present only the branching of the first two steps.

At the two extremes of views on abortion, religiosity is what separates the students. In the middle of the spectrum, however, tradition is the differentiating predictor. On same-sex marriage, tradition is almost always the most important differentiating predictor.

The flowcharts not only illustrate the gaps in attitudes toward same-sex marriage vs. abortion (Dillon 2014) but also their interactions with the country of studies, which represent the cultural distinctions of the YARG participants. The CHAID identified different clusters of countries emerging in support of same-sex marriage vs. the support of legal abortion. For instance, Israel and Turkey emerged together in support of same-sex marriage, yet Israel, Japan and India are grouped together in support of legal abortion.

The flowcharts detected predictors beyond country/culture, namely level of religiosity and expression of traditional values. Again, we found little consistency in the various countries (or groups of countries). For example, students in Poland are divided in their support of same-sex marriage by expressions of traditional values, while they are divided in their religiosity level by their support of legal abortion.

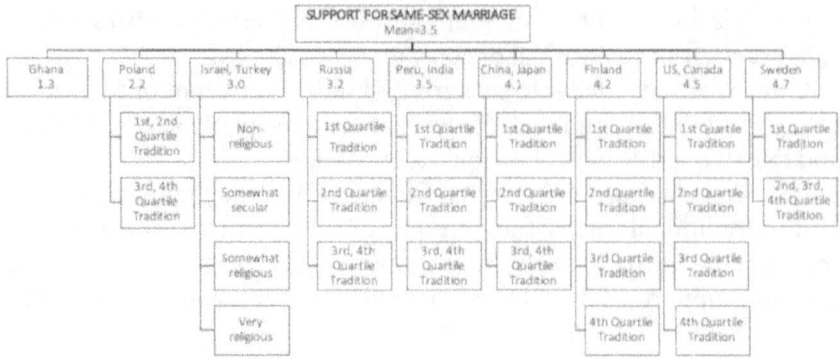

Figure 4. CHAID tree for support for same-sex marriage.

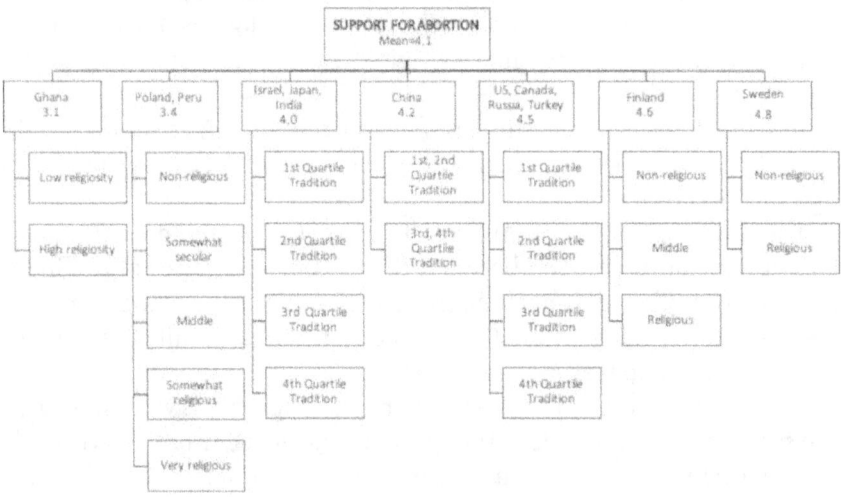

Figure 5. CHAID tree for support for legal abortion.

A Complex Lived Reality

In research we tend to focus on general patterns and publicly significant issues. This is reflected in our analyses above, where we have investigated how heteronormativity is associated with religion in different ways. Our results have expressed the relevance of reflectively moving between the universal and the particular. When we zoom in from our bird's eye view, we realise that the reality we explore is complex. Consequently, we need to account for the fact that this is also the reality that individuals face. The relevance in their lives, for example of the association of religion with heteronormativity, can be straightforward in a way that allows us to sidestep variations, nuances and ambiguities. There is maybe also a demand for this, letting everyday reality and the private rest in the shadows. Still, everyday life is messy and fluid. It is formed by – but also forms – identities, subjectivities, experiences, emotions, bodies and desires that are lived out on individual and collective levels of spaces and politics (Yip and Nynäs 2012). A close-up look at everyday life uncovers a new level of complexity involving a range of dynamics and strategies: people conform to, appropriate, negotiate, transgress, challenge and resist social organisations and power structures (e.g. May 2011; Pink 2012). This is also a matter of how heteronormativity gains cultural, social and individual relevance and weight.

As the last part of our triangulation, we will briefly look at this through the lens of individuals living in a strongly heteronormative society, namely Ghana: the most heteronormative case in the YARG study in terms of attitudes towards same-sex relations. This is interview data from a separate case study with a local LGBTQI-community, a sub-study of the YARG project (Meijer 2022). The interviews were collected through snowball sampling in collaboration with a LGBTQI organisation and the call for participants addressed "young adults between 18 and 30 years who would identify as LGBTQ or have same-sex romantic relationships and have a background in tertiary education". Conducting a study like this with highly vulnerable subjects required a lot in terms of both methodological and ethical considerations and precautions.

In this part of the chapter we will only account for some relevant variations of how heteronormative attitudes are conformed to and managed, and present three sets of examples or themes. They take the form of three different themes that have emerged through a qualitative analysis that was carried out in the sub-study which focused on sexual stigma, religiosity and strategies and agency among young adults who identified as sexual minorities in Ghana (Meijer 2022). The first theme is about adjusting to heteronormativity, the second is about accepting heteronormative ideals, and the third is about internalisation of homo-negative views. After some short extracts from the interviews, we briefly discuss the themes. It should be emphasised that these do not exemplify either the complex reality of how people conform to, appropriate, suffer from or challenge heteronormative views. In many cases such dichotomies are only one corporeality; during the interviews many participants would share different views on heterosexism that could sometimes be seen as conflicting, which relates to the complexity of dealing with being stigmatised in everyday life. We can see that the examples illustrate (1) heteronormative adjustments as a strategy, (2) acceptance of heteronormative ideals and (3) self-stigmatisation through internalisation of homo-negativity.

Example 1 – Heteronormative Adjustments to Avoid Stigmatisation

Participant A – young woman (28) who identifies as lesbian:

> I have never been threatened before. Because, I know my right. I know where to act as a lesbian and where not to act as a lesbian. [...] When I am in a LGBT meeting, I act as a lesbian. But when I am out with my family, on church programmes, I don't act like that. I'll ignore you. I change my language, how I speak. When I am in a LGBT meeting, I can speak anyhow, I speak with you – I am telling you what I am. I am a lesbian. But when I move with other people, I don't tell them I am a lesbian. I don't even raise the topic that comes with LGBT, something, no, no, no. 'Cause I don't want them to say something bad, that would affect me.

Participant B – non-binary person (20) who identifies as being queer:

> Yeah, they know I dress like a lady, I do my things like a lady, but they don't see bad, but outside there is talk. So, sometimes they advise me to come and I know how to – I should – [sigh] compromise, because the ways some people speak outside, it is not nice.

Participant C – young man (21) who identifies as homosexual:

> I know how to take care of myself. Like, you know, how to handle yourself. [...] Me, being a Christian, when I go to a place and you are Christian and there, I know how to compose myself for them. Not coming out, being my sexual preference or something. [...] When I go to church activities, I can just come in and I can be very feminine. But when it comes to churches in Ghana here, they do not, they cannot just say to you straightforward because you are feminine, you cannot set a foot [inside], like that. But they think maybe, they will leave me, because I am thin, that is why I am being feminine. So they won't say anything. But when they see you in key activities, social gatherings, then they attack you as a gay person.

Participant D – young man (23) who identifies as homosexual:

> When it comes to religious communities, because it is not a norm that has been accepted, we are kind of cautious. To prevent stigma and humiliation. I think it is best to stick to our own beliefs.

These four participants are affirmative of their own sexuality and have not internalised stigmatising beliefs against homosexuality. But as they explain in these fragments, they adjust their behaviour, especially in their religious communities, as a strategy to avoid sexual stigma. Doing this, they fulfil heteronormative expectations. They avoid discussing anything related to non-normative issues, such as homosexuality. Their life is shaped by a social matrix which requires them to perform multiple identities, or at least context-specific identifications (Richardson and Monro 2012).

Participant A is conscious of the stigmatisation and navigates it by adjusting her way of acting towards her family and in her church. Participant B, who is assumed to be a homosexual by people in their neighbourhood and religious community, is often advised by their parents to "compromise" with their style of clothes and behaviour to avoid stigmatisation. Participant C views these issues in a similar way to participant A; he is conscious of the stigmatisation and "knows how to take care" of himself. He knows in which religious gatherings he can allow himself to be feminine and in which, especially larger ones, he cannot. Participant D exemplifies this too by arguing that sexual minorities have to be "cautious" to avoid stigma. Even though these participants do not internalise heteronormativity, their adjustment to avoid stigmatisation demonstrates how heteronormative behaviour is publicly viewed as the norm and anything that deviates risks stigmatisation, a stigmatisation that is supported with religious homo-negative discourses.

Example 2 – Acceptance of Heteronormative Ideals

Participant E – young woman (23) who identifies as lesbian:

- I: Um, so and what are the things that you think that are the biggest obstacles?
- P: Being a lesbian.
- I: Why do you think that?
- P: Because, you know, in Ghana here it is not accepted. And if it is not accepted in your – you are just dreaming this – you are just being with your fellow woman and like – you can't just be like that. That means, you are not doing anything. Yes. Because you have to get married, and also get kids. Who will be there to replace you when you are gone one day?
- I: Is this what your family wants for you?
- P: That's what I want.

[...]

- I: What if it would be possible to get married with a woman?
- P: It is not possible. Here in Ghana, it is not possible. Yeah.
- I: But would you like to if it was possible?
- P: No.
- I: Why, why not?
- P: Because it is not right. Yeah.

Participant F – young man (25) who identifies as homosexual:

  I: What about marriage, do you want to get married at some point?
  P: Marriage. Even my bible says that marriage is not very important. It is either you get married or you live single forever. With no attachments at all.

Participant G – young woman (23) who identifies as lesbian:

  P: I think if you are a les [lesbian], it does not mean when you get engaged to your partner, that it shows that you're both lesbian or you love the person. I just believe that if you are a les [lesbian], you should be real, you should not add anything to it.
  I: Why do you think that?
  P: Because, although we are a lesbian, I know it is a sin. Because we do not have to, but we did not decide to do it. So, we do not have to add more to it, to get engaged or something. You should be real.

These three fragments from interviews show how heteronormativity underpins stigmatisation against homosexuality and how heteronormativity is internalised by non-heterosexual persons through religious values. These participants identify as religious and are active in their religious communities; they attend religious ceremonies once or twice a week. Their families are involved in these communities as well. However, homo-negative religious discourses are shared and spread by religious authorities within the communities they are part of. Dominant beliefs, such as that homosexuality is the biggest religious sin, are often discussed and repeated by religious leaders. Homosexuals are viewed as people who do not live righteously and therefore will never have a successful, happy and healthy life. At the same time, heteronormative values are seen as the opposite: the way to achieve a successful life. These participants accept heteronormativity, in the sense that they aim for heteronormative ideals such as a heterosexual marriage.

For the first participant, E, a young woman who identifies as a lesbian, this means that she holds that she must change and become a heterosexual woman in order to get married and start a family. Participant F, a young man who identifies as a homosexual man, sees it a little differently. For him the choice is either to get married or stay single as a homosexual man. Either way, he cannot have any romantic relationships with other men and has to conceal his sexuality. The third participant, G, a young woman who identifies as a lesbian, holds similar views to the first participant. She has internalised the idea that homosexuality is a sin and therefore there is, according to her, no subjective right to wish for equal rights and ceremonies, such as marriage or engagement; these romantic, politically important and often religiously significant ceremonies are viewed as exclusively heterosexual. Young adults who belong to religious communities and identify as sexual minorities are automatically excluded from marriage or starting a family, and view abstinence or living a life as a heterosexual as the only options to harmonise their religiosity and to be accepted by their religious communities. They come to embrace these ideals to a great extent.

Example 3. Self-stigma through Internalisation of Homo-negative Beliefs

Participant H – young woman (21) who identifies as bisexual:

> That place, the first time I went there, I felt sick. [...] 'Cause, I felt as, I don't know, I don't know how to explain it. [...] That place could be destroyed any time, any moment. [...] I did not feel good, because of everything that was going on there. 'Cause it was like, the reflection of what, I don't know.

Participant I – young woman (28) who identifies as lesbian:

> Because I am a lesbian, it has blocked my way. So I don't get a chance to work. [...] Everything is like, it is an evil [thing], so I should stop. Yes, so my mom does not talk to me.

Participant J – young man (25) who identifies as homosexual:

> I cannot just wake up and say I am normal to this. Unless I keep on meditating the word of God, for him, to be guiding me. Change – leading me to the right path. And I know one day, one day, I will get rid of it [the homosexual feelings].

Participant K – young woman (19) who identifies as lesbian:

> That is what I know, I believe there is a God. [...] I do not do anything bad aside from the lifestyle I am living. So, I think, when I will stop with that one [homosexuality], I will be fully a Christian.

These participants present examples of internalisations of homo-negative religious beliefs. The last three participants, I, J and K, discuss not only how they cannot embrace their sexuality, as the participants in the previous example do, but also experience themselves as deviant. They believe that they must change because homosexuality is an "evil" thing and is not righteous. Often these ideas are discussed repeatedly by family members and religious authorities, who sometimes address these beliefs personally. At the same time, religious leaders promise success, health and financial gain in the future through "change", or practices related to "conversion therapy", all with the aim of becoming a heterosexual.

If family members or close friends share these kinds of views, the risk of self-stigma increases, as people tend to internalise strongly shared ideas. As participant K says, when she rejects her sexuality and can pass as a heterosexual, she can be "fully a Christian". These short interview extracts show how stigmatising religious beliefs are reinforced by heteronormative structures. The participants have internalised these beliefs and are convinced they need to change to have a successful and righteous religious life.

Participant H provides another example of feeling sick after she visited a queer bar. She seems anxious that the place could be destroyed at any time, by God, because there were so many queer people there. During the discussion of the bar, she refers to the story of Sodom and Gomorrah as if the queer bar was a place that should be punished and destroyed. Her description of the bar and her feelings are another example of how homo-negative religious beliefs are aligned with heteronormativity; anything deviant should be punished and is seen as evil.

In these examples the cultural and social idealisation of heteronormativity turns into active efforts to suppress alternatives – including one's own self. Participants in this study who want to change their sexuality often refer to places or friends they have to cut off, in order to dissociate themselves from homosexuality. Heteronormative places or friends – in contrast – are seen as a way to progress their change. People who hold homo-negative views in this sub-study were often friends with each other. People with similar views would support each other in changing. However, for "masculine" women or "feminine" men, this idea of change and strategies to avoid stigma was often not seen as an option as they cannot "adjust" their appearances to pass as heteronormative. They are perceived to be homosexual women or men because of their appearances. Heteronormativity is thus related to the alignment between gender and sexuality, where women are supposed to be feminine and men masculine. For masculine women or feminine men this leaves few or no strategies to navigate stigmatisation in religious communities. Often these participants rejected their religious communities and distanced themselves from anyone who held homo-negative beliefs. They were forced into a life with no other alternatives than being excluded from the heteronormative mainstream culture and society.

Concluding Discussion

In this chapter we have explored the association between heteronormativity and religion by using a form of triangulation. Our study is not representative; rather, it serves the purpose of amplifying some observations and comprehending them in relation to each other, thereby nuancing and broadening our understanding. From a bird's eye view, using some descriptive results and a cluster analysis based on our respondents' agreement with items that measure heteronormativity, we have confirmed the association between religiosity and heteronormativity. The association between heteronormativity and religion is consistent with many previous studies, but we find the results interesting given that our sample consists of young adults, university students. However, both national GDP/capita and female-labour participation also seemed, with some noteworthy exceptions, to be part of the general picture. People affirming tradition as a value are also more likely to exhibit more heteronormative attitudes. The secular are, in light of the results from our cluster analysis, generally more open-minded and less in-group oriented.

Nevertheless, our results indicate not only the association between religiosity and heteronormativity, but also the significance of accounting for basic values. The traditional value in Schwartz's theoretic model is particularly negatively correlated with attitudes towards abortion and same-sex relations. This is, however, an intricate association. Our multi-variate CHAID analysis showed how religiosity and tradition can be clearly related but also work independently of each other. With respect to this there are considerable variations between countries, and contextual variations surface. The same complexity was observed with regards to how attitude towards same-sex relations and abortion varied on a country level, came together or disconnected. CHAID revealed sometimes surprising clusters of nations. For example, across continents, students in India and Peru with shared traditional values express similar attitudes towards same-sex relations, while students from the USA, Canada, Russia and Turkey with shared traditional values express similar attitudes towards abortions.

The third part of our triangulation exemplified how LGBTQI persons themselves can affirm and reproduce rather strong heteronormative attitudes, regardless of the extent to which they have internalised these on a private level. The way they managed this privately could differ enormously, from finding refuge in alternative spaces where they could resist heteronormative violence to turning this violence on themselves. Our examples illustrated a scale from identity-concealment to acceptance of heteronormativity to self-rejection as internalisation of homo-negativity. In these examples too, religion was reproduced as traditionalism, authoritarianism and institutionalism, with a relationship to alternative gender and sexuality characterised by excluding attitudes and practices as an intrinsically constraining and restrictive force, policing gendered and sexual subjectivities and practices. However, these are the results we receive when we turn to the most heteronormative and religious context in our study, and even here, we find islands of resistance and transgression, perhaps with the capacity, to some extent, to transform society and culture.

In short, our study of the association between religion and heteronormativity among young adults in several countries worldwide does not present new or surprising results as such. Rather, our findings and observations are in general consistent with previous research. Nevertheless, the methodological triangulation that we have applied to the data from our global study shows that each level of analysis in itself presents a limited set of observations that are in need of additional nuances and recognition of variations. In cases where we deal with multi-dimensional phenomena such as religion, gender and sexuality we need to be able to approach complexity methodologically and avoid reductionism and relativism. This is even more crucial in cross-cultural studies, but such approaches are also decisive in our effort to resist simplifications that feed into simplified political agendas such as putting trust in modernity or secularity. The decline of religion may empower individual and social agency to produce spaces for non-heteronormative alternatives and challenge the patriarchal kernel of power. Yet, we have shown how such alternatives may also themselves reproduce heteronormativity and that heteronormativity is in some contexts sustained by primarily dominant value profiles and not necessarily by religion. And finally, thinking of the decline of religion as a "solution" means that we disregard other dimensions that produce heteronormativity, and that heteronormativity is not a stable phenomenon, but manifest in many ways and is constantly reinforced and reconfigured cross-culturally.

Peter Nynäs, Dr Theol., is a professor of the Study of Religions at Åbo Akademi University (ÅAU), Finland, and dean of the Faculty of Arts, Psychology and Theology. He is the director and PI of the Åbo Akademi University Centre of Excellence in Research Young Adults and Religion in a Global Perspective Project (2015–19) and earlier the Centre of Excellence in Research Post-secular Culture and a Changing Religious Landscape in Finland Project (2010–14). Among the books he has edited are *On the Outskirts of "the Church": Diversities, Fluidities, and New Spaces of Religion in Finland* (with R. Illman and T. Martikainen, LIT-Verlag, 2015), *Religion, Gender, and Sexuality in Everyday Life* (with A. Yip, Ashgate, 2012), and *The Diversity of Worldviews among Young Adults: Contemporary (Non)Religiosity and Spirituality through the Lens of an International Mixed Method Study* (with A. Keysar, J. Kontala, B.-W. Kwaku Golo, M. Lassander, M. Shterin, S. Sjö and P. Stenner; Springer, 2021). See https://research.abo.fi/en/persons/peter-nynäs.

Dr Ariela Keysar, a demographer, is a recipient of the 2021 Marshall Sklare Award, given by the Association for the Social Scientific Study of Jewry to "a senior scholar who has made a significant scholarly contribution to the social scientific study of Jewry". She is senior fellow in public policy and law at Trinity College, Hartford, Connecticut. She is co-principal investigator, The Class of 1995/5755 Longitudinal Study of Young American and Canadian Jews (1995–2019); and US principal investigator, Young Adults and Religion in a Global Perspective (2015–19). She was associate director of the Institute for the Study of Secularism in Society and Culture at Trinity College (2005–19). She is co-author of *Religion in a Free Market* and *The Next Generation: Jewish Children and Adolescents*. She has co-edited volumes on secularism in relation to women, science, and secularity. She holds a PhD in demography from the Hebrew University of Jerusalem, Israel.

Clara Marlijn Meijer has a PhD in the Study of Religions from Åbo Akademi University in Finland. Her doctoral thesis explores how Ghanaian young adults identifying as sexual minorities negotiate their sexuality and religious identity in everyday life. Her research was part of the Doctoral Training Network for Minority Research and the international research project Young Adults and Religion in a Global Perspective led by Professor Peter Nynäs.

Sofia Sjö, Dr.Theol., works as research librarian at the Donner Institute, Turku, Finland. Her research focuses on religion, popular culture, media and gender and has been published in a number of journals and edited volumes. She was a senior researcher in the YARG project and has co-edited three volumes within the project: a thematic issue on socialisation published in *Religion* 49(2), *Digital Media, Young Adults, and Religion: An International Perspective* (Routledge, 2020) and *The Diversity of Worldviews among Young Adults: Contemporary (Non)Religiosity and Spirituality through the Lens of an International Mixed Method Study* (Springer, 2022).

References

Beit Simchat Torah. 2021. "CBST History". Retrieved from www.cbst.org/. Accessed 21 October 2021.

Berlant, Laurent, and Michael Warner. 1998. "Sex in Public". *Critical Inquiry* 24(2): 547–66.

Boisvert, Donald L., and Carly Daniel-Hughes, eds. 2017. *The Bloomsbury Reader in Religion, Sexuality, and Gender*. London: Bloomsbury Academic.

Brooks, Clem, and Catherine Bolzendahl. 2004. "The Transformation of US Gender Role Attitudes: Cohort Replacement, Social-structural Change, and Ideological Learning". *Social Science Research* 33(1): 106–33.

Browne, Kath, Sally R. Munt and Andrew K.-T. Yip. 2010. *Queer Spiritual Spaces: Sexuality and Sacred Places*. London: Ashgate.

Chambers, Samuel A. 2007. "'An Incalculable Effect': Subversions of Heteronormativity". *Political Studies* 55: 656–79

Connolly, William. 2005. *Pluralism*. Durham, NC: Duke University Press.

Datta, Neil. 2018. "Restoring the Natural Order: The Religious Extremists' Vision to Mobilize European Societies against Human Rights on Sexuality and Reproduction". Retrieved from www.epfweb.org/publications.

Dennis, Jeffery P. 2003. "Heteronormativity". In *Men and Masculinities: A Social, Cultural, and Historical Encyclopaedia*, ed. Michael, S. Kimmel and Amy Aronson, 382. Santa Barbara, CA: ABC CLIO.

Dillon, Michele. 2014. "Asynchrony in Attitudes toward Abortion and Gay Rights: The Challenge to Values Alignment". *Journal for the Scientific Study of Religion* 53(1): 1–16.

Edelman, Lee. 2004. *No Future: Queer Theory and the Death Drive*. Durham, NC: Duke University Press.

Fusch, Patricia, Gene E. Fusch and Lawrence R. Ness. 2018. "Denzin's Paradigm Shift: Revisiting Triangulation in Qualitative Research". *Journal of Social Change* 10(1): 19–32.

Greene, Jennifer C., and Jori N. Hall. 2010. "Dialectics and Pragmatism: Being of Consequence". In *Mixed Methods in Social and Behavioral Research* (2nd edn), ed. Abbas Tashakkori and Charles Teddlie, 119–43. London: Sage.

Hunt, Stephen J., and Andrew K.-T. Yip. 2012. *The Ashgate Research Companion to Contemporary Religion and Sexuality*. Farnham: Ashgate.

ILGA. 2021. *Annual Review of the Human Rights Situation of Lesbian, Gay, Bisexual, Trans and Intersex People in Europe and Central Asia*. Brussels: ILGA Europe. Retrieved from https://ilga-europe.org/report/annual-review-2021/

Jakobsen, Janet, and Ann Pellegrini. 2008. *Secularisms*. Durham: Duke University Press.

Kitzinger, Celia, Sue Wilkinson and Rachel Perkins. 1992. "Theorizing Heterosexuality". *Feminism and Psychology* 2(3): 293–324.

Krok, Dariusz. 2015. "Value Systems and Religiosity as Predictors of Nonreligious and Religious Coping with Stress in Early Adulthood". *Archives of Psychiatry and Psychotherapy* 17(3): 21–31.

Lassander, Mika, and Peter Nynäs. 2016. "Contemporary Fundamentalist Christianity in Finland: The Variety of Religious Subjectivities and their Association with Values". *Interdisciplinary Journal for Religion and Transformation in Contemporary Society* 2(3): 154–84.

McCormack, Mark. 2012. *The Declining Significance of Homophobia: How Teenage Boys are Redefining Masculinity and Heterosexuality*. Oxford: Oxford University Press.

McCormack, Mark, and Eric Anderson. 2010. "'It's Just Not Acceptable any more': The Erosion of Homophobia and the Softening of Masculinity at an English Sixth Form". *Sociology* 44(5): 843–59.

MacKinnon, Catharine. 1982. "Feminism, Marxism, Method, and the State: An Agenda for Theory". *Feminist Theory* 7(3): 515–44.

Maio, Gregory, R. 2017. *The Psychology of Human Values*. New York: Routledge.

May, Vanessa. 2011. *Sociology of Personal Life*. Basingstoke: Palgrave Macmillan.

Meijer, Clara Marlijn. 2022. *Sexuality, Stigma and Religion: The Negotiation of Sexuality and Religion among Sexual Minorities in Ghana*. Åbo: Åbo Akademi University Press.

Moore, Laura M., and Reeve Vanneman. 2003. "Context Matters: Effects of the Proportion of Fundamentalists on Gender Attitudes". *Social Forces* 82(1): 115–39.

Nastasi, Bonni Kaul, John H. Hitchcock and Lisa M. Brown. 2010. "An Inclusive Framework for Conceptualizing Mixed Methods Design Typologies: Moving Toward Fully Integrated Synergistic Research Models". In *Mixed Methods in Social and Behavioral Research* (2nd edn), ed. Abbas Tashakkori and Charles Teddlie, 305–38. London: Sage.

Nynäs Peter, Eetu Kejonen and Pieter Vullers. 2020. "The Changing Relation between Sexual and Gender Minorities and Religion in Finland: Some Observations in the Light of Postsecularity". In *Public Discourses about Homosexuality and Religion in Europe and Beyond*, ed. Marco Derks and Mariecke van den Berg, 171–96. Basingstoke: Palgrave Macmillan.

Nynäs, Peter, Ariela Keysar and Martin Lagerström. 2022. "Who are they and what do they value? The Five Global Worldviews of Young Adults". In *The Diversity of Worldviews among Young Adults: Contemporary (Non)Religiosity and Spirituality through the Lens of an International Mixed Method Study*, ed. Peter Nynäs, Ariela Keysar, Janne Kontala, Ben-Willie Kwaku Golo, Mika T. Lassander, Marat Shterin, Sofia Sjö and Paul Stenner, 47–71. Cham: Springer. https://doi.org/10.1007/978-3-030-94691-3_3

Nynäs, Peter, Janne Kontala and Mika Lassander. 2021. "The Faith Q-Sort: In-Depth Assessment of Diverse Spirituality and Religiosity in 12 Countries". In *Assessing Spirituality in a Diverse World*, ed. Amy L. Ai, Paul Wink, Raymond F. Paloutzian and Kevin A. Harris, 554–73. Cham: Springer.

Nynäs, Peter, and Mika Lassander. 2015. "LGBT Activism and Reflexive Religion: A Case Study from Finland in the Light of Social Movements Theory". *Journal of Contemporary Religion* 30(3): 453–71.

Nynäs, Peter, and Andrew K.-T. Yip, eds. 2012. *Religion, Gender, and Sexuality in Everyday Life*. Farnham: Ashgate.

Onwuegbuzie, Anthony J., and Julie P. Combs. 2010. "Emergent Data Analysis Techniques in Mixed Methods Research: A Synthesis". In *Mixed Methods in Social and Behavioral Research* (2nd edn), ed. Abbas Tashakkori and Charles Teddlie, 397–430. London: Sage.

Page, Sarah-Jane, and Heather Shipley. 2020. *Religion and Sexualities: Theories, Themes, and Methodologies*. New York: Routledge.

Perales, Francisco, and Gary Bouma. 2019. "Religion, Religiosity and Patriarchal Gender Beliefs: Understanding the Australian Experience". *Journal of Sociology* 55(2): 323–41.

Perreault, William D., and Hiram C. Barksdale. 1980. "A Model-free Approach for Analysis of Complex Contingency Data in Survey Research". *Journal of Marketing Research* 17: 503–15.

Pink, Sarah. 2012. *Situating Everyday Life: Practices and Places*. London: Sage.

Rahman, Momin, and Stevi Jackson. 2010. *Gender and Sexuality: Sociological Approaches*. Cambridge: Polity Press.

Rich, Adrienne. 1980. "Compulsory Heterosexuality and Lesbian Existence". *Signs* 5(4): 631–60.

Richardson, Diane. 2010. "Youth Masculinities: Compelling Male Heterosexuality". *British Journal of Sociology* 61(4): 737–56.

Richardson, Diane, and Surya Monro. 2012. *Sexuality, Equality and Diversity*. Basingstoke: Palgrave MacMillan.

Saroglou, Vassilis, Vanessa Delpierre and Rebecca Dernelle. 2004. "Values and Religiosity: A Meta-analysis of Studies Using Schwartz's Model". *Personality and Individual Differences* 37(4): 721–34. https://doi.org/10.1016/j.paid.2003.10.005.

Schwartz, Shalom H. 1992. "Universals in the Content and Structure of Values: Theoretical Advances and Empirical Tests in 20 Countries". *Advances in Experimental Social Psychology* 25: 1–65.

Schwartz, Shalom H. 2017. "The Refined Theory of Basic Values". In *Values and Behavior: Taking a Cross-cultural Perspective*, ed. Sonia Roccas and Lilach Sagiv, 51–72. Cham: Springer.

Schwartz, Shalom H., Jan Cieiuch, Michele Vecchione, Eldad Davidov, Ronald Fischer, Constanze Beierlein, Alice Ramos, Markku Verkasalo, Jan-Erik Lönnqvist, Kursad Demirutku, Ozlem Dirilen-Gumus and Mark Konty. 2012. "Refining the Theory of Basic Individual Values". *Journal of Personality and Social Psychology* 103(4): 663–88.

Schwartz, Shalom H., and Sipke Huismans. 1995. "Value Priorities and Religiosity in Four Western Religions". *Social Psychology Quarterly* 58(2): 88–107.

Seguino, Stephanie. 2011. "Help or Hindrance? Religion's Impact on Gender Inequality in Attitudes and Outcomes". *World Development* 39(8): 1308–21

Taylor, Charles. 2007. *A Secular Age*. Cambridge, MA: Harvard University Press.

Taylor, Yvette, and Ria Snowdon, eds. 2014. *Queering Religion, Religious Queers*. New York: Routledge.

Trappolin, Luca, Alessandro Gasparini and Robert Wintemute. 2012. *Confronting Homophobia in Europe: Social and Legal Perspectives*. Oxford: Hart.

Weeks, Jeffrey. 2007. *The World We Have Won: The Remaking of Erotic and Intimate Life*. London: Routledge.

Yip, Andrew K.-T. 2008. "The Quest for Intimate/Sexual Citizenship: Lived Experiences of Lesbian and Bisexual Muslim Women". *Contemporary Islam* 2(2): 99–117.

Yip, Andrew K.-T. 2010. "Coming Home from the Wilderness: An Overview of Recent Scholarly Research on LGBTQI Religiosity/Spirituality in the West". In *Queer Spiritual Spaces: Sexuality and Sacred Spaces*, ed. Kath Browne, Sally A. Munt and Andrew K.-T. Yip, 35–50. Burlington, VT: Ashgate.

Yip, Andrew K.-T. 2012. "Homophobia and Ethnic Minorities in the UK". In *Confronting Homophobia in Europe: Social and Legal Perspectives*, ed. Luca Trappolin, Alessandro Gasparini and Robert Wintemute, 107–30. Oxford: Hart.

Yip, Andrew K.-T., Michael Keenan and Sarah-Jane Page. 2011. *Religion, Youth and Sexuality: Selected Key Findings from a Multi-faith Exploration*. Nottingham: University of Nottingham. Retrieved from www.religionandsociety.org.uk/uploads/docs/2011_03/1298990240_rys-research-report.pdf

Yip, Andrew K.-T., and Peter Nynäs. 2012. "Re-framing the Intersection between Religion, Gender and Sexuality in Everyday Life". In *Religion, Gender, and Sexuality in Everyday Life*, ed. Andrew K.-T. Yip and Peter Nynäs, 1–16. Burlington, VT: Ashgate.

Yip, Andrew K.-T., and Sarah-Jane Page. 2016. *Religious and Sexual Identities: A Multi-faith Exploration of Young Adults*. London: Routledge.

Young, Pamela and Heather Shipley. 2020. *Identities under Construction: Religion, Gender, and Sexuality among Youth in Canada*. Montreal: McGill-Queen's University Press.

– 5 –

The Multiplicity of Chinese and Indian Religions

A Critical Reappraisal of the Notion of "Eastern Religion"

MÅNS BROO AND RUBY SAIN

Despite devastating criticism from post-colonial scholars over recent decades, the distinction between "Eastern" and "Western" religion is still used as a generic model for comprehending basic distinctions in the study of religion as well as in relation to debates on religious change in the West. Colin Campbell discussed the Western understanding of "Eastern religions" as marking a watershed in contemporary religious change. But what really are these "Eastern" religions, outside the desk of scholars? This chapter explores Campbell's basic model and in particular questions the inherent stereotypical assumption of "Eastern" or "Asian" religion still powerfully resonant in the West. Embedded in the rich mixed-methods material, the chapter points to the inherent and neglected diversity in the Asian countries of the People's Republic of China and India. Our results show that while categories such as "Muslim", "Buddhist" and "Taoist" are naturally useful in many ways, they tell us little about the types of worldviews that the young university students studied here hold as additional and relevant crossings of the lines of religious affiliation are significant.

Theorising Asian Religion

While the study of religion as an academic discipline was born in a Western context, many of the early theorists had much to say about Asia as well. Max Weber famously saw primitive religion as fundamentally magical and animistic. Once society developed enough for the appearance of a priestly class, religion was transformed into one of two alternative forms. One posited an immanent divinity, always part of the world and to which humankind in some way can "adapt" itself, and the other a transcendental divinity, fundamentally different from the world. The first form, characterised by Weber as the "Eastern religious world view", is one that rejects dualism altogether (Campbell 2007, 85). There is a paradox here, often articulated in overviews of Indian religion (e.g. Babb 1975, xvii–xviii): this non-dualism or unity emerges from a tradition bewilderingly varied and manifold.

Weber's "Eastern religious world view" has recently been picked up by Colin Campbell (2007) in the context of his idea of an "easternisation of the West". But what exactly does this monistic Eastern world view look like? In a critical article, Malcolm Hamilton (2002, 244–5) summarises Campbell's – or perhaps rather Weber's – view: in the Eastern view humanity and nature are one; the spiritual and physical are one; mind and body are one; a human being should recognise his or her basic oneness with nature, the spiritual and the mental, rather than attempt to analyse, label, categorise, manipulate, control or consume the things of the world; because of his or her oneness with all existence, a human being should feel "at home" in any place and with any person; science and technology at best create an illusion of progress; enlightenment involves achieving a sense of oneness with the universal; it is a state where all dichotomies vanish; meditation, a special state of quiet contemplation, is essential for achieving enlightenment.

The Western view is the opposite of this. Here, humans have characteristics which set them apart from nature and the spiritual; humans are divided into a body, a spirit and a mind; there is a personal God who rules over humanity; humans must control and manipulate nature to ensure their survival; rational thought and an analytical approach to problem-solving should be emphasised; science and technology have given us a good life and provide our main hope for an even better future; action and the competitive spirit should be rewarded.

Now, the very term "Asian religiosity" is of course extremely universalist and reductionistic, even colonial in tone. As articulated by Edward Said (1980), one of the goals of post-colonial theory is to articulate the ways in which colonising nations make universal claims, whereby those of the colonised become tentative and provisional (Deal and Beal 2004, 143). Gayatri Chakravorty Spivak and other post-colonial theorists remind us about the dangers of essentialist categories such as "Asian religiosity", "Chinese culture" or "Indian religion". As social constructs they are far more unstable than they may sound, since such labels were applied within a colonial discourse, with significant ideological and hegemonic implications. The subaltern was forced into a position not of his or her own choosing, but one that he or she often assumed later on (Deal and Beal 2004, 149).

Randall Nadeau (2013, 245) further reminds us that the very existence of Asian religions as distinct traditions, as opposed to their being part of a general "heathendom" or "paganism", was recognised in the West only in very recent times. The first English usage of the term "Boudhism" occurred in 1801, "Hindooism" in 1829, "Taouism" in 1839 and "Confucianism" in 1862. To a large extent, these are terms constructed in the West (for an excellent discussion on the history of the term "Hinduism", see Pennington 2005), that only later came to be aassumed by Asians themselves. The extent to which they apply to any kind of empirical reality "out there" is debatable, as there is an enormous internal diversity within the two countries studied in this chapter as well. Nadeau (2013, 13) cites a linguistic diversity index, according to which there is a 92 per cent likelihood that any two random Indians will speak mutually incomprehensible languages. In China, the same number is 51 per cent. This could be contrasted with only 2.7 per cent in Japan.

Rather than finding a generic "Eastern religion" within the rich YARG material, we should therefore expect to find a great diversity and methodological tools for systematically mapping and describing this diversity. That much is obvious. But what does this diversity look like and how does it relate to earlier studies on religion in these countries when we explore the results from using Q-sort and interviews from the YARG project (see Chapter 1)?

China

While C. K. Yang (1961) understood Chinese religion in general (rather than merely as "Buddhism", "Taoism" and so on) as "diffused religion" in contrast to institutional religion, Fenggang Yang's (2012) comprehensive overview of religious change under Communist rule in China suggests a more nuanced approach, showing the great variety of Chinese religion.

While officially atheist and demanding open denunciation of gods, spirits and ghosts from its members (Yang 2016, 438), the Chinese Communist Party has historically applied different strategies towards religion. Since the end of the violently anti-religious Cultural Revolution in 1979, China has seen a dramatic resurgence of religion – but one that is carefully monitored by the state. Lily Kong and Junxi Quian (2019, 262) posit three reasons for the present liberal policy towards religion. First, religions have been made part of the state's mission of constructing "spiritual civilisation" and a "harmonious society". Second, religions give the state a new edge of soft political power in both domestic and international affairs. Third, religions have been used as resources and assets for regional development.

Using a political-economic approach to understanding religion in contemporary China, Fenggang Yang presents a model of three "markets" of religion. The first is the "red" or officially approved, legal one, the second is the "black" or illegal one and the third is the "grey" one with explicit religion (illegal activities of legal groups etc.) and implicitly religious matters in the form of culture or health. Until recently, because of a dispute between the Vatican and the Chinese government, two-thirds of Chinese Catholics fell into the black market, together with Falun gong and many Christian sects (Yang 2012, 100). Yang further writes (2012, 118–19) that 100 million of the 1.4 billion Chinese belong to the red market and another 200 million to the black market, but that another study shows that 85 per cent have some religious beliefs or practices.

Many studies, however, estimate the religiosity in China to be considerably lower than that. According to the 2000 World Value Survey (Yang 2012, 130), only 13.7 per cent of respondents in the People's Republic of China considered themselves "a religious person" (compared to 72.2 per cent in Taiwan five years earlier), and only 6 per cent were members of a religious denomination (again compared to 79.1 per cent in Taiwan). This can be compared to the combined memberships of the Chinese Communist Party, the Chinese Communist Youth League and the Chinese Young Pioneers of about 20.7 per cent of the total population, more than that of any organised religion (Yang 2016, 437–8).

Confucianism, whether seen as a religion or not (Sun 2013), has seen a revival during the last few decades and is often claimed to form the very backbone of Chinese culture (Nadeau 2013, 5). It puts an emphasis on education, political authoritarianism, family values, filial piety, civic values, public support for the arts and civil religion, ceremonial living, politeness and decorum. The holistically hierarchical social structure of China has is in fact much in common with that of India, even though one is based on Confucian principles and the other on the caste society (Saavala 2010, 14).

India

Early studies of Indian religion and particularly Hinduism were heavily based on Sanskritic, Brahminical sources, often giving scholars the appearance of an unchanging tradition, or of a glorious ancient tradition in decline (Pennington 2005). Overviews of Hinduism have often retained some of this approach until recent times (e.g. Brockington 1981). At the same time, as Swapan Pramanik (2013, 59–60) notes, the writings of European travellers and missionaries in the nineteenth century emphasised the multiplicity of beliefs and practices in India in contrast to the perceived monochromatic normative structures of (particularly) Protestant Christianity. Such writings eventually led to early ethnographic studies not only of Hindu communities but also tribes and people belonging to other religions. A particularly striking example of this kind of work (though one naturally dated in terms of method and theory today – particularly in regard to notions of "race") is the exhaustive *Tribes and Castes of Bengal* by H. H. Risley (1998 [1891-2]). Such early sociological work, generally by colonial administrators, was eventually followed by studies by Indian sociologists, such as M. N. Srinivas (1952), G. S. Ghurye (1953), L. P. Vidyarthi (1961) and many others.

In trying to make sense of the vast variety of lived Hinduism, several models have been suggested. Lawrence Babb (1975) saw popular religion in India as a complex system of divine and human hierarchies. C. J. Fuller (2004), on the other hand, saw the complex relationship between humans and a multitude of divine figures as being central for understanding popular Hinduism. Others have focused on the interrelation between purity and impurity as well as auspiciousness and inauspiciousness (e.g. Carman and Marglin 1985).

In contrast to China, India has often been seen as an intensely religious country, where religious differences – particularly between the Hindu majority and the large Muslim minority – influence politics, economy and social life. Further, the division between "religious" and "secular" is said to be notoriously difficult to draw in India, not least in relation to Hindutva, Hindu nationalism (e.g. Pramanik 2013, 68). Nevertheless, the concept of a "secular state" is both an important and a contested one in India. Originally a Western concept, it has been reframed and is constantly renegotiated in India, where "secularity" generally is understood as being religiously neutral instead of non-religious (for a discussion, see e.g. Prasad and Kumar 2000).

Using the FQS Statements to Test the Thesis of "Eastern Religion"

Before moving on to the FQS prototypes from China and India, let us see whether or not the global YARG material can say anything about Campbell's theory of Eastern and Western religion. Table 9 below

Table 9. FQS Statements as sorted in four countries (scale: –4 to 4).

Country	N	FQS9	FQS11	FQS44	FQS53	FQS70	FQS75	FQS86
India	45	1.89	–0.36	–0.40	–0.47	0.93	0.40	0.13
China	46	1.26	1.54	–1.22	–0.37	–0.04	1.22	1.20
Sweden	30	0.90	0.30	–0.13	0.67	1.63	1.27	0.57
USA	49	0.61	0.45	0.22	0.20	0.47	0.84	0.53

shows how the FQS interviewees, independent of prototypes they fall under, rated the FQS statements (Appendix 2) most closely dealing with Campbell's dichotomy. Of the thirteen countries included in the YARG survey, we chose the USA and Sweden to reflect the West, while China and India represented the East. USA and Sweden are examples of cultural areas where (Protestant) Christianity and the study of religions have developed in parallel, while China and India represent two rather different parts of what is usually referred to as the East. Two of the FQS statements deal with how to understand the ultimate being. FQS9, "Thinks about the ultimate as a life force rather than a supernatural being", and FQS53, "Believes in a divine being with whom one can have personal relations", can be understood as describing pantheism or theism, or an Eastern and Western understanding of the divine, respectively.

In this case, there does indeed seem to be a difference between East and West. Viewing the ultimate as a life force rather than as a person (FQS9) scored significantly higher in India (1.89) and China (1.26) than in Sweden (0.90) and USA (0.61). Similarly, the theist opposite view (FQS53, viewing the divine as a being with whom one can have personal relations) scored higher in the West (USA 0.20 and Sweden 0.67) than in the East (India –0.47 and China –0.37).

However, things were less clear with the other statements. For FQS11, "Has a strong sense of a spiritual or higher order of reality in the midst of the natural world (e.g. a forest or the ocean)", which comes close to Campbell's "man should recognise his basic oneness with nature, the spiritual and the mental", the results are ambiguous. China ranks highest (1.54), but India ranks lower (–0.36) than Sweden and USA (0.30 and 0.45, respectively). The same is the case with FQS86, "Is committed to following a spiritual path that is in harmony with the environment", where again China comes first (1.20) but India last (0.13). Also, FQS75, "Feels a sense of peace even in the face of life difficulties", corresponding to Campbell's "because of his oneness with all existence, man should feel 'at home' in any place and with any person", shows Sweden first (with 1.27), followed by China (1.22), USA (0.84) and last again India (0.40).

With FQS44, "Senses a divine or universal luminous element within him- or herself", corresponding with Campbell's "spiritual and physical are one", we find USA taking the lead (0.22), followed by Sweden (-0.13), India (-0.40) and China (-1.22).

Finally, FQS70, "Rejects religious ideas that conflict with scientific or rational principles", corresponding to Campbell's Western "rational thought and an analytical approach to problem solving should be emphasised" or Eastern "science and technology at best create an illusion of progress", shows Sweden as being most "Western" (1.63) – but then comes India (0.93), followed by USA (0.47) finally China (-0.04).

What we thus see from the FQS interviewees is that attributing national differences to some essential difference between East and West does not work very well. Of course, the FQS was not primarily constructed to measure or test a difference between Eastern and Western religiosities. There are, for example, no statements that directly assess the monism or "oneness" that figures so prominently in Campbell's Eastern religiosity, a surprising oversight considering the great variety of worldviews otherwise present among the statements – an oversight that shows that creating an instrument that captures 100 per cent of worldviews is very difficult. Neither can the Western or Eastern samples be said to be representative for all Western or Eastern university students, let alone the "West" and "East" in any strict sense. Finally, as noted by Minna Saavala in her ethnographic study of middle-class Hindus in the South Indian city of Hyderabad, interviews and surveys are not always so useful in studying the worldviews of the middle class. Saavala argues (2010, 3, 24–5) that the need for keeping up appearances in the midst of a struggle over prestige and propriety means that the interviewees may not always disclose their personal opinions.

Nevertheless, we find little support for Campbell's dichotomy in the material at hand. Instead, let us take a closer look at the young students interviewed in China and India. What kinds of worldviews do they hold?

The FQS Prototypes: China

The Chinese FQS interviews were all conducted by Yiwen Ji and Juan Cao at Fudan University in Shanghai. With almost 30,000 students, Fudan University is one of the most prestigious Chinese universities today. It is also an extremely selective university, with less than 0.2 per cent of National College Entrance Examination takers being accepted (*Times Higher Education* 2019a). As a comprehensive university, Fudan has a strong tradition in humanities, social sciences and fundamental sciences.

Nearly one-third of the students come from the Yangtze Triangle – Shanghai, Jiangsu and Zhejiang Province. The other students come from all over China, most of them having at least a middle-class background. The students at Fudan therefore do not represent young people in China in general, but rather a very privileged elite – an elite that will be instrumental in building the China of the future.

Six prototypes emerged from the Chinese FQS samples. This is a lot; within the global YARG sample, most countries had three or four prototypes and only India had more (eight). Appendix 2 The YARG Prototypes describes these prototypes using the terminology of their distinguishing FQS statements, that is, statements scoring +4 or –4 or that were otherwise statistically distinctive. These short descriptions were created within the YARG project based on longer descriptions by Dr Sofia Sjö with the assistance of Professor Peter Nynäs and Måns Broo. In the interest of saving space, we have had to contend with a more general, contextualising commentary below, including some illustrative quotations from interviewees flagged as representing the particular prototype.

China 1: "Non-religious This-Worldly Activist"

China 1 is a secular prototype, similar to the first prototype of most cases within the YARG project, though it is noteworthy that the first Chinese prototype is not against religion *per se*. This ties in well with the current (comparatively) liberal view on religion in the People's Republic (Yang 2012, 262). In common with many other secular first prototypes, China 1 is also male-dominated (Sjö *et al.* 2022).

China 1 is open to some type of belief, even though not necessarily one that involves some kind of transcendent other. As one interviewee (YCHYJ164) says:

> Because, after all, what gives life dignity is really nothing but faith. It could be a religious belief, or it could be a faith. Anyway, it is by faith that we are empowered. And this power itself – I do not want to ascribe it to religion. It is more like to take personal responsibility for the person himself. Religion, on the other hand, seems to me like a spiritual comfort. [...] Because, you know, people are too weak to take on some responsibilities. By positing the existence of a divinity, they have someone to bear much of the weight. In this way, when I do wrong, I can attribute my mistakes to the will of the divinity, or, I can console myself that I shall be forgiven after all. That is to say, when I find it hard to forgive myself, I invite, say, a god, to do the forgiving for me so that I can go on with my life without feeling guilty. [...] But all this sounds to me like a self-comforting excuse. I think religion is something like spiritual marijuana.

China 2: "Open-Minded and Spiritually Engaged"

China 2 expresses a personal interest in spiritual and religious matters. In many countries, prototype 2 represents a traditionally theistic worldview. In distinction, this prototype is indeed interested in religion and spirituality, but is not committed to any particular community. This open-mindedness is well illustrated by the following interviewee (YCNJT002):

> Yes, because I think I don't have a fixed or unique religious faith, but I'm very interested in this. I think all kinds of religious theories are quite interesting. I have a good friend who is a Muslim. We usually discuss some Islamic doctrines. I don't quite agree with some Islamic things, because he is very devout and very traditional, but I still think that his experience can give me some inspiration. For example, Muslims spend almost a month fasting. They can't eat anything during the day, so he can only eat at midnight. He had a hard time because of his habit, especially at the end of the semester. When he expresses to me his faith, it seems to me unique. It is very different from that of non-believers or non-Muslims, because he doesn't take this as a burden but accepts it as granted. This is very interesting. In fact, many religions have this tradition of asceticism, but when time goes by, it has received some criticism or been compromised by secularism. [...] I've attended a lot of Christian lessons before, and I am also very interested in Buddhism. I feel it is good to get all kinds of religious traditions together and to compare and inspire each other.

The open-minded view on religion and spirituality of this prototype combined with the importance placed on individual freedom of choice comes out nicely in the following citation by another interviewee (YCHYJ170):

> Actually, I think all the religions share some things, such as we should be kind to the world. However, that is the manner of dealing with people. As for dealing with our own heart, I think we should follow the spirituality and explore by ourselves. Everyone had his own way and we just need to find one ideal for ourselves.

Being open-minded does not mean that this prototype has no strong opinion. One such is rejecting the idea of men and women by nature having different roles in society. As one interviewee says (YCNJT002):

> I: What do you think of gender roles?
> P: I think this is quite interesting. Buddhism believes that all beings are equal. Anyway, I think, first, men and women should be equal. As for their responsibilities in the society, there is no much difference except giving birth to children. But I think that giving birth to children should be a common responsibility of both men and women. It isn't only a responsibility of women alone. From the feminist point of view, I can't

accept the concept in Muslim tradition. They have such a tradition. I think that since religion always talk about universal fraternity, it should treat everything equal. If it confines different duties of men and women, it is easy to cause discrimination or inequality.

China 3: "Committed and Communally Engaged Believer"

China 3 represents the traditionally theist prototype, with a particular emphasis on community. Only women made up this prototype (Sjö *et al.* 2022). As a Catholic woman (YCNJT205) says, when talking about religious memories from her childhood:

> Then my mum brought me to the church where there was a summer class. There were about 20 or 30 Catholic kids there, and there were people explaining the Bible and teaching us to sing. My mum was busy at work and had no time to pick me up from this class. And one day she even forgot to order me lunch. That was really sad. Then the church teacher cooked noodles for me. This is something I find special and remember deeply. I felt that I belonged there, or there was someone other than my friends who would care about me. This is what I remember the deepest.

Nevertheless, in common with all the other prototypes so far, this one supports individual freedom of choice and matters of faith and morality. As the same Catholic woman (YCNJT205) says, when answering the question whether or not her parents as well are Catholics:

> Yes, my mum is, and my dad might be as well, theoretically speaking. There used to be regulations like decades ago that said that in a couple both must be believers [in order to get married in the church], and my dad started to believe in Catholicism due to this reason. But now he doesn't care much about it, he's like hanging around the outer circle yet doesn't interfere in me and my mum's belief. Furthermore, since Chinese people have been Buddhists long ago, like there are a lot of Buddhists and there are people in my dad's family who believe in Buddhism, he likes to burn incense [at Buddhist altars]. We tried to talk him out of it, but we eventually decided to ignore it, because he never interferes in our belief, and he'd go to church when we drag him with us, so we let it be.

Also, the idea of taking comfort in thinking that those who do not live righteously will suffer is foreign to this prototype (globally, in the whole YARG sample, only one Hebrew Israeli prototype rates this statement highly). As the same person says (YCNJT205):

> I: Then would you think that those who don't believe in God, they will go to hell no matter if they are good people.
> P: No.

I: You don't think this way?

P: No, I don't think this way. First of all, even if you believe in God, you wouldn't be able to enter heaven without being a good person, so the main thing is that one needs to be a good person in the first place. I think this matters more.

China 4: "Experience-Oriented and Spiritually Inclined Traditionalist"

For China 4, spiritual experiences are essential. Somewhat like China 2, the spiritual experiences of China 4 need not be linked to traditional religion *per se*. One interviewee (YCNJT200) exemplified the FQS statement on liking "paradox and mysteries" (FQS91) with Harry Potter and the film, *Pan's Labyrinth*. Nonetheless, an interesting aspect of China 4 is that while there is little or no religious or spiritual engagement here, some religious ideas figure in the background. As one young man says (YCHYJ166) with regard to who taught him the spiritual ideas he holds to:

> No one taught me. There is a line by Su Dongpo [1037–1101]. [...]. It goes something like this: those whose names are remembered by history were invariably born at troubled times, by which he meant social upheavals. At times of peace, fame is meaningless. He goes on to say that, if you start to read and learn at this life-time, you are already too late, which means that things like reading and learning must be begun in a previous life and it is invariably too late if you realise your want to learn only in this life. I count myself as one of those who did some reading in their previous lives.

China 5: "Disengaged Relativist"

China 5 presents a shifting outlook. Religion and spirituality are distant from the daily life of China 5. As one interviewee (YCNJT182) says, talking about her own childhood:

> I knew nothing about [religion] when I was young. Uh, if you want me to say something, does the belief of folk religion count? Actually I didn't get touch with it, either. But my grandmother believed. Does the tomb-sweeping count? I knew well about that when I was a child. And my grandmother believed in ghosts and spirits and often told us some horror stories. Afterwards, when I went to senior high school, my father followed Buddhism, and he sometimes took me out to do religious activities together with them. In fact, I didn't get what they were doing then. Sometimes, they may recite or sing the scriptures while I stood by

at a loss. Maybe my father also showed me some lectures delivered by the masters of Buddhism. In fact, these masters told some great truths, which I had heard about in my daily life, but the difference was that they were in a religious form. That's it. Besides, there was something in it out of contact with our times which I couldn't believe in. And then I went to college and took courses. One title for our midterm paper was Chinese beliefs. I read many relevant things preparing for that.

The doubt about whether or not folk religion counts as religion is shared by others as well (e.g. YCNJT200), and harks back to the way in which all beliefs not explicitly part of organised religions such as Buddhism or Islam were in the People's Republic of China categorised as harmful "feudal superstitions" (*fengjian mixin*), sometimes with the exception of annual festivals and ancestor worship. Only during the 1990s did Chinese scholars start writing about "popular beliefs" (*minijan xinjang*) instead, but the negative attitude towards folk religion largely still persists (Overmyer 2001).

Beside relatives and college courses, another source of religious knowledge is the internet. As one interviewee (YCNJT182) recalls, tying in with the feeling of loss of faith or divine presence also characteristic of this prototype:

> I: The first time when I logged in to Zhihu [a Chinese website for questions and answers] was to read some funny answers. Then I found someone in the year 2013 maybe. I was then in the third year of my senior high school and always did badly in writing compositions. This person wrote many articles then, and I would log in to Zhihu and read them. He was already dead but his articles influenced me a lot.
> I: In which aspect?
> P: The pure things. The purest beauty, the simplest things. I think he really lived a simple life, maybe even poor, but that time I was totally touched. Now I have lost that feeling, but I was really happy then.

Nevertheless, what really characterises this prototype is the shifting, uncertain nature of its worldview. It represents very much a young person still searching for his or her identity. As one interviewee (YCNJT201) says:

> I: Do you have some kind of dream for your future?
> P: No, I don't have special belief or ideal, I think.
> I: Have you thought about what you are going to do in the future, have you?
> P: I'm still thinking, I don't know what exactly I'm going to do yet, because I'm only at my second year, so it is not something in a hurry, I can first ... first write my thesis.

China 6: "Self-realisation and Experience-Focused Humanist"

China 6 takes leave of religion, focusing on self-realisation instead. China 6 is similar to the secular China 1, though there is more room for spiritual experiences here, with the proviso that the word "spiritual" should not be taken to mean something transcendent. The main thing is self-realisation, or self-actualisation, as the following interviewee (YCHYJ161) understands the term:

> I: Why do you agree with this card, "Sees personal self-realisation as a primary spiritual goal in life" [FQS93]?
> P: [...] Because my experience in school and among friends tells me that only self-actualisation can be defined as the primary goal of life.
> I: What does that really mean?
> P: Self-actualisation is to realise your own value.
> I: Then what is your value in your opinion? Have you thought about that?
> P: Everyone is good at something and can do something better than others. They can bring change to some people or to a small group. Though I'm an economics major, I don't think I will go into a consulting firm or other companies that people usually think economics majors go to. Perhaps I will make some money, try to get financially independent and then draw, sketch and paint. That is my dream.

Nevertheless, there is some connection to religion even here. The same interviewee connects the idea of symmetry, harmony and balance as reflections of ultimate truth that she approves of with Buddhism, the religion of her grandparents.

Taken together, these prototypes reveal some interesting facts about the students interviewed at Fudan University. With a few exceptions, these urban, elite students are not religiously very committed and much of the information they have about religion comes from university courses they have attended, often on Chinese classical literature. This is also one reason why Buddhism figures so much more prominently than Taoism in the interviews. The Confucian value of honouring one's parents does not come out clearly in the FQS, but it is heavily present in the interviews, where many mention the expectations their parents have of them – almost all of the interviewees are single children.

While some criticise specific religious customs (mostly in relation to gender differences), almost nobody is against religion *per se*. Many of the students mention religious friends, parents or grandparents, a fact suggestive in itself: being associated with religion is something worth mentioning. Even if being actively associated with religion oneself is not the norm, religion in itself is thus seen as an important part of Chinese culture (for an overview of Christianity and Chinese culture, see Ruokanen and Huang 2010). Nevertheless, actively searching for a personal religious identity is not a part of the lived experience of these students, as FQS statement 72 "Has moved from one group to another in search of a spiritual or ideological home" is the only consensus statement in the whole Chinese sample, where all the prototypes ranked it negatively.

Further, with the possible exception of the Catholics, Yang's "black market" of religion does not figure in the interviews. Probably this is because these students have no connection with illegal religious groups, but it may also be a strategic choice to not mention such ties, as they might endanger the elite status of the students. Finally, even though Chinese scholars are turning away from the trend of calling popular beliefs "superstitions", that concept is still very much alive among these students.

The FQS Prototypes: India

The data from India were gathered by research assistants Sohini Ray and Mallarika Sarkar in the state of West Bengal. Having more than 91 million inhabitants (as of 2011), West Bengal is one of the most populous states of India. Hindus at 70.5 per cent make up the majority in the state, according to the latest Census of India (Government of India 2011). Muslims comprise 27 per cent of the population, making them a large minority. Among the smaller religious minorities, Christians (0.72 per cent) and Buddhists (0.31 per cent) are the most noteworthy. The capital of West Bengal is Kolkata (Calcutta), often called (particularly by its inhabitants) the cultural capital of India. Nevertheless, West Bengal is predominantly an agricultural economy.

To capture the diversity of West Bengal, the FQS interviews were conducted at three universities of West Bengal: the elite Jadavpur University in metropolitan Kolkata (ranked tenth in all of India, *Times Higher Education* 2019b), the University of Kalyani in semi-urban Nadia and the University of Gour Banga in rural Malda. While Muslims are a minority in West Bengal as a whole, they form the majority (54 per cent) in Malda, and are therefore well represented at Gour Banga University as well. According to Arijit Das (2017), the Muslim population of Malda is nevertheless lagging behind in almost all the parameters of elementary education.

Eight prototypes emerged from the Indian FQS interviews, the maximum number allowed by the software used to create them. This in itself indicates the great variety found within the Indian material. Three prototypes were represented by only women (3, 7 and 8), but unfortunately, the Indian FQS material in general was rather heavily skewed towards women (more than 70 per cent of the respondents were women, see Sjö *et al.* 2022), making this difference less important than it might have been.

We will below briefly describe these prototypes in the same way as we did for China.

India 1: "Progressive Secular Humanist"

Rejecting religion, India 1 is positive towards both personal and worldwide human progress. Interestingly, all the students flagged as representing this prototype are students at metropolitan Jadavpur University, with a Hindu background. Secularism has a long tradition among the intellectuals of Bengal (Chaudhuri 2012), and actively championed among the students of Jadavpur University, often considered heavily influenced by Marxist activists (Thakur and Yasmeen 2015). This secular Hindu prototype is particularly worthy of note in a world where preconceived categories of Hindus are often the idealised spiritual one, the incompetent otherworldly one or the feared nationalist (Saavala 2010, 150).

The Hindu students at Jadavpur University are in many ways a typical example of the Bengali *bhadralok*, "respectable people", the Hindu middle class with its origins in the late-eighteenth-century colonial enterprise that was the first group to gain entry to urban professional occupations. Having its origin in high-caste groups, the *bhadralok* is today a more heterogeneous social group. They are characterised by the great emphasis they place on education (often English-medium, such as at Jadavpur) for their children and an appreciation of writing, music and the arts (Ganguly-Scrase 2003, 551). Minna Saavala (2010, 152) found that while the new middle class in Hyderabad have increasingly become conscious of the importance of religion, the same does not appear to be true for the "old" middle class of Kolkata (see Broo *et al.* 2019, 226–7).

Compared to the similarly secular China 1, India 1 is much more critical of religion, no doubt at least in part because, for Indian students, religion is such a publicly polarising factor, compared to their Chinese counterparts. Being critical of the religion of one's people and distancing oneself from the idea that religion should rule the nation are very important here. One female interviewee (YINSR023) mentions the Babri Masjid case, when in 1992 Hindu activists demolished a mosque built over the site held to be the birthplace of the Hindu god Rama, leading to riots claiming at least two thousand deaths all over India and prolonged litigation over the ownership of the site. Linking such religious violence with ISIS of Syria and Iraq, she says,

[Religion] affected me in a very bad way in the Babri Masjid case. That was horrible. Like I was young back then when the verdict came out [in 2000], I think I was fourteen, and I remember the day because we were supposed to go on a school trip on that day. But the school trip was cancelled because the Babri Masjid verdict came out and there was huge social turmoil all around. I do consider myself lucky that all the time that I was in the city I never witnessed riots or bombings or stuff like that that religion triggers, bad stuff that happens all around the world. [...] Every Indian that day I think was moved by that in a very negative way. And there are many international things like that that take place. I think what the ISIS is trying to do does affect me very badly because I always imagine myself being there in Syria or in any Middle Eastern country and I don't know what to say right now. I feel that I am lucky that I have been born here, but if I was born there I wouldn't have any guarantee of life. I can say that tomorrow I am going to live and go to the university regularly now but not there. People my age, boys and girls my age are living in fear and all because of how the deformed idea of religion, this perverted idea of religion is affecting us.

Something else that leads India 1 to take exception to religion is the idea of giving up bodily pleasures for religious or spiritual reasons. As the same interviewee says,

That's just stupid because we only get one life and in this one life I think we should live our life to the fullest! Because we are humans, we are also, we have good and bad in us. So in order to achieve something I can not give up a part of me because that would only hinder the natural balance. We are supposed to do some things in our lives, there are certain things that humans do and for that, nature has set us in this way. So if I give up a natural instinct for some other spiritual or religious thing that I want to achieve, that is not natural to me.

Another student (YINSR024) follows a similar naturalistic discourse in explaining why she disapproves of religious regulations on sexuality:

The next card [FQS59] says "his or her sexuality is strongly guided by a religious or spiritual outlook". Okay, I have to strongly disagree with this because sexuality is again a very personal choice and religion or spirituality can never guide such personal choices because sexuality stems from a very different perspective altogether. It's related to biological and hormonal things. So your religion can't really say that it's not ok to do this or not ok to do that.

While the critical view of religion held by these students is often inherited from a parent (see Kwaku Golo *et al.* 2019, 189–90), they also usually have at least one parent they consider religious, and if they consider their families as being not religious at all, they still celebrate some

Hindu festivals in their homes. After all, they support individual freedom of choice in matters of faith and morality. As one male interviewee (JISR008) says,

> Religion is a personal matter. My girlfriend is quite a religious person. If she wishes to pursue that in our home, that wouldn't pose a problem. Only Lakshmi Puja is celebrated at my home. [...] My father is a member of this group of singers. He does it at leisure, as it gives him pleasure. He does it because he likes it. He has been doing this for the past five years. My father is a farmer. He used to play cards after returning from work, but then he thought he must put a stop to this kind of activity and therefore he took to singing devotional songs.

India 2: "Non-active Believer"

India 2 is comfortable with his or her own religion but does not actively practise it. As discussed in connection with China 2 above, in the broader YARG national samples, the second prototype is often a traditionally theist one. India 2 is a believer, but one that for various reasons does not actively engage in religious observances. What that means varies – one Muslim woman (YINMS032) does not see herself as an actively religious person since she misses some of the daily prayers. Another woman (YINMS039) likewise strongly considers herself a Hindu, but she distances herself from ideas such as reincarnation or a personal god. Unlike India 1, this prototype thus includes both Hindus and Muslims.

India 3: "Progressive Security-Motivated Pluralist"

India 3 is socially engaged and turns to religion only for security. Like India 1 above, India 3 also consists only of Hindus from Jadavpur University. Like India 1 again, this prototype also has strongly secular and progressive values. However, unlike India 1, there is some place for religion here, especially when it comes to prayers for solace and personal protection. As one interviewee (YINSR007) says:

> I do pray, but not like standing in front of an idol and praying or repeating mantras and fingering *jap malas* [rosaries], those are things that I don't do, but I do definitely pray from within. Maybe before going to sleep, I do have an interaction with God, God in a very abstract sense, in the sense that that is the part of the day when I find peace and solace. I do find the cosiness and comfort which I deliberately seek.

In contrast to parents often viewed as being very religious, individuals of this prototype thus do not see themselves as being that religious, especially when it comes to religious observances. One interviewee (YINSR056) says the following in answer to whether she considers herself to be religious or not:

> Somewhere in the middle. Being religious means that you have to go to temples, know all the rituals; my parents are very religious. They actually keep fasts and do all the rituals but I am not religious in that way. But I have a strong belief in a super power and know that there is something positive, a positive vibe. So I don't know whether I am religious or not, somewhere in the middle because I don't believe in all the practices, all the beliefs and all the sayings of what the scriptures say.

One of these "beliefs" that this prototype takes exception to is holding that man and women are intended for different roles. As one interviewee (YINSR069) says:

> This statement [FQS54], "thinks that men and women are by nature intended for different roles" I consider not at all relevant for me, because women and men are not to be considered different. They are different by gender, not by roles. Roles are assigned by society.

India 4: "Emotionally and Scripturally Directed Adherent"

India 4 combines an emotionally and scripturally based religiosity. India 4 includes again only Hindus, but not only urban ones. This profile is religiously committed, having a special connection with the sacred scripture (the Bhagavad-Gita came up often in the interviews) but also with emotionally powerful experiences. As one interviewee (YINMS050) says:

> [FQS] card number 14 says that one feels good when visiting a sacred place. This feeling is particularly strong while visiting a place of worship such as a mosque or a church. It feels, while visiting such places, as if we are in a different place altogether and there is a distinct urge to pray to the deity housed there. The whole feeling is somewhat different, something mystical.

The importance of visiting religious places is interesting, considering the importance placed by practically all Hindu interviewees on the yearly festivals celebrated in the home. Saavala (2010, 156) claims that the domesticity of religious life is a uniting feature of all middle-class Hindu religiosity, something this prototype challenges. Another interviewee (YINMS092) spoke at some length about the way in which she finds inspiration in painting and writing poetry.

Interestingly, though the individuals flagged for the prototypes are all Bengali Hindus, famous for their worship of goddesses such as Durga,

Kali or Lakshmi (Fell McDermott 2011), this prototype does not agree with the statement that one understands or relates to the divine as feminine (FQS19). As the interviewee above (YINMS050) said:

> I think that female goddesses and male gods are both the same for me. Though I am a female, I still have these views instilled in me. I believe that both female and male goddesses are equal to me.

Another interviewee (YINMS092) brought out another statement this prototype does not like:

> P: "Prays chiefly for personal protection". No, I don't pray only for myself but for others too. My family has taught me that.
> I: You mean for your whole family?
> P: No, I mean in general. My father taught me that if I can make others happy I will be happy too. That's what my father taught me. He taught me to pray for the good for others.

India 5: "Tradition-Oriented Universalist"

The interviewees flagged for India 5 are all practising Muslims that focus on the importance of tradition. While some of the statements characterising this prototype seem ambiguous, such as holding that the world's religious traditions point to a common truth while thinking that one should remain loyal to the religion of one's nation, these ambiguities usually stem from how particular terms are used. For example, the "religion of one's nation" is generally understood among these students (e.g. YINMS004, but this idea is not exclusive to this prototype) as relating to one's own "people", so that the religion of the "nation" of these interviewees is Islam. Here, the minority position of Islam in West Bengal and India as a whole makes sticking to the religion of one's community particularly important (see Broo *et al.* 2019). Similarly, one interviewee (YINMS013) interpreted "holding that the world's religious traditions point to a common truth" to mean that all religions point to Islam, the only true religion.

As in India 4 above, this prototype does not agree with understanding and relating to the divine as feminine. One interviewee (YINMS004) says:

> P: I know that God can never be a female.
> I: According to you, is God male then?
> P: That I don't know, but God can't be female.
> I: Okay. That means you are saying that God is male, but at the same time you are not sure about it, right?
> P: No. But I know God can't be female.

Another interviewee (YINM104) points out that as God is almighty, God can have no particular shape or gender. Others (YINMS058, YINMS031) see God as not only not being feminine, but beyond such gender distinctions altogether. Neither Hindus nor Muslims in our sample thus seem to agree with this statement, though the arguments against it differ.

While all the persons interviewed spoke at length about the different religious activities they engage in, several evinced a doubt to whether or not they really could call themselves "religious", often because of a failure to keep up to a very high standard of perceived proper Muslim behaviour. As one female interviewee (YINMS004) replied as to her own prayers:

> P: If I stay at home and have time then I do perform. But now I cannot read as I go to the university. And while at work, girls can't read *namaz* [prayers]. But I try to read Qur'an every day.
> I: Ok. Does your father perform the daily prayer?
> P: Yes. My father does his *salat* five times a day. He is very particular about it and pressurises us to read the Qur'an daily, wear purdah as well as hijab but I cannot follow it.

India 6: "Privately Religious and Socially Engaged"

India 6 gives religion a social importance but is mostly privately engaged. In contrast to India 5, where religion mostly plays a social role for inter-minority solidarity, for India 6, religion is mostly a private affair. For this prototype, the same number of Hindus and Muslims are flagged. What are then the religious or spiritual practices one engages in privately? For one Hindu woman (YINMS047), this means repeating a forty-line prayer for Hanuman every day, or at least on Tuesdays and Saturdays, and being vegetarian those days as well. Another Hindu (YINMS058), who is formally initiated by a Vaishnava guru says that she worships at her home altar every morning.

Another distinguishing feature of this prototype is spending much time reading or talking about one's convictions. One Hindu woman (YINMS058) studies the Bhagavad-Gita regularly, and one Muslim woman (YINMS031) follows the TV-channel of a popular Salafist preacher, where she learns many things related to society as well, as this prototype is not only privately religiously engaged but has a social interest as well. For example, this woman has strong opinions on wearing the veil.

> P: I support all the religious principles written in Qur'an. Like for example, if you consider the practice of *purdah* [veiling], it is for our own safety that women should follow this practice.

I: So, do you support the practice of *purdah*?
P: Yes definitely, because I believe that if a girl is in jeans, she might become a victim of physical abuse but it is not the case with us [veiled Muslims]. We can move freely anywhere when we veil ourselves.

India 7: "Religiously Disconnected and Security-Inclined"

India 7 is religious only on special occasions, and where a need for security takes precedence. India 7 consists of both Hindus and Muslims. This prototype is not against religion, but has either little time or little interest to engage seriously with it. Viewing everything from a religious or spiritual framework is foreign to these students. Often this is connected to topical issues in Indian society. One Hindu interviewee (YINM036) said:

> There are some events that do not need to be viewed from a religious framework. For example, if a Hindu man marries a Muslim woman, they might be killed in some families, because for these families, religion comes first and only then human life. To a human being, it is life that comes foremost and not his religion, and this needs to be understood.

Nevertheless, this lack of religion sometimes leads to a sense of inadequacy, as we have seen in prototypes 2 and 5 already. As one Muslim interviewee says (YINMS001):

I: So you feel guilty if you are not able to perform the prayers five times a day?
P: Yes Ma'am. Sometimes [laughter]! God is after all like the teachers who listens to the students who study all year and not to the ones who open the book just two days prior to the exam.

India 8: "Tradition-Oriented and Confidently Religious"

India 8 is grounded in religion but modestly engaged. This final Indian prototype holds many liberal values in common with India 1 and 3, such as supporting individual freedom of choice in matters of faith and morality but is also secure in his or her traditional religion albeit only being modestly engaged religiously. India 8 includes only Hindu and Buddhist individuals and is the only Indian prototype where reincarnation is seen as important – an interesting find in itself, considering the way in which the belief in reincarnation is often seen as being one of the cornerstones of Hinduism. One Buddhist interviewee (YINSR006), linking belief in rebirth with Buddhism rather than the Hinduism around her, says:

> I liked card number ninety [FQS90], which says, "affirms the idea of reincarnation, the cycle of birth and rebirth". I truly believe in this because it really touched me. Most of the people I have encountered so far don't believe in reincarnation or rebirth but I strongly believe in this because the religion that I follow is Buddhism which strongly believes in reincarnation. I have read books, I have seen videos on this whole process. So, I strongly believe in karma. It is said that what you do in this life will fructify in the next life, after you die, in the cycle of rebirth. So, if you do good in this life, you will have a better life in the next after rebirth. I strongly believe in this.

The eight Indian prototypes together reveal some of the wide variety of worldviews present among university students in West Bengal today. The largely secular prototypes 1 and 3 consist of urban, middle-class Hindus alone. The Muslims of the sample are found in half of the prototypes (2, 5, 6 and 7), and likewise, half of the prototypes (2, 6, 7, 8) include students from different religious traditions (Hinduism, Islam and Buddhism). No doubt the great religious and social plurality behind the Indian sample is one reason for the great number of sometimes rather similar prototypes. Nevertheless, the prototypes show us clearly that simply classifying these students as "Hindus", "Muslims" or "Buddhists" would have reduced the variety found both within and without these labels.

There were no consensus statements in the Indian sample. Nevertheless, some commonalities appear. While the Chinese sample showed most students to have some connection with religion, the Indian sample is chock-full of religion, with almost all students having at least one religious parent and all kinds of experiences of religion in their quotidian life, both positive and negative. This is certainly one reason for the strong positions taken and the frequent critical notes even by persons that deem themselves religious in general.

Even though Bengali Hinduism is often seen as focused on worshipping goddesses, and most Hindu interviewees mentioned celebrating festivals connected with goddesses such as Durga, Lakshmi and Saraswati, neither Muslims nor Hindus approved of the idea of seeing the divine in feminine terms. Reincarnation, likewise considered central to Hinduism and sometimes identified as a typical Hindu idea by Muslim interviewees (e.g. YINM010), finds little support among the Hindu interviewees.

Finally, the religiosity of the Muslim students interviewed is very much tied up with their minority status, a status that they are very conscious of and that affects their lives in various ways (see Broo *et al.* 2019).

Concluding Discussion

With the exception of the difference between pantheistic and theistic views of the ultimate being, the global YARG sample showed little support for any essential difference between East and West. However, the methodological approach of the YARG project uncovers in a clarifying way that the variety of worldviews found among the young university students in China and India is unusually large, comprising as it does six and eight prototypes, respectively, compared to a maximum of five in any other country within the YARG sample. Further, these prototypes often cross the lines of religious affiliation. This shows us that while categories such as "Muslim", "Buddhist" and "Taoist" are naturally useful in many ways, they tell us little about the types of worldviews that the young university students studied here hold.

With a few exceptions, the Chinese students were not religiously very committed, and none had independently searched for a religious identity. Still, while some criticised specific religious customs (mostly in relation to gender differences), few were negative towards religion in general. Many mentioned religious friends, parents or grandparents, a fact suggesting that being associated with religion is something worth mentioning and that religion is seen as an important part of Chinese culture.

In contrast to their Chinese counterparts, the Indian students were surrounded by religion on all sides and acutely aware of the social implications of religion. This, together with their middle-class background, led many, in particular the urban students, to an active critique of religion. We could report some interesting findings regarding e.g. lack of support for the idea of reincarnation, and seeing the divine in feminine terms. Finally, the religiosity of the Muslim students interviewed is very much tied up with their minority status, a status that they are very conscious of and that affects their lives in various ways (see Broo *et al.* 2019).

In this chapter, we have seen how essentialist categories can be deceiving. Before closing, let us return to Chakravorty Spivak's point about how the subaltern is forced into a position not of his or her own choosing but assuming it in time. Nevertheless, the position assumed may not look the way the armchair scholar supposes. Consider the following statement by a Buddhist woman (YINSR006) in reply to the question about what Buddhism is:

> Um ... in Buddhism, we pray to Lord Buddha who is actually, what should I say, something like – Lord Buddha is like Jesus, in the sense that he was the one who showed us the path. Ok? Actually, he was the son of a Raja.

He gave up all his worldly life and his family. He was seeking what to say, peace, OK? He believed in non-violence. Our [religion] is like "Ahimsa, Karma, Dharma", that is what we believe in and so, Lord Buddha showed us the path. We follow him. OK? But there are two sects in Buddhism, one is Hinayana and one is Mahayana. We follow [...] Guru Padmasambhava, who is also known as Guru Rinpoche. He is our main deity whom we worship, OK? So in Buddhism we worship Lord Buddha but for us Guru Padmasambhava is the main deity, he is the main person whom we worship. So, that's it. What else would you like to know?

Originally spoken in English, this summary of Buddhism is full of terminology taken from Christianity (praying, Jesus, sects, worship, deity), but it looks nothing like how Buddhism is "supposed" to be presented (see e.g. Robinson and Johnson 1982). The merit of the FQS method, whatever its flaws, is that it brings out the seeming idiosyncrasies that make up everyday religion.

Dr Måns Broo is a lecturer in the study of religions at Åbo Akademi University, Finland, and an associate research fellow at the Oxford Centre for Hindu Studies. His research interests include historical and contemporary forms of yoga, Gaudiya Vaishnavism and globalised Hinduism. His most recent monograph is a Finnish translation of the Shandilya- and Narada-bhakti-sutra (Gaudeamus, 2021).

Professor Ruby Sain completed her studies at the University of Kalyani (BA, MA, PhD), since which she has been serving the profession of sociology for over thirty years at Jadavpur University and then joined Adamas University as Emeritus Professor. She established the Centre for the Study of Religion and Society at Jadavpur University and founded the Jadavpur University Journal of Sociology. In addition she has served as guest faculty member at the University of Manitoba, Lund University, Gothenburg University, the University of California and Grand Valley State University, and has been a visiting fellow at The Oxford Centre for Hindu Studies; she has developed research collaborations with many of these and other universities. She has published several articles and book chapters. Her many edited or authored books include volumes on the sociology of religion, the future of religious studies in India and religion in India in general, particularly relating to religious pluralism and contemporary social problems.

References

Babb, Lawrence A. 1975. *The Divine Hierarchy: Popular Hinduism in Central India.* New York: Columbia University Press.

Brockington, John L. 1981. *The Sacred Thread: Hinduism in its Continuity and Diversity*. Edinburgh: Edinburgh University Press.

Broo, Måns, Sawsan Kheir and Mallarika Sarkar. 2019. "Two Cases of Religious Socialization among Minorities". *Religion* 49(2): 221–39.

Campbell, Colin. 2007. *The Easternization of the West: A Thematic Account of Cultural Change in the Modern Era*. Boulder, CO: Paradigm.

Carman, John B., and Frédérique A. Marglin, eds. 1985. *Purity and Auspiciousness in Indian Society*. Leiden: E. J. Brill.

Chaudhuri, Rosinka. 2012. *Freedom and Beef-Steaks: Colonial Calcutta Culture*. New Delhi: Orient BlackSwan.

Das, Arijit. 2017. "Educational Development and its Determinant in Minority Concentrated Districts (MCDs) of West Bengal: A Case Study of Malda District". *International Journal of Child Health and Human Development* 10(1). Retrieved from www.questia.com/library/p439807/international-journal-of-child-health-and-human-development/i4163262/vol-10-no-1-2017. Accessed 1 December 2017.

Deal, William E., and Timothy K. Beal. 2004. *Theory for Religious Studies*. New York: Routledge.

Fell McDermott, Rachel. 2011. *Revelry, Rivalry, and Longing for the Goddesses of Bengal: The Fortunes of Hindu Festivals*. New York: Columbia University Press.

Fuller, C. J. 2004. *The Camphor Flame: Popular Hinduism and Society in India*. Princeton, NJ: Princeton University Press.

Ganguly-Scrase, Ruchira. 2003. "Paradoxes of Globalization, Liberalization and Gender Equality: The Worldviews of the Lower Middle Class in West Bengal, India". *Gender and Society* 17(4): 544–66.

Ghurye, G. S. 1953. *Indian Sadhus*. Bombay: Popular Prakashan.

Government of India. 2011. "Census of India". Retrieved from https://censusindia.gov.in. Accessed 20 March 2021.

Hamilton, Malcolm B. 2002. "The Easternisation Thesis: Critical Reflections". *Religion* 32: 243–58.

Kong, Lily, and Junxi Quian. 2019. "Dialogue with Religious Life in Asia". In *Routledge Handbook of Postsecularity*, ed. Justine Beaumont, 258–68. London: Routledge.

Kwaku Golo, Ben-Willie, Måns Broo, Slawomir Sztajer, Francis Benyah, Sohini Ray and Mallarika Sarkar. 2019. "Primary Religious Socialization Agents and Young Adults' Understanding of Religion: Connections and Disconnections". *Religion* 49(2): 179–200.

Nadeau, Randall L. 2013. *Asian Religions: A Cultural Perspective*. Chichester: John Wiley & Sons.

Overmyer, Daniel L. 2001. "From 'Feudal Superstition' to 'Popular Beliefs': New Directions in Mainland Chinese Studies of Chinese Popular Religion". *Cahiers d'Extrême-Asie* 2001(12): 103–26.

Pennington, Brian K. 2005. *Was Hinduism Constructed? Britons, Indians, and the Colonial Construction of Religion*. Oxford: Oxford University Press.

Pramanik, Swapan. 2013. "The Sociology of Religion in India". In *The Sociology of Religion in India: Past, Present and Future*, ed. Ferdinando Sardella and Ruby Sain, 59–71. New Delhi: Abhijeet Publications.

Prasad, Ganesh, and Anand Kumar. 2000. "The Concept, Constraints and Prospect of Secularism in India". *The Indian Journal of Political Science* 67(4): 793–808.

Risley, Herbert Hope. 1998 [1891–2]. *The Tribes and Castes of Bengal* (2 vols.). Calcutta: Firma KML.

Robinson, Richard H., and Willard L. Johnson. 1982. *The Buddhist Religion. A Historical Introduction* (3rd edn). Belmont: Wadsworth Publishing Company.

Ruokanen, Miikka, and Paulos Huang, eds. 2010. *Christianity and Chinese Culture*. Grand Rapids: Eerdmans.

Saavala, Minna. 2010. *Middle-Class Moralities. Everyday Struggle over Belonging and Prestige in India*. Hyderabad: Orient BlackSwan.

Said, Edward. 1980. *Orientalism*. London: Routledge & Kegan Paul.

Sjö, Sofia, Maria Klingenberg, Ben-Willie Kwaku Golo and Clara Marlijn Meijer. 2022. "Gendered Views among Young Adults in a Global Study: Male and Female Worldview Prototypes". In *The Diversity of Worldviews among Young Adults: Contemporary (Non)Religiosity and Spirituality through the Lens of an International Mixed Method Study*, ed. Peter Nynäs, Ariela Keysar, Janne Kontala, Ben-Willie Kwaku Golo, Mika T. Lassander, Marat Shterin, Sofia Sjö and Paul Stenner, 175–95. Cham: Springer. https://doi.org/10.1007/978-3-030-94691-3_9

Srinivas, M. N. 1952. *Religion and Society among the Coorgs of South India*. New Delhi: Oxford University Press.

Sun, Anna. 2013. *Confucianism as a World Religion. Contested Histories and Contemporary Realities*. Princeton and Oxford: Princeton University Press.

Thakur, Somdev, and Summia Yasmeen. 2015. "Can Jadavpur University Be Saved?". Retrieved from www.educationworld.in/can-jadavpur-university-be-saved. Accessed 17 May 2019.

Times Higher Education. 2019a. "The Best Universities in China 2019". Retrieved from www.timeshighereducation.com/student/best-universities/best-universities-china. Accessed 7 May 2019.

Times Higher Education. 2019b. "The Best Universities in India 2019". Retrieved from www.timeshighereducation.com/student/best-universities/best-universities-india. Accessed 7 May 2019.

Vidyarthi, Lalita Prasad. 1961. *The Sacred Complex in Hindu Gaya*. Bombay: Asia Publishing House.

Yang, Ch'ing k'un. 1961. *Religion in Chinese Society*. Berkeley, CA: University of California Press.

Yang, Fenggang. 2012. *Religion in China: Survival and Revival under Communist Rule*. New York: Oxford University Press.

Yang, Fenggang. 2016. "Religious Awakening in China under Communist Rule: A Political Economy Approach". In *The New Blackwell Companion to the Sociology of Religion*, ed. Brian S. Turner, 431–56. Chichester: John Wiley & Sons.

– 6 –

Conceptualisations of the "Sacred Individual"

A Comparative Study of Russian and Finnish Young Adults

POLINA VRUBLEVSKAYA, MARCUS MOBERG AND
KAROLIINA DAHL

This chapter explores data gathered among young adults in Russia and Finland in light of the Durkheimian notion of the "sacred individual". This notion is grounded in the contention that accelerating modern-day processes of individualisation and pluralisation have given rise to a situation where the personal autonomy, rights and self-determination of the individual have accrued non-contingent, "sacred" status. By identifying and exploring Russian and Finnish respondents' scores on a smaller set of Faith Q-Sort (FQS) statements – referred to as the "sacred individual subset" – the chapter explores the extent to which the FQS data can be used to empirically test and elaborate on broader theoretical perspectives. In so doing, it also aims to demonstrate how the mixed-methods data can usefully be approached and analysed from multiple theoretical perspectives. The FQS analyses are further combined with the Finnish and Russian interview data in order to further illustrate how the notion of the sacred individual provides a particular lens for making sense of respondents' repeated emphasis on the importance of respecting and tolerating the viewpoints and outlooks of others.

Introduction

Over the past couple of decades, inspired in particular by the "new cultural sociology" of Jeffrey Alexander (2003), scholars in the humanities and social sciences have paid renewed attention to the "sacred". Scholars of religion have been particularly keen on highlighting the ways in which the concept of the sacred offers a useful way of moving beyond the many limitations associated with the category of "religion" (e.g. Lynch 2012) and simplistic dichotomies between "religion" and the "secular" (e.g. Knott 2013). As is outlined in more detail in Chapter 1 in this volume, the YARG project's mixed-methods framework was consciously designed to both avoid and interrogate predefined conceptions of religiosity, spirituality and values. The project's employment of Q-methodology and semi-structured interviewing resulted in a rich body of data that can readily be examined through various theoretical lenses, including perspectives on the sacred. Indeed, the full potential of the data gathered in YARG is realised only when viewed and examined in light of different theoretical approaches and perspectives. Taking a primarily inductive approach, this chapter explores select portions of this data in light of the originally Durkheimian theory of the sacred. More specifically, drawing on the FQS and interview data gathered within the project, this chapter engages in an explorative comparative analysis of the ways in which the idea of the "sacred individual" is formed, expressed and conceptualised among young adult respondents in Russia and Finland. The principal aim of the chapter is to identify and analyse the main ways in which the idea of the "sacred individual" is narratively constructed and conceptualised among these two sets of respondents from notably different socio-cultural and religious backgrounds.

Finland and Russia are very differently located on the Inglehart-Welzel "Cultural Map of the World" (World Values Survey Association 2020), which provided the principal macro-theoretical justification for the choice of countries included in YARG. On the map's horizontal axis of survival vs. self-expressive values Finland and Russia are located at diametrically opposite ends: while Finland counts among the most self-expressive of countries, Russia counts among the countries that most strongly emphasise survival values. On the map's vertical axis of traditional vs. secular-rational values, however, both countries are situated relatively closely to each other in the secular-rational category. The religious landscapes of both countries remain dominated by historical institutional churches that each represent a major Christian tradition: the Evangelical Lutheran Church of Finland in Finland and the Russian Orthodox Church in Russia. Both countries have, however, become increasingly diverse when it comes to religious dispositions and values over the past two to three decades.

This chapter consists of two main sections. In the first section we introduce the theory of the sacred with detailed elaboration on two topics: the idea of the "sacred individual" and conceptual expressions of the sacred. The second section is devoted to the analysis of the case we have studied. The chapter closes with a brief discussion of the findings presented therein.

The Theory of the Sacred

The concept of the sacred occupies centre-stage in Émile Durkheim's social theoretical thinking. It stems from his more general assertion that all societies "create systems of symbolic classification to make sense of the world" (Lynch 2012, 21). For Durkheim, the sacred refers to those phenomena, things, practices, ideas, persons, etc. that are endowed with a non-contingent, non-negotiable and absolute character by members of a particular community. Cultural constructions of the sacred are typically formed in direct opposition to the *profane*, i.e. classes of phenomena that members of a particular community perceive as belonging to the contingent world of everyday life. Since the sacred plays a particularly central function in upholding established social order (e.g. Paden 2000, 211), it is typically surrounded and protected by rules and prescribed behaviours designed to safeguard it from profanation. Sacred phenomena thus "exert a profound moral claim" (Lynch 2012, 11, 25–30; Paden 2000, 211) over people's lives by underpinning many of the categories people use to organise and structure their life and values as a community. Hence, through providing the basis for moral order and solidarity among individuals, the community itself becomes the epitome of the sacred (Pickering 2009, 132).

In Durkheim's perspective, ritual plays a central role in a community's reproduction of its sense of the sacred by providing shared moments of collective effervescence. As Durkheim explains, by regularly bringing individuals together in common concerted action that refers to and articulates the community's sense of the sacred, ritual serves to revitalise individual community members' perceptions of the sacred by inducing experiences of *sui generis* social reality, thereby also strengthening feelings of mutual identification and solidarity (cf. Rawls 2004; Lynch 2012, 31). Although they are closely related, Durkheim makes a general distinction between rituals and collective *representations* as means of generating and expressing the sacred. Collective representations of the sacred take verbal, visual and textual form (e.g. stories, myths, artwork, symbols, etc.). Such representations serve to secure the continuity of particular understandings of the sacred across generations and to extend the core values of a community both spatially and temporally.

The sacred is thus not to be understood in terms of an ontologically fixed category. Rather, the sacred is organised by cultures into historically and contextually specified manifestations, or so-called "sacred forms", which change over time according to the changes of social life and shifts in the cultural contours of the societies in which they are constructed (Alexander 2003, 27-84; Lynch 2012, 32-3). Sacred forms thus communicate the core values on which particular social orders are based at particular points in time (Durkheim 1995, 425). Although this chapter focuses on conceptual expressions and narrative constructions of the "sacred individual" as derived from the particular data gathered in YARG against the backdrop of a particular reading of Durkheim, we acknowledge the equal validity of other approaches and readings (e.g. Alexander 2003; Anttonen 1999; Taves 2009; Lynch 2012; Knott 2013). We also acknowledge that the cognitive approach to the sacred was ardently contested by Georges Bataille (i.e. Winfree and Mitchell 2009), whose arguments we also find persuasive.

The Sacred and Religion

While the sacred has traditionally been closely tied to religious frameworks and typically been entwined with religious discourses, it extends well beyond these. Religion should therefore by no means be regarded as constituting the "source" of the sacred. Nor should religion be seen to enjoy any privileged position in defining the sacred and the profane. In sharp contrast to earlier usages classified as essentialist, popularised by scholars such as Rudolf Otto and Mircea Eliade, an understanding of the sacred that remains true to its Durkheimian inheritance would insist on its metaphysically neutral and non-ontological character and maintain that nothing should be regarded as being inherently sacred in and of itself, but rather that any construction of the sacred should always be understood as the outcome of historical social processes (e.g. Paden 1991, 11, 14-15). Religion in all its variations therefore provides but one among many representational repertoires for the expression of the sacred (Lynch 2012, 21). The distinctive line between sacred and profane classes of phenomena is, moreover, always conditioned and structured by the logics of social life itself (Durkheim and Mauss 2009). Hence, the sacred is not to be confused with the category of "religion" (Stausberg 2017), just as the "secular" should not be conflated with the "profane" (Knott 2013, 148). The increasing institutionalisation of ever more areas of social life in complex modern societies gives rise to new systems of classification and new sacred forms for the maintenance of social order. This results in a diffusion of new systems of classification and sacred forms across different institutional sites in society (e.g. the political, scientific, educational, legal, etc.), which often develop their own specific interpretations of the sacred that contain both "religious" and "secular" elements (Lynch 2012, 11; Heider and Warner 2010). Notable examples of some of the principal sacred forms in modern societies include human rights, nature and the environment, the sanctity of childhood and various notions pertaining to particular nation-states.

The "Sacred Individual" and "Moral Individualism"

Durkheim's intellectual legacy comprises two potentially very useful ideas for exploring the character of contemporary sacred forms and their ideational impact on both broader societal and individual levels. Derived from his major works *The Division of Labor in Society* (1991 [1893]) and *The Elementary Forms of the Religious Life* (1995 [1912]), as well as his essay on "Individualism and Intellectuals" (1973 [1898]), the first of these ideas is his contention that, while the core of traditional society lies in "the idea it has of itself" as a *collective* (Durkheim 1995, 425), modern society instead tends to consolidate around what he terms the "cult of the individual" ("culte de la personne"; Durkheim 1991, 396). The "cult of the individual" is varyingly referred to as "individualist faith", the "religion of humanity" and the "religion of the individual", and freedom of thought is described as its main ritual (Durkheim 1973, 49). This "religion", argues Stausberg (2017, 560), is built around a notion of the sacredness of humanity, which centres on three closely interrelated propositions: that the sacredness of humanity is (1) *natural* and inherent in all human beings, (2) *equally applicable* to each and every person, and (3) *universal* and applicable to all contexts, times and places (Hunt 2007, 30; cf. Miller 1996, 234; Kurakin 2015, 391). The rise and perpetuation of the notion of the sacredness of the individual is therefore inextricably connected to the development of modern societies and the gradual transition from "ascending" to "descending" models of political legitimacy, that is, a general relocation of power from the single sovereign or social class to the "people" (Calhoun 1997). Indeed, as Paden (2000, 219) observes, under such social and cultural conditions, "sacredness becomes invested in basic freedoms, equality of opportunity, the dignity of human persons, and self-determination rather than with duties and allegiances or the protection of rank and status" (Paden 2000, 119–220; cf. Lynch 2012, 20). This view amounts to a highly cognitive and individualised understanding of the sacred (Durkheim 1995, 438). In modern society, intense affective collective experiences of effervescence give way to logical thought that, despite being rooted in the individual, extends beyond "fleeting representations" and invites individuals "to conceive a whole world of stable ideals, the common ground of intelligences" (Durkheim 1995, 437).

In "Individualism and Intellectuals", Durkheim (1973 [1898]) expands further on the notion of "moral individualism", arguing that it gradually solidifies through the development of ever more complex and differentiated societies. As a general moral orientation, moral individualism comes to substitute traditional religious frameworks that were built on principles of collectivity and the perceived homogeneity of communities' members. Because the development of increasingly large, complex and differentiated societies makes it ever more difficult to uphold a generally shared social moral order, modern societies instead are compelled to accept and recognise the heterogeneity of its members (Durkheim 1973, 44). The moral order of modern society thus ceases to rest on an ideal of sameness and instead finds a new basis in "encountering and honoring otherness" (Cladis 2005, 407). This results in a new moral order based on the primacy of humanity, coupled with the abandonment of previous bases of social worth or status, such as the hereditary, religious, national, ethnic, etc. In sharp contrast to "utilitarian egoist" and Social Darwinist perspectives that were prevalent at the time, Durkheim argued that moral individualism principally flowed from abstract notions about universal laws and was directed towards fellow humans, i.e. others than the self (Joas 2008, 137). In this view, which essentially constitutes a sociological elaboration of Kantian ethics (never treat others as means to an end but as ends in themselves), mutual respect and recognition emerges as the key motive of moral conduct and being moral becomes a matter of rejecting social injustice and working towards eradicating it. We can therefore understand Durkheim's moral individualism "as a cluster of dynamic beliefs and practices, symbols and institutions that support the dignity and rights of the individual" (Cladis 2005, 385). The notion of the "sacred individual" has subsequently been further elaborated by Hans Joas (2013) who provides an illustrative account of the ways in which modern sacred forms tend to be infused with both religious and secular elements. Joas analyses in detail the extended process whereby originally Christian categories gradually became generalised as universal values and were eventually integrated in the notion of human rights. Donald N. Levine (2006) has, in turn, explored how historical developments in liberal education contributed to the rise of the sacredness of the "individual mind" in the collective representations of modern Western societies.

While the notion of the sacred individual has indeed been explored in broader sociological and socio-historical perspective, it has to the best of our knowledge not yet been explored in direct relation to empirical data generated on the basis of research with living subjects. Several connections can, however, be observed between the findings of the YARG project and the longitudinal research project "The National Study of Youth and Religion", carried out in the United States between 2001 and 2015 under the leadership of Christian Smith. Among many other things, this project revealed that American young adults typically tend to make moral judgements without making any explicit references to any particular moral authorities or without considering their moral judgements to be guided by any particular understandings of history, heritage, revelation, tradition or the like (Smith and Snell 2009, 280). The YARG survey results also lend clear support for the notion that people belonging to the present young adult generation tend to approach social morals through an individualistic frame, typically without recourse to tradition, heritage or the like. For instance, when Russian and Finnish respondents were asked, "Which of the following do you rely on for guidance as you live your life and make decisions?", the vast majority of them (93 per cent of Russian and 95 per cent of Finnish respondents) answered that they relied only on their "own reason and judgement".

Conceptual Expressions of the Sacred

In the conclusion to *Elementary Forms*, Durkheim posits that the sacred in modern society is mainly expressed and "grasped" through linguistic concepts rather than through collective ritual action. In Durkheim's essentially social-evolutionary framework, linguistic conceptual forms of the sacred thus become increasingly prevalent as society becomes ever more *rationalised*. The rationalisation of society also affects developments in language and language use. The development of "sacred language" and the compiling of corpora of "sacred texts" therefore also mark the start of a general rationalisation of the sacred (Gane 1983; Miller 1996, 235). Because of its relatively fixed and impersonal character – extending over both space and time and the personal experiences of any particular individual – language hence offers the most stable form for the expression and articulation of the sacred in modern society (Durkheim 1995, 434–5). Increasingly grounded in language, "the modern collective conscience has [thus] been transformed to encompass increasingly abstract and generalized sentiments" (Grusky and Galescu 2005, 328). In modern society, shared perceptions of the sacred are thus primarily both generated and expressed through linguistic concepts that increasingly emerge out of the exchange of thoughts and "communication between minds" (Durkheim 1973, 49; Anttonen 2000; Stedman-Jones 2012). In this view, people's perceptions of the sacred consequently need to be understood in relation to a view of society as a cognitive or a discursive system (Stedman-Jones 2000, 71).

Empirical Data and Analysis

As elaborated in more detail in Chapter 1 in this volume, the FQS was specifically designed for the purpose of researching various types of (both positive and negative) interconnections between people's beliefs, values and views on religion and faith-related issues. Each factor (i.e. prototype or general "mind-set") that the FQS analysis yields can be approached through various theoretical lenses. What follows is an exploration of how the Russian and Finnish prototypes can be seen to reflect the notion of the sacred individual, as underpinned by moral individualism. As noted earlier, our analysis is pursued in an exploratory spirit and directly based on the particular type of data that the FQS instrument generates. The following exploration can therefore also be viewed in terms of a further exploration of the utility and possibilities of Q-methodology itself. We begin with the assumption that the notion of the sacred individual should be empirically observable in the data generated by the instruments employed in YARG, and in this case especially the FQS prototypes (Appendix 2) and interviews with Finnish and Russian respondents (for details on the interview model, see Appendix 4). It is crucial to note, however, that neither the concept of the sacred nor the notion of the sacred individual occupied any position whatsoever in either the initial research design or basic terminological apparatus of the YARG project as a whole. The YARG project did not, therefore, contain any type of predetermined understanding of either of these concepts or notions. Furthermore, there were no mentions of "the sacred" in the interview guide. We are thus bringing the theoretical question of the conceptual and narrative construction of the sacred individual to the data in a *post hoc* fashion, albeit following an initial stage of interpreting the results of the FQS.

In total, the YARG FQS analysis yielded fifty-six prototypes across fourteen cultural contexts, with an average of three to five prototypes per context. The Finnish sample yielded three prototypes, and the Russian five. An initial FQS data analysis of three main types of FQS statements (for the FQS statements, see Appendix 1) was conducted in relation to both the Finnish and Russian samples: (1) consensus statements that represent common ground between all prototypes within a particular sample; (2) defining statements that represent positions that are peculiar to particular prototypes; and (3) distinguishing statements that point to significant differences between the prototypes regarding positions on certain issues. On explicitly theoretical grounds, among these groups of statements, a smaller subset of statements that directly express or articulate elements that pertain to the Durkheimian notion of the sacred individual was identified:

51 Actively works towards making the world a better place to live.
52 Lives his or her earthly life in conscious anticipation of a life hereafter.
77 Is profoundly touched by the suffering of others.
93 Sees personal self-realisation as a primary spiritual goal in life.
99 Takes comfort in thinking that those who do not live righteously will face suffering or punishment.
100 Supports individual freedom of choice in matters of faith and morality.

Statements FQS77 and FQS99 stand in some form of opposition when it comes to the basic attitude and disposition towards others, sympathy and "broader pity" (or lack thereof), that make up the defining characteristics of moral individualists (Durkheim 1973, 48). Apart from its specific content, statement FQS51 also provided Finnish and Russian respondents with an opportunity to ponder what a "better place to live" might actually mean. We assume that the statement served to prompt respondents to articulate their efforts to battle injustices that cause human suffering; the idea of (in)justice being closely connected to a recognition of human dignity and a willingness to safeguard it (Fournier 2005, 53). Statements FQS93 and FQS100 most explicitly relate to the idea of human dignity, personal integrity and self-determination. Agreement with these statements thus equals a general recognition and respect for a commonly shared humanity. Lastly, statement FQS52 articulates a rejection of the widely established modern notion of earthly human life as valuable in and of itself as well as of the notion that the sanctity of each life essentially rests on a recognition of its fragility and finitude.

While our selection of statements is thus fundamentally theory-driven, it is simultaneously also directly informed by the empirical data. As noted, as a first general stage, we identified the statements that appeared as consensual, defining or distinguishing for all prototypes from Finland and Russia. On the basis of our theoretical focus, this was followed by a second stage, where we identified a particular smaller subset of statements that together, in their various ways, pertain directly to the Durkheimian notion of moral individualism and the sacred individual. We choose to call this the "sacred individual subset". It is important to note, however, that this particular subset is peculiar to the Finnish and Russian samples. Explorations of the FQS data for other national samples included in YARG that followed the same analytical procedure would probably end up with a different set of statements making up the "sacred individual subset". As a third stage, we compared all prototypes across the two chosen samples in order to identify the relevance of our subset of statements for each of them (see Table 10). The subset emerged as particularly relevant for two of the eight prototypes under consideration: "Active and Confident Believer" (Finnish Prototype 2) and "Individual Pluralist" (Russian Prototype 2). While the Finnish prototype

Table 10. Scores for the "sacred individual subset" in FQS (for Finnish FQS Prototype 2 and Russian FQS Prototype 2). Abbreviations: dis = distinguishing; def = defining; con = consensus; dash = irrelevant.

FQS statement (N)	Prototypes – Finland				Prototypes – Russia			
	Confident Rationalist	Active and Confident Believer	Emotionally Motivated Pluralist	Progressive Secular Rationalist	Individual Pluralist	Environmentally Concerned and Spiritually Inclined Non-Religious	Critical and Unengaged Religious Conformist	Anxious Believer
Supports individual freedom of choice in matters of faith and morality (100)	+4, def	+3, dis	+4, def	+4, con				
Is profoundly touched by the suffering of others (77)	–	–	+4, dis	–	+4, def	–	–	–
Takes comfort in thinking that those who do not live righteously will face suffering or punishment (99)	–2, dis	–4, def		–	–4, dis	–	–	–
Lives his or her earthly life in conscious anticipation of a life hereafter (52)	–2, dis	+1, dis	–2, dis	0, con	–2, con	–1, con		
Actively works towards making the world a better place to live (51)	–	+2, dis	–	+1, con				
Sees personal self-realisation as a primary spiritual goal in life (93)	–	–1, dis	–	–	+4, def	–	+4, def	

can be described as "conventionally religious", the Russian prototype is instead characterised by a generally eclectic attitude towards religious and spiritual matters. In spite of these differences, these two prototypes share many commonalities when it comes to the notions of the sacred individual and moral individualism.

The whole subset of six statements is present only in one prototype: "Individual Pluralist" (Russian Prototype 2). Five of these six statements are also present in "Active and Confident Believer" (Finnish Prototype 2).

At the final stage of analysis, we move to the interviews conducted with Finnish and Russian respondents who scored higher on either one of the two prototypes under consideration. The analysis thus focuses on how the notion of the "sacred individual" finds linguistic expression as part of respondents' comments on the statements included in the "sacred individual" subset. In doing so, our aim is to further test our theoretical assumption that the selected statements are particularly indicative of "mind-sets" for which the ideas and values related to moral individualism constitute an integral part. In combining an analysis of prototypes with an analysis of the accounts of respondents themselves as expressed in interviews, our aim is also to highlight the particular expressions that Finnish and Russian young adults use when they talk about their values and ideas in ways that connect to the notion of the sacred individual. This analysis could also be understood in terms of a broader elaboration of the commentary-style descriptions of the prototypes (see Appendix 2) that cover the whole range of relevant statements for each prototype while altogether avoiding all and any theoretical interpretations.

Initially, the interviews were analysed in their original languages (Finnish, Swedish and Russian) by the researchers who conducted them. In this chapter, the interviews appear in their English translations, and we are aware of the limitations that this entails in terms of linguistic analysis. In the following, we treat individual respondents' views as expressed in the interviews as illustrative of a broader whole constituted by one of the particular prototypes under consideration. Our focus therefore does not lie on the views of individual respondents, but the extent to which these are shared and expressed among representatives of the prototypes through shared collective linguistic concepts.

The Cases

Like the vast majority of respondents in the YARG project, the Finnish and Russian respondents were all aged between 18 and 28 at the time when the interviews were conducted in 2016. With respect to gender, females dominate in both prototypes under consideration (10 out of 13 respondents for the Russian prototype and 8 of the 13 respondents for the Finnish prototype).

Since the collapse of the Soviet Union in the early 1990s, Russia has been experiencing dramatic religious change. Today, approximately 71 per cent of Russian citizens have been baptised into Russian Orthodox Christianity (Pew Research Center 2017). Among these, however, only around 10 per cent could be described as "religiously active" in terms of church attendance, and both public and private religious practice (Prutskova 2015; Zabaev et al. 2018; Markin 2018). In comparison to the other Russian prototypes, the prototype we are focusing on here is neither strongly religious, nor non- or anti-religious. Rather, it reflects a fleeting, "seekership"-like outlook, or an inclination to embrace elements from various religious and spiritual "traditions". For this prototype, morality is not perceived to be grounded in religion, with self-realisation instead standing out as the primary life-goal. With one exception, all other respondents whose FQS sorts contributed to the forming of this prototype were baptised into Orthodox Christianity. However, only three of them were active church members, while the others held either "in-between" (2) or distant (8) attitudes.

While the Evangelical Lutheran Church of Finland (ELCF) still retains the status of majority church, it has experienced progressive long-term decline by all conventional sociological indicators since the early 1970s, especially among younger generations. ELCF membership rates have slowly but surely continued to decrease (from 93 per cent of the population in 1974 to 65.1 per cent in 2023), church attendance has declined sharply, traditional mechanisms of religious socialisation have been progressively weakening, people have become less and less interested in church teachings and activities, and so on. Currently approximately 32 per cent in 2022 of the Finnish population do not belong to any religious community (Official Statistics of Finland 2022). While the Finnish religious landscape has gradually become increasingly diverse, Finnish religiosity remains highly privatised. The prototype focused on in this chapter (Active and Confident Believer), however, constitutes the most "conventionally religious" of all three Finnish prototypes. This prototype is characterised by an expressed and active religious/spiritual identification and engagement. Twelve of the respondents whose FQS sorts contributed to the formation of this prototype were members of some Christian congregation (including one who was a member of both the ELCF and the Krishna movement), while one was a Finnish Neopagan.

Case Study 1: Russian Prototype 2 "Individual Pluralist"

This prototype is the only one out of the eight prototypes studied that includes all of the statements we refer to in terms of the "sacred individual subset". FQS100 was strongly agreed with and emerged as a consensus statement for all Russian prototypes. In the case of this prototype, however, FQS100 is positioned in direct relation to all other statements that were identified above as pertaining to the notion of the sacred individual. FQS100 therefore also becomes centrally embedded as part of the narrative constructions of the sacred individual that can be found among the respondents whose FQS sorts contributed to the forming of this prototype. Individual freedom of choice (in matters of faith and morality) is expressed in relation to a wide range of thoughts and sentiments such as personal *wishes, likes, interests, opinions, decisions*, etc. that are typically directly juxtaposed to things like *imposition, pressure, judgement (disapproval), restriction*, etc.

> Well, I think that everyone must choose independently what he or she, what he or she – likes more, finds more interesting, what he or she believes in, and there mustn't be any pressure or – disapproval, and he or she should make a choice regardless of other people's opinion, so to say.
> (YRUPV028)

In this constellation, support for *individual freedom* goes along with *self-realisation* as a main spiritual goal in life. Self-realisation is often put into effect as following one's freely chosen wishes and convictions.

Individual freedom is also often directly related to various possibilities and prospects, as well as broader conditions that are either conducive to self-realisation or work to curtail it.

> It seems to me that personal self-enhancement is impossible under strict limitations or strong influence of a definite, a definite religious, again, model from which there is no way out.
> (YRUPV041)

Respondents often illustrate what they mean by self-realisation by connecting it to the accumulation of life experiences and developing certain skills. This would be expected considering that they all engaged in higher education and that they also all found themselves in the transitional life-phase of "emerging adulthood" at the time of the interview. However, the narratives also reveal broader understandings of self-realisation.

> For me to self-realise in a lot of things, I need to do something good for humanity, I don't know what exactly, but I want to do something like that,

as it seems to me that everyone must make his or her own contribution, even a small one, even if it helps just a single person. Right.

(YRUPV004)

In this account, self-realisation is described as a matter of becoming a better fellow human, or as something that is crucial for both individual and collective solidarity and well-being. In other cases, self-realisation is instead described in terms of a gradual *process* of personal improvement.

> There are certain goals I'd like to achieve right now so as to understand, that is, so as to become a happier person. That is – how shall I put it – there is always room for improvement right now. I do not know; it is no good to settle for what you have already achieved.
>
> (YRUPV043)

Throughout the interviews with respondents whose FQS sort contributed to the formation of this prototype, individual well-being is typically described in relation to notions such as *happiness*, *self-enhancement*, etc., which all presuppose social and cultural conditions that are conducive to, or at least do not curtail, individual freedom and self-realisation. In what generally reflects a Kantian view of human dignity, the freedoms required for self-realisation to become possible are described in uncompromising terms as something given *naturally*. In some cases, this view is also related to *respect* and *tolerance* for others.

> I am quite tolerant, that is, to other religions, because, well, and to other convictions, naturally, because everyone is entitled to his or her own opinion. Right. That is, due to a certain set of circumstances, every person has an outlook – and it does not matter whether it is similar to mine or different from it.
>
> (YRUPV013)

This excerpt provides a general illustration of the ways in which respondents typically talk about *freedom of choice, conscience, opinion*, etc., as a way of highlighting the inherent dignity and self-determination of each and every person. As is explicitly highlighted by some respondents, this inherent dignity and self-determination is crucial for everyone's pursuit of happiness.

> We were born to be happy, to bring joy to our parents and ourselves. Probably actually ourselves first of all, good as it is to keep your parents happy, and I'm really glad that mine are happy.
>
> (YRUPV024)

Respondents also highlight the *sanctity* of human life through direct negation of FQS52 "Lives his or her earthly life in conscious anticipation of a life hereafter".

> If you live in anticipation of an afterlife, it means that you do not live this life in full and therefore suffer from it, er, doing harm to yourself. It is not, well, I do not think it is acceptable, either.
>
> (YRUPV011)

In this account, the idea of living one's life in constant anticipation of an afterlife is rejected because it results in a devaluation of earthly life, which then comes to stand in contradiction to the notion of the right of every human being to a dignified *good life*. The very same idea stands behind the acknowledged importance of treating fellow humans with respect and without resorting to any forms of violence, be it physical or psychological.

> As for me, I have kind of never had any hard feelings against anyone, in terms of wishing something, let alone seeking revenge. Right. So I want to raise my children in the same way, so that they don't feel any urge to harm anyone. Well, first of all, for us, for me at least, harming someone, avenging or something makes me feel bad in the first place, I reckon.
>
> (YRUPV004)

> P: However, there are things I cannot accept in any form, of course.
> I: Such as?
> P: I don't know, violence to weak people or animals, that is, to people who have done nothing to deserve such an attitude, right. Or some kind of betrayal. I don't know how to put it, letting down someone who had expectations of you. That is, um, not unconsciously, but intentionally – I don't know, any betrayal in general.
>
> (YRUPV043)

Respondents' accepting, compassionate and sympathetic attitudes towards others are also recurrently expressed with the help of FQS77, as in the following two accounts.

> I get very affected if someone is dying, or grieving, or has some tragedy going on, I get very anxious and try to help.
>
> (YRUPV004)

> I get very worried when someone is suffering, especially a relative or a friend, but I worry about strangers too. This is why – I have a profound sympathy for them.
>
> (YRUPV028)

Strong agreement with FQS77 also entails opposing any types of actions that cause harm or suffering. An expressed desire to reduce the suffering of living creatures often takes the form of *helping* in some way or *sharing in (co-experiencing)* the suffering. This further highlights the value that respondents attach to the pursuit of happiness in life. FQS51 serves to further reinforce such sentiment and to transform it into something pro-active, i.e. "making the world a better place to live". Although FQS51 only constituted a consensus statement with a less significant +1 score, it nevertheless served to generate discussion among Russian respondents who scored high on this prototype.

> P: I have a few traits I do not like. Right. And, well – I just don't know how to change them, but yeah, I'd like to. That is, change is better.
> I: Why is it better?
> P: Well, because it is kind of – What I have now prevents me from, uh – how shall I put it, feeling perfectly happy. Or, uh – um – feeling that, uh, I only bring joy to others. That is, I do not offend them, I do not, well, how shall I put it, I do not hurt them. That is, I understand I need to change; I need to change some things about myself so as not to do it.
> (YRUPV043)

Thus, an acknowledgement of the intrinsic worth of each individual life as such and the belief that everyone deserves to be happy serves to inspire attentiveness and care towards others. This realisation may also inspire self-improvement.

Apart from sympathy as a principal attitude towards others, an additional *principle of non-judgement* also comes into play through a strong disagreement with FQS99, which also distinguishes this prototype.

> Well, I am generally convinced that every person has his or her own views and we have no right to be judgemental about them or, uh, set him on the right path, the path which we think is right but he thinks otherwise.
> (YRUPV024)

Further, FQS99 also serves to actualise notions about *human inviolability*.

> The fact that someone "will face suffering or punishment", even for some wrongful deeds, is kind of outrageous; I have never enjoyed anyone's suffering, not once in my life, even if the person is bad. If a person is bad, it is already a punishment, leave him be.
> (YRUPV004)

Lastly, it is important to highlight that despite the fact that this prototype does not represent a strictly religious one, the moral ideals of its representatives are nonetheless often expressed by means of Judaeo-Christian vocabulary.

> Well, common values, moral ones, such as do not do anything evil, honour thy father and thy mother, thou shalt not kill, thou shalt not steal, thou shalt not lie or something. Right, so in general, nothing too specific, just things any normal person should follow, in my opinion, just to lead a normal life, not to do any harm, to be useful to other people or to himself at least, right.
> (YRUPV004)

Case study 2: Finnish Prototype 2 "Active and Confident Believer"

This prototype includes five of the six statements contained in the "sacred individual subset". Although FQS77 does not figure as either a defining, distinguishing or consensual statement for this prototype, the interviews nevertheless reveal the position of its representatives on this statement in five out of thirteen cases. The representatives of this prototype express an intolerance of violence that causes human suffering. These views are accompanied by the expression of high levels of *sympathy* that makes it difficult for the respondents to be confronted by injustices and *evil*.

> I can't watch the news because I can't like, I can't sort of handle this evil and that, that sort of agony that humans go through [...] you're not like a cold person when you do it because you just like can't, you just can't, it's just so sad that you just can't, but you also have to live your own life and do the best you can to help other people.
>
> (YFIKD124T)

As already demonstrated, the concepts that respondents use to express their views on this statement are very similar to the ones that they also use to express their views on FQS99. In what most probably reflects the liberal "mainline" Protestant religiosity of these respondents, they are horrified by the notion that anyone could take comfort in someone else's suffering. This is illustrated by the accounts below.

> This is in my opinion like a horrifying idea.
>
> (YFIKD124T)

> That I would take comfort in thinking that someone else is suffering, this is a completely preposterous idea.
>
> (YFIKD133T)

However, the representatives of this Finnish prototype express their disagreement with FQS99 in notably different ways from the representatives of the Russian prototype discussed above. These respondents do not so much speak of adopting a less judgemental attitude, but rather about trying to overcome injustices and evil deeds, and avoiding getting into or "feeding a spiral of hate".

> Of course, often when you are angry if you hear, for instance, news about someone who was hurt, these violent thoughts of revenge come to you but, at the end of the day, it does not really bring you any comfort. It mostly just feeds the spiral of hate.
>
> (YFIKD143T)

For the representatives of this prototype, this non-judgemental attitude is directly linked to a strong belief in the providence and will of God and notions about the limits of human understanding.

> It is not possible for a human being to understand Him completely. Somehow I feel that I do not even have the right to say who is completely right or wrong, or who receives salvation and who does not, so like, with a certain type of respect, I would, like, leave those kinds of decisions to God to deal with.
>
> (YFIKD146T)

For some respondents, encounters with people who do not live righteously also serve to induce feelings of *distress*, *sadness* and *sorrow*.

> I really don't experience any kind of joy or sense of elation from someone else receiving punishment. On the contrary, I tend to experience, well, not sorrow unless it is experienced by someone close to me, but it gets me thinking of the idea that everyone else could discover Jesus as well.
>
> (YFIKD060PT)

> It is not like the people in the Christian circles feast on the thought of the pagans suffering damnation. You do always pray for those people, nonetheless, and you pray that, for example, those friends who do not believe could find God [...] it is more likely to make you a little sad, I don't wish for anyone to suffer damnation.
>
> (YFIKD159T)

> That type of thought just seems too rough to me somehow. So I myself am more like, if I would be thinking to myself that someone else would end up in perdition or would have to face suffering or punishment, whether it would be physical in this type of world that we live in or some type of transcendental punishment for example, so, so um, I would much rather become sad because of it than receive consolation from that thought.
>
> (YFIKD146T)

Considering the liberal Protestant, but nonetheless clearly conventionally religious, character of this prototype, it is not surprising that its individual representatives frequently express their sentiments on human well-being and suffering through religious idioms, drawing on terms and concepts such as transcendental punishment (hell), damnation and/or salvation, a personal turn to righteousness ("discovering Jesus"), and so on. Indeed, their reasoning with regard to both FQS77 and FQS99 often takes the form of "hopes for the better". In addition, an emphasis on the *finitude of life* also appears in connection with the theme of suffering.

> I try not to cause suffering to anyone, to any form of life. You also do not disparage other life forms because you see the equal standing that they all

have in the end. Then again, it also, maybe, slightly calms down my own [suffering] – or it helps you understand the suffering that you see around you.

(YFIKD126T)

Apart from openly recognising the equal value of all living creatures in the face of death, an additional emphasis on earthly life also often emerges in relation to FQS52.

> The idea of anticipating death [FQS52], I guess that one doesn't really describe me so well since I agree to gladly go through this one life here first. But it isn't for me, like, a thing which I would be contemplating with horror.
>
> (YFIKD060PT)

As with the Russian case above, here again emerges the idea that one's earthly life ideally should be a good life and lived to the fullest. The achievement of a "good life" is often directly related to being a good person.

> It is also fairly easy to identify with the suffering and experiences of all the unknown people and hope to be able to help.
>
> (YFIKD143T)

The distinguishing statement FQS51 frequently acts to further reinforce this sentiment.

> I have got so much that I want to pass on the joy and love and this carefree attitude, so I feel that I have also been called upon to pass this thing on. It clearly is part of a Christian's life. It cannot, you cannot just be staring at yourself. And I mean we clearly have been called upon to make the world a better place to live in. [...] I try to influence the world mainly within my immediate surroundings.
>
> (YFIKD133T)

Here, an expressed intention "to pass on the joy and love" is shaped by the religious convictions of this respondent and conceived as "part of a Christian life". Notably, the same logic of care for others also clearly emerged in the interviews with representatives of the Russian prototype under consideration, although without overt religious connotations. Still, when the desire to remain helpful and work towards reducing suffering seems not to lead to any tangible results, this may serve to provoke a sense of helplessness.

> At times, you start to experience this type of feeling of helplessness perhaps, in a sense that you wish that you could do more, but then again in practice, you don't necessarily find any means to do so, maybe.
>
> (YFIKD146T)

> I would love to do a lot of all kinds of things that would reduce their suffering but I can't do everything.
>
> (YFIKD135T)

Finally, agreement with the statement on individual freedom of choice in matters of faith and morality (FQS100) is also distinctive of this prototype. As with the Russian prototype discussed above, it is articulated by the help of several concepts, including personal *rights, decision, choice*, etc. Support for the notion of individual freedom is also frequently expressed through *negation*, or through highlighting that which is perceived to constitute a threat to individual freedom.

> It's self-evident that each individual needs to be allowed personally to choose their own faith and their own morals. It's a little like it's no use trying to force anyone to do anything they wouldn't voluntarily do. Even if it was possible to force someone into doing something, it would only be apparent rather than genuine.
>
> (YFIKD143T)

Nevertheless, there are issues and situations that the respondents find it difficult to tolerate.

> I wouldn't say that it's about me being intolerant, it's more about me wanting to say out loud that these are my own values, and that this is how I think about things, but that I also do hold respect for people who think differently from myself.
>
> (YFIKD146T)

> When you've actually seen that like people are just, just like crazy then that just changes it. But, but in general this is like part of that tolerance idea that everything should be tolerated, but then if you have a different opinion then you've seen like you feel contempt towards it all even though you don't really.
>
> (YFIKD124T)

In comparison with the Russian case, in the Finnish prototype, concepts pertaining to the notion of the "sacred individual" emerge more frequently in connection with common Christian notions, thus embedding the "sacred individual subset" more firmly within a particular (mainly Lutheran) religious discourse. This results in a fascinating merger of conceptualisations of the sacred as represented by God (Jesus) on the one hand, and by humanity on the other.

Concluding Discussion

In a decidedly explorative fashion, this chapter has attempted to take a step forwards in Durkheim-inspired theorising on the "sacred individual". It has identified a set of key concepts illustrative of the notion of moral individualism in direct relation to a particular body of empirical data. We have presented two particular conceptualisations of the "sacred individual" derived from one Finnish and one Russian FQS prototype as well as their connected interviews. Two particularly notable observations with regard to the notion of the sacred individual emerge from our explorative analysis in this chapter.

First, in both of the cases explored, *respect* emerged as a key motive of moral conduct. Along with respect comes the concept of *tolerance* that appears problematic because it risks being reduced to either indifference (which would be immoral) or an avoidance of expressing moral judgements out of a fear of coming across as intolerant. This problem emerges quite explicitly in the conventionally religious Finnish case. In this particular case, a certain tension can be discerned between the general ideal of tolerance and the sacred commitments of a particular religious understanding. Second, both prototypes display a strong intention of "doing good and resisting bad". The accounts of representatives of both prototypes display a clear connection between feelings of sympathy for others and a desire to reduce harm or suffering in a way that reflects the key tenets of moral individualism as outlined by Durkheim. Furthermore, the intention of doing good and resisting evil often serves as inspiration for becoming a better person who is more considerate of others. In the accounts of representatives of the Russian prototype, this primarily takes the form of work on oneself devoid of any specific ideological attachments. In the accounts of representatives of the Finnish prototype, by contrast, self-enhancement and becoming a better person is primarily understood and expressed through a religious idiom.

Throughout the interviews with representatives of both the Finnish and Russian prototypes, we can observe a strong orientation among respondents towards the rights and well-being of others. It is important to point out, however, that out of eight country-specific prototypes (three in Finland and five in Russia), only two of them were marked by statements included in what we identified as the "sacred individual subset" (i.e. as consensual, defining or distinguishing statements). The values and moral judgements expressed by representatives of these two prototypes might therefore not be particularly representative for other young adults that were interviewed for the YARG project in either Finland or

Russia. We could, of course, speculate about where exactly the moral ideals expressed by our respondents come from and the various reasons why they become integrated as part of the outlooks of some of these individuals but not others. In the case of the Finnish prototype discussed in this chapter, the answer seems to suggest itself: it comes mainly from the tradition of Lutheran Christianity. When it comes to the Russian prototype, however, it appears that the question has to remain unresolved, at least for the time being. In terms of final remarks, we therefore cordially encourage and invite further firmly empirically grounded research on representations of the Durkheimian notion of moral individualism and expressions of the notion of the "sacred individual".

Polina Vrublevskaya is a research fellow of the sociological laboratory "Sociology of Religion" at St Tikhon's University in Moscow, Russia. She holds a joined master's degree in Sociology at Moscow School of Social and Economic Sciences and University of Manchester (2014). Her main research interests include community policies, sociological theory of sacred and field studies of Russian Orthodox Church. Vrublevskaya served as research assistant for the Åbo Akademi University Centre of Excellence Young Adults and Religion in a Global Perspective Project (2015–19) in Russia and is currently working on a doctoral dissertation in Study of Religions at Åbo Akademi University (ÅAU) (2018–). Her main publications are found at https://research.abo.fi/en/persons/polina-vrublevskaya/publications.

Dr Marcus Moberg is professor in the study of religions at Åbo Akademi University. His main research interests include the sociology of religion, religion and media, and discourse theory and analysis in the Study of Religion. Moberg acted as Senior Researcher in the Centre of Excellence Young Adults and Religion in a Global Perspective at ÅAU (2015–19). Recent publications include *Religion, Discourse, and Society* (Routledge, 2021) and *Digital Media, Young Adults and Religion: An International Perspective* (co-edited with Sofia Sjö; Routledge, 2020).

Karoliina Dahl, MA, is a doctoral student of the Study of Religions at Åbo Akademi University (ÅAU), Turku, Finland. Dahl worked as a research assistant in Finland and member of the core team of the Centre of Excellence Young Adults and Religion in a Global Perspective at ÅAU (2015–19), and she gathered the data in Finland. Her dissertation project focuses on continuities and changes in Finnish young adults' religious, nonreligious and spiritual views of life.

References

Alexander, Jeffrey. 2003. *The Meanings of Social Life: A Cultural Sociology*. New York: Oxford University Press.

Anttonen, Veikko. 1999. "Toward a Cognitive Theory of the Sacred: An Ethnographic Approach". Annual Meeting of SSSR in Boston, Massachusetts, USA, 5-7 November. Retrieved from www.folklore.ee/folklore/vol14/sacred.htm.

Anttonen, Veikko. 2000. "Sacred". In *Guide to the Study of Religion*, ed. Willi Braun and Russell T. McCutcheon, 271-82. London: Continuum.

Calhoun, John C. 1997. *Nationalism*. Minneapolis, MN: University of Minnesota Press.

Cladis, Mark S. 2005. "Beyond Solidarity? Durkheim and Twenty-first Century Democracy in a Global Age". In *Cambridge Companion to Durkheim*, ed. Jeffery Alexander and Paul Smith, 383-409. Cambridge: Cambridge University Press.

Durkheim, Émile. 1973. "Individualism and the Intellectuals". In *Émile Durkheim: On Morality and Society*, ed. Robert N. Bellah, 43-57. Chicago, IL: University of Chicago Press.

Durkheim, Émile. 1991. *De la division du travail social*. Paris: Quadrige.

Durkheim, Émile. 1995. *The Elementary Forms of Religious Life*. Florence, MA: The Free Press.

Durkheim, Émile, and Marcel Mauss. 2009. *Primitive Classification* (Routledge Revivals). London: Routledge.

Fournier, Michael. 2005. "Durkheim's Life and Context: Something New about Durkheim?" In *Cambridge Companion to Durkheim*, ed. Jeffery Alexander and Paul Smith, 41-69. Cambridge: Cambridge University Press.

Gane, Mike. 1983. "Durkheim: The Sacred Language". *Economy and Society* 12(1): 1-47.

Grusky, David, and Gabriela Galescu. 2005. "Is Durkheim a Class Analyst?" In *Cambridge Companion to Durkheim* ed. Jeffery Alexander and Paul Smith, 322-59. Cambridge: Cambridge University Press.

Heider, Anne, and Stephen R. Warner. 2010. "Bodies in Sync: Interaction Ritual Theory Applied to Sacred Harp Singing". *Sociology of Religion* 71(1): 76-97.

Hunt, Lynn. 2007. *Inventing Human Rights: A History*. New York: Norton.

Joas, Hans. 2008. *Do We Need Religion? On the Experience of Self-Transcendence*. Boulder, CO: Paradigm Publishers.

Joas, Hans. 2013. *The Sacredness of the Person: A New Genealogy of Human Rights*. Washington, DC: Georgetown University Press.

Knott, Kim. 2013. "The Secular Sacred: In Between or Both/And?" In *Social Identities between the Sacred and the Secular* (AHRC/ESRC Religion and

Society Series), ed. Abby Day, Giselle Vincent and Christopher R. Cotter, 145–60. Farnham: Ashgate.

Kurakin, Dmitriy. 2015. "Reassembling the Ambiguity of the Sacred: A Neglected Inconsistency in Readings of Durkheim". *Journal of Classical Sociology* 15(4): 377–95.

Levine, Donald N. 2006. *Powers of the Mind: The Reinvention of Liberal Learning in America.* Chicago, IL: University of Chicago Press.

Lynch, Gordon. 2012. *On the Sacred.* Durham: Acumen.

Markin, Kirill. 2018. "Between Belief and Unbelief: Non-practicing Orthodox Christians in the Context of the Russian Sociology of Religion". *Monitoring of Public Opinion: Economic and Social Changes* 2: 274–90. doi: 10.14515/monitoring.2018.2.16.

Miller, William W. 1996. *Durkheim, Morals and Modernity.* New York: Routledge.

Official Statistics of Finland. 2022. "Population structure / 11rx - Belonging to a religious community by age and sex, 1990-2022." Retrieved from https://pxdata.stat.fi/PxWeb/pxweb/en/StatFin/StatFin__vaerak/statfin_vaerak_pxt_11rx.px/

Paden, William E. 1991. "Before 'the Sacred' became theological: rereading the Durkheimian Legacy". *Method and Theory in the Study of Religion* 3(1): 10–23.

Paden, William E. 2000. "Sacred Order". *Method and Theory in the Study of Religion* 12(1): 207–25.

Pew Research Center. 2017. "Religious Belief and National Belonging in Central and Eastern Europe". Retrieved from www.pewforum.org/2017/05/10/religious-belief-and-national-belonging-in-central-and-eastern-europe/

Pickering, William S. F. 2009. *Durkheim's Sociology of Religion.* Cambridge: James Clarke & Co.

Prutskova, Elena. 2015. "Связь религиозности и ценностно-нормативных показателей: фактор религиозной социализации" [Association of Religiosity with Norms and Values.The Factor of Religious Socialisation]. *Вестник ПСТГУ. Серия I: Богословие. Философия* 59(3): 62–80.

Rawls, Ann W. 2004. *Epistemology and Practice: Durkheim's "The Elementary Forms of Religious Life".* Cambridge: Cambridge University Press.

Smith, Christian, and Patricia Snell. 2009. *Souls in Transition: The Religious and Spiritual Lives of Emerging Adults.* Oxford: Oxford University Press.

Stausberg, Michael. 2017. "The Sacred, the Holy, the Numinous – and Religion: On the Emergence and Early History of a Terminological Constellation". *Religion* 47(4): 557–90.

Stedman-Jones, Susan. 2000. "Representations in Durkheim's Masters: Kant and Renouvier. II: Representation and Logic" In *Durkheim and Representations*, ed. William S. F. Pickering, 59–79. London: Routledge.

Stedman-Jones, Susan. 2012. "Forms of Thought and Forms of Society: Durkheim and the Question of the Categories". *L'Année sociologique* 62(2): 387–407.

Taves, Ann. 2009. *Religious Experience Reconsidered: A Building-Block Approach to the Study of Religion and Other Special Things.* Princeton: Princeton University Press.

Winfree, Jason K., and Andrew J. Mitchell, eds. 2009. *The Obsessions of Georges Bataille: Community and Communication.* New York: State University of New York Press.

World Values Survey Association. 2020. "Inglehart–Welzel Cultural Map". Retrieved from www.worldvaluessurvey.org/WVSContents.jsp.

Zabaev, Ivan, Yana Mikhaylova and Daria Oreshina. 2018. "Neither Public nor Private Religion: The Russian Orthodox Church in the Public Sphere of Contemporary Russia". *Journal of Contemporary Religion* 33(1): 17–38.

– 7 –

Secular Identities in Context: Emerging Prototypes among Non-religious Young Adults

JANNE KONTALA, ARIELA KEYSAR AND SAWSAN KHEIR

The number of "nones", people who do not identify with a religion, is increasing in many countries. Many are forming new worldviews. While "nones" are estimated to account for between 16 and 33 per cent of the global population, and are most common among young adults, we still lack a coherent perspective on non-religious identities. In this chapter, we uncover a spectrum of these identities. Utilising a mixed-methods approach in several diverse cultures, we rely on surveys and interviews with young adults to shed light on the complexity of their non-religious choices. This global research delves into critical research questions: What are the emerging non-religious prototypes among contemporary young adults? Do they form a single global identity or are they influenced by their specific national contexts, and if so, how? What is the role of their religious/non-religious upbringing? We found that the major non-religious outlook is fairly secular, but we also unveiled notable openness towards religion. Somewhat surprisingly, one-third of the respondents that define the prototypes were associated with outlooks that in various ways indicated some engagement with religion or spirituality. The quotations sprinkled through this chapter illuminate this seeming contradiction with personal narratives.

Introduction

Non-religion is a complex, layered concept whose meaning varies by individual and by culture. It can be defined as lack of belief, or as lack of identification with a particular religious group, or as lack of religious behaviour, such as attendance at services (Keysar and Kosmin 2007).

There are people who participate in religious rituals without believing, as well as the opposite (Davie 1994; Sherkat 2014). Even along the single dimension of belief there is diversity, from resolute atheists to agnostics to deists to individuals who are spiritual but not monotheistic (Keysar 2014). Non-religion can also be perceived as a presence rather than an absence – for example, a set of values that does not require anchoring to a deity (Day 2011). Further complicating matters is the fact that secularity can be defined at the individual level as lack of religiosity, or at the societal level as tolerance by the state of religious diversity (Kosmin 2007; Keysar and Kosmin 2008).

"No religion" and "not religious" vary by culture and context around the globe (Pew 2012; Keysar 2017). We might contrast the situation in Japan and Scandinavia, for instance: in the former case secularisation has taken place on the societal level, whereas on the individual level the situation is complicated, and persons who deny the existence of supernatural beings are rare (Roemer 2010). In Scandinavia, on the other hand, there is a close alliance between state and the church, whereas Scandinavian individuals are relatively secularised (Lüchau 2010).

The World Value Survey (WVS) (2014) asked respondents in more than fifty countries (including the most populous, India and China), "Independently of whether you attend religious services or not, are you a religious person, not a religious person, or an atheist?" According to WVS 2014, 53 per cent of people worldwide defined themselves as "religious", 33 per cent as "not religious", and 11 per cent as "atheists" (3 per cent provided no answer). At the top we find Japan and China with 60 per cent calling themselves "not a religious person", followed by 50 per cent in Sweden. These can be contrasted with these countries in our sample: 30 per cent in Russia, 18 per cent in India, 12 per cent in Peru and Turkey and less than 5 per cent in Ghana.

Being non-religious does not preclude people from having opinions about religion. A majority (68 per cent) of people who call themselves "not religious" believe religion has "to make sense of life in this world", while a minority (32 per cent) believe that its meaning is "to make sense of life after death". "Religious" and "not religious" people disagree on other meanings of religion: for the "not religious", religion is far more about doing "good to other people" than about following "religious norms and ceremonies" (Keysar 2017). Religiosity also differs by demographics (Keysar 2007; Zuckerman 2007). The religious gender gap is well documented: women tend to be more religious (Beit-Hallahmi 2007, 2014). Globally among the religious, the male to female ratio is 47/53 and the opposite among the non-religious: 53/47 (Keysar 2017). Women are more likely than men to affirm their belief in God and to attend religious services (Sherkat and Ellison 1999; Sherkat 2014). Some of the biggest gender gaps in disbelief are found in Japan (22-point gap), Russia (15-point gap), and Sweden (14-point gap) (Keysar 2015). Age is an important factor as youth is often associated with challenging authority, including religious institutions. In Sweden, for example, the age pattern of atheism is linear and the likelihood of declared atheists under the age of 30 is double that of those aged 50 and over (Keysar 2015).

Atheism, by both identification and belief, is associated with higher educational level, primarily with a university degree (Keysar 2015). The national level of education has been found to correlate positively with secularity (Braun 2012) and disbelief in God (Azarvan 2013). National contexts matter, however, and there are countries where higher education correlates negatively with atheism (Keysar and Navarro-Rivera 2013). On the individual level, a non-religious person is found to be educated above average (Hadaway and Roof 1988; Feigelman, Gorman and Varacalli 1992; Keysar and Kosmin 2007; Keysar 2017; Phillips 2007; Bainbridge 2009; Argyle 2000). Even here, going into details may complicate matters: Keysar (2007) finds agnostics to be the best educated group out of atheists, agnostics and those with no religion, the educational level of the atheists being closer to the national mean. Kosmin et al. (2009) found that the educational attainment of the non-religious is similar to the national mean, whereas Cragun (2014) found individuals associated with the New Atheist movement to be significantly better educated than the national mean. What counts as religion may also influence the outcome. Mayrl and Oeur (2009) found college experience to have a negative effect on religious practice, whereas the effect on beliefs was more complex. The global research delves into critical research questions: What are the emerging outlook types among contemporary young adults, who consider themselves as non-religious, or secular? Do they form a single global identity or are they influenced by their specific national contexts, and if so, how? What is the role of their religious/non-religious upbringing?

This chapter utilises a mixed-model approach to shed light on the worldviews of young adults who identify themselves as "not religious". Based on surveys and interviews with college students in twelve diverse cultures, we discovered a spectrum of identities and non-religious choices. Thus, the chapter uses research methodologies, quantitative and qualitative, which were designed to probe religious subjectivities instead of studying the opposite, non-religion. This study is part of a larger research project, Young Adults and Religion in Global Context (YARG). YARG respondents are religiously diverse. Scattered globally, they include secular societies, such as Sweden and Canada, as well as religious

Ghana. They also represent multiple religions; for instance, Catholics in Poland, Jews and Muslims in Israel, Hindus and Muslims in India, Lutherans in Finland, and no religion in China. Noteworthy in regard to previous studies that have found non-religion to correlate negatively with age and positively with education, the respondents of our study are under the age of 30 and college students.

Non-religious Outlooks

In this study, we identify four worldview prototypes tied to non-religious self-identification and examine their occurrence by gender, nationality and other characteristics. We develop the prototypes using the Faith Q-sort method.[1] Developed by David Wulff (2019), the method combines quantitative and qualitative features to assess interpersonally shared preferences in the domain of worldview. Previous studies have discovered outlook variation among non-religious individuals (Schnell and Keenan 2011; Pasquale 2010; Cotter 2011; Silver *et al.* 2014; Pew 2018). Arthur Nilsson's (2007) Q-methodological study identified a decidedly non-religious type amongst its four worldview types. Studies specifically utilising FQS have found a secular-humanistic outlook to recur in various contexts, with some internal variation (Wulff 2019; Kontala 2016).

We apply the prototypes to quantitative survey data from twelve countries. We include quotations from in-depth interviews to enrich understanding of the young adults. In the YARG 2016 survey, respondents were asked about their religiosity: "Regardless of whether you consider yourself as belonging or close to a particular religious group, community, or tradition, how religious would you say you are?" 0 means "not at all religious", 10 means "very religious". Our analysis focuses on the least religious, or most secular individuals, YARG respondents who chose 0, 1 or 2. This group can be classified as relatively non-religious.[2] For the purposes of this study, we let 0 stand for "highly non-religious", 1 for "moderately non-religious" and 2 for "somewhat non-religious". In all, there were 197 non-religious students who completed both the survey and participated in the Faith Q-sort statements selection.

How does self-identification relate to other dimensions, such as theistic beliefs, belonging to a religious group or behaving according

---

1. See Appendix 1.
2. One might argue that it is questionable whether a person choosing anything but 0 can stand for non-religion. We should keep in mind that sometimes even public spokespersons for New Atheism do not self-identify with the most extreme values available on the scale. See McAnulla (2012, 88–9).

to religious doctrine? Non-religious self-identification does not always mean disbelief or non-religious behaviour (Keysar 2007, 2017; Sherkat 2014; Pew 2015). We investigate the relationships between religious self-assessment, the Faith Q-sort and the survey results for gender, nationality, being raised with religion and current religious adherence and behaviour.

Our method of selection allows respondents to decide what religion means to them. Non-religious identification can be understood in terms of a flexible model of multiple wheels rather than a fixed and absolute construct (af Burén 2015). The idea of the wheel comes from the analogy of rotation. The person is surrounded by an inner wheel of different identifications, and an outer wheel of circumstances. Since circumstances change, one's identification may change as well. Consequently, a respondent may think of herself as non-religious regarding A and in situation X, whereas the same person might show signs of religiosity regarding B, or in situation Y. She may think of his or her non-belief when she thinks of her identification, despite being a member of a religious community. Or the person may think of himself or herself as non-religious compared to others in the same community, yet feeling more religious than members of another community. Instead of deciding what religion means for the respondents, we explore what kinds of worldviews and demographic indicators are associated with non-religious self-identification.

We choose to call our respondents' outlooks worldviews, and the emerging shared patterns worldview prototypes (or just prototypes). The precedent of worldview, *Weltanschauung*, was first connected with German idealism. The English version "worldview" has been used and theorised in various ways: for interpersonally shared ideologies, for privately held outlooks, for explicitly formulated philosophies and for implicit and intuitive structures (Naugle 2002; Nilsson 2013; Kontala 2016). We use it as a parent term that can incorporate religious, spiritual or non-religious outlooks. This is a practical choice we make at the outset, to accommodate all kinds of emerging viewpoints that could reject, accommodate, approve or doubt religion or spirituality. The interpersonally shared preferences are called worldview prototypes. As such, they arise from the data, and involve no preconceived notions about existing non-religious worldview types. The prototype names reflect the internal distinctions found in this study. We make no claims about the validity of these names outside our study, even though we believe similar preferences may arise in other studies with similar samples.

The global exploration presented here is of young adults, sometimes referred to as millennials but in some cases representatives also of the succeeding Generation Z. Our data from twelve diverse countries of the

East and the West derive from primarily Catholics in Poland, Jews and Muslims in Israel and Hindus in India, as well as from countries undergoing religious transitions, such as China and Russia. In Ghana, for instance, there were no respondents with religious identity scored below 2. This means that while the respondents from Ghana were the least *religious* in that area, they represent the least *non-religious* respondents of our sample.

The Emerging Prototypes

Starting with factor extraction with Principal Component Analysis, we went on with Varimax rotation for eight factors.[3] We manually added fourteen sorts,[4] wrote out factors with at least two defining respondents and concluded by running the Qanalyzis feature.[5] The analysis yielded four factors, explaining 41 per cent of the total variance.[6] The factors are associated with 117 defining respondents, with all twelve countries being represented.

We can now take a look at the four main factors, the emerging worldview prototypes. Let us start with their common ground. The prototypes show non-religious tendencies. Persons of these prototypes do not dedicate their lives to serving the divine (FQS36). They are not active or contributing members of religious or spiritual communities (FQS97), nor do they believe that religion should play the central role in the governance of the nation (FQS77). These preferences combine with a humanistic orientation. Persons associated with these prototypes believe that one can be deeply moral without being religious (FQS83) and support individual freedom of choice in matters of faith and morality (FQS100). Profoundly touched by the suffering of others (FQS77), they actively work towards making the world a better place to live (FQS51). Emotionally and experientially, they feel spiritually moved and deeply sustained by music, art or poetry (FQS33).

---

3. We used the project software PQMethod by Peter Schmolk, freely available online.
4. The highest bias on a factor would have to be at least 50 per cent more than on the next highest one for the sort to be flagged manually.
5. A defining respondent is a person who scores at least 50 per cent more on one prototype than on others. Non-defining respondents hold viewpoints that are not clearly associated with any of the prototypes, or their viewpoint may be nearly equally associated with two prototypes.
6. To compare, a seven-factor solution would explain 52 per cent, but three of the factors would be associated with only one respondent. It is therefore meaningful to speak about shared preferences with only four factors.

We shall now examine in more detail the particular characteristics of each prototype.

Prototype 1: Secular Humanist

The major prototype is the first, named the Secular Humanist. This prototype comprises 40 per cent (80) of the respondents. Their humanism is of an activist type, which is expressed by their emphasis on statements that talk about societal change and making the world a better place (FQS56; FQS51). However, they see no higher purpose or ultimate destiny for the human species (FQS96). They are the most consistent of all prototypes in rejecting religion: divinity, practices, beliefs, scriptures, traditions, authorities and institutions are systematically rejected.[7] In the words of a person who was born and grew up in a Nordic country, with nominally religious immigrant parents: "No religious conviction at all, I would claim" (a Swedish student with immigrant parents, YSEJK020). Another person underwent confirmation, mainly to learn more about Christianity. And it never made any sense: "how can [people] believe in this since I feel it is a little nonsensical" (a Swedish student with secular parents, YSEJK013).

Some respondents from Nordic countries indicated that they wanted to give religion a chance by trying out confirmation, yet the experience did not lead to a less pronounced non-religious stance. In Nordic countries, growing up secular often goes hand in hand with being nominally Christian. The cultural setting accommodates religiosity in terms of formal membership or participation in major rites of passage, but that is as far as it goes. Otherwise, it seems there was little or no religious influence in the upbringing of the Nordic respondents. Scandinavian secularisation can be regarded as a precondition for being religiously indifferent – something that would be a more difficult stance to take if there was social pressure in religious matters (Bagg and Voas 2010; Quack 2017a, 2017b).

Somewhat surprisingly, the Secular Humanists are positively interested in other people's religions (FQS81). One woman says nothing

---

7. Lack of interest in religiosity and spirituality: FQS16; FQS22; FQS52; FQS79. Rejection of religious rules and practices: FQS12; FQS23; FQS59; FQS67; FQS98. Rejection of religious authorities and scriptures: FQS18; FQS20; FQS32. Rejection of religious ideas in general: FQS15; FQS60; FQS70; FQS87; FQS92. No relationship to nor experiences of divinity or holy figures: FQS36; FQS45; FQS53; FQS55; FQS66; FQS74; FQS78. Rejection of religion as a social phenomenon: FQS31; FQS46; FQS71; FQS97; FQS101.

negative about religion during the whole interview (a Swedish student who grew up without religion, YSEJK009). Others go further than that. A young Swedish man talks about his multi-cultural student apartment, with different cultural and religious influences. Despite his experimentation, he has so far not come across anything resembling a religious experience:

> we had a Buddhist who had meditation with us for some months ago, and it was really interesting [...] there was a Hindu who had yoga, not like yoga when you go to student gym [...] but there was more focus on yoga as a religious activity. I think it is interesting, to test these things still and especially when it is someone who really believes in it.
>
> (YSEJK004)

Emotionally, they express stability (FQS75, FQS80), feeling inspired by paradox and mystery, and music, art or poetry (FQS33, FQS91).

Prototype 2: Religion-Approving Humanist

The second prototype, the Religion-Approving Humanist, differs from all prototypes, but it differs from the first one most. The major difference is that the Religion-Approving Humanists express considerable openness towards religion. With nineteen defining respondents, this outlook is minor, but not marginal. It shows that a non-religious identification can combine with a surprisingly religion-accommodating outlook. Compared with the previous prototype, there is a notable difference of opinion about the means to progress: this prototype holds religion to be a central means for becoming a better and more moral person (FQS3), as stated by an Israeli Druze student: "my personal belief is that – that all religions are alike, I mean, there is no difference" (YILSK276).

Thinking that the world's religious traditions point to a common truth (FQS4), this prototype does not find it difficult to believe in a benevolent divine being in the face of evil (FQS85). Persons of this prototype also view the divine as a protecting, guiding and nurturing parent (FQS41; FQS74). In the words of an Israeli female Druze:

> because I firmly believe in God, not a little ... like, I feel as if there was not even one time when I felt that I was annoyed in my life and God didn't give me something better in return, not once in my life [...] in all domains.
>
> (YILSK107)

Engaging in charitable acts (FQS27), and praying for protection (FQS62), they value and safeguard their personal purity (FQS48). Two Israeli Arab students exemplify this disposition as follows:

> like, have sexual relationships [...] before marriage, among us this is for example forbidden [Interviewer: "Among us" you mean the Bedouins?] Among the Bedouins, in Islam [in general] [...] this is forbidden.
> (YILSK278)

> I do not do that thing because my religion forbids me to drink wine.
> (YILSK143)

Instead of seeing religion as an illusory creation of human fears and desires (FQS60), this prototype values the continuity of the religion of one's family or ancestors (FQS58). Even though they express stability, contentment and a lack of negative impulses (FQS35, FQS61, FQS63, FQS69, FQS75, FQS80), persons of this prototype long for a deeper faith (FQS8), and become more religious at times of crisis (FQS17). We may ask if it is appropriate to call this prototype "just" Religion-Approving, or if it would be more appropriate to name the prototype "Religious Humanist". Our choice is based on the respondents' self-identification, choosing 0–2 on a scale of 0–10 about religious identity. This needs to be kept in mind with all prototype names. They are meant to reflect distinctions internal to this particular study, and to honour the self-identification of the respondents. The prototype names, hence, may need modification if the results are compared with other samples.

Prototype 3: Spiritual but not Religious

The third prototype is called Spiritual but not Religious. With its fifteen associated respondents it is slightly smaller than the second one. It differs from the Secular Humanists by showing openness towards spirituality, yet unlike the Religion-Approving Humanists, not so with traditional religiosity.

Persons associated with this prototype have an activist outlook (FQS51, FQS56). Having undergone a change in their faith (FQS37), they believe in some way without considering themselves religious (FQS28). Rejecting group-based religion and practices (FQS7, FQS21, FQS31, FQS46), they value personal self-realisation (FQS93). They find inspiration in music, art or poetry (FQS33), and take delight in paradox and mystery (FQS91). There is a notable interest in personal spirituality that distinguishes this prototype from the others, exemplified by the following respondent, an Israeli Jewish student who has maintained an interest in personal growth for a long time:

> The desire to be more, this desire, like, to be more than this flat level of the tradition and the religion, and the normal life, where I grew up and the

environment I was born into. But real desire to – to reach my full potential. To achieve what I am capable of.

(YILAM107)

The Spiritual but not Religious report having used methods for attaining altered states of consciousness (FQS50). This is illustrated by the words of a Jewish Israeli student as follows:

> almost every day I do an hour of meditations, relaxation, relaxation before sleeping, guided imagery […] in the meditation slowly, slowly the body relaxes, it's getting quieter, more blood flows to the ears so you can hear more of that small sound of silence. And then slowly, slowly I achieve a distance from all those things that allegedly defines me at that moment, but they don't. There is some sort of smarter part, more peaceful. Suddenly, in the middle of the meditation, the idea popped up for me.
>
> (YILAM107)

Instead of being alienated from divinity (FQS55, FQS39), the divine or a higher reality is seen as a deep mystery that can be pointed to but never fully understood (FQS88). There is a strong sense of a spiritual or higher order of reality (FQS11) and the ultimate is thought of as a life force or creative energy (FQS9), as highlighted by the following American and Peruvian students:

> what is the higher power in my mind? It's like whatever enables us to all coexist. So I don't know. I feel like in a way the world is all very connected […] The higher power is just like existence as a concept for me […] that is very baffling.
>
> (YUSTP016)

> what nature represents, I don't know, a very important entity, right? […] it is almost as it were almost a living being, that is, a being – or just that type of creative force.
>
> (YPESC072P)

Taking interest in religious or spiritual matters (FQS24), they spend much time reading or talking about their convictions (FQS6), which they are not reluctant to reveal to others (FQS82).

Prototype 4: Vaguely Non-religious

The fourth prototype is called Vaguely Non-religious, because of their shifting and ambiguous outlook. It is the smallest of the four, with only three defining respondents. The shifting nature of their outlook (FQS17, FQS84) is captured by an American student, who considers herself to be agnostic: "I have a very shifting religious outlook. So, if like I hear like something about like one religion, they may be right. And like if I hear something with others, like, oh they may be right, too" (American student, YUSTP019).

Persons of this prototype are open to the idea of a higher purpose or an ultimate destiny for the human species (FQS96). Consistently rejecting all religious and spiritual practices, they are ambiguous about the divine. Despite feeling distant from the divine (FQS45), they consider the ultimate as a life force or energy (FQS9) and feel protected and guided by a spiritual being (FQS74). In the words of a self-identified agnostic: "It's like I can't really confirm God, but I know there's something driving this thing, like this world [...] it is like sometimes things are not really explainable by science or anything" (American student, YUSTP019).

A Polish student with a religious familial background contemplates on the nature of her beliefs:

> I believe in some way that there is something, that something guides us – for instance, it happened that I came here or something like that. But I do not think I am a religious person because I do not express it in terms of sort of God's existence as it is seen in Poland. Maybe there is something like this, but – somehow – I have not experienced it and somehow I know there is something, but I cannot specify it, so I am not a religious person who believes only in it.
>
> (YPLSS063PT)

Believing in some way (FQS28), they reject what conflicts with science and rationality (FQS70), but not all religious content (FQS32). While communal religiosity is not important to them (FQS30, FQS97), and they reject the idea of religion playing a role in national politics (FQS71), they have a favourable disposition towards the plurality of religious traditions (FQS4, FQS29, FQS81), as the same student explains:

> there is a particular religion and we somehow believe in it or something, but do not seek it. It is not the case that I seek, because for me, all religions constitute a unity. It does not matter what we call them; it does not matter what figures will be there and so on. For me it is nevertheless one thing.
>
> (YPLSS063PT)

Socially they do not feel closest with those with the same outlook (FQS47), and are reluctant to reveal their convictions to others (FQS82). Feeling uncomfortable with death (FQS80), they report experiences of the presence of spirits, demons or saints (FQS68):

> I sense the presence of someone when I am somewhere, just in some sacred places. However – um – well, I don't know, for instance, at a cemetery, I just sense that it surrounds me – not in a sense that I see something or

that something moves, though I know there is something like that and it is somehow real and – um, I believe in it.

(YPLSS063PT)

There does not seem to be anything threatening about the reported experience. It is likely that the felt presence is not about demons, as persons of this prototype do not feel threatened by evil forces at work in the world (FQS61).

Prototype Summary

We have given a detailed description of the four prototypes. We first established that there is a common ground consisting of agreement with some humanistic preferences, and rejection of religion in terms of serving the divine, being active or contributing as members of religious or spiritual communities and believing that religion should play the central role in the governance of the nation. Beyond this, the prototypes differ from each other. Table 11 summarises how the prototypes differ from each other by the various dimensions expressed by the items of the FQS-set.

Interestingly, one topic where the prototypes differ, yet also seem to share something, is the attitude towards other faiths. They differ since they do not unanimously affirm the following statements. Yet all prototypes agree with at least one of the following statements, and they do not reject any of them:[8]

- "Thinks that the world's religious traditions point to a common truth" (FQS4; P2 agrees).
- "Is inclined to embrace elements from various religious and spiritual traditions" (FQS29, P3 and P4 agree).
- "Is positively engaged by or interested in other people's religious traditions" (FQS81; P1, P3 and P4 agree).

---

8. Agreement here means that the rank of a particular statement is at least amongst the 25 most agreeable statements. Lack of rejection means none of the prototypes had any of the three statements within the bottom half.

Table 11. Non-religious prototype summary.

	P1	P2	P3	P4
Humanism	• activist outlook • no higher purpose for the human species	• religion a central means for becoming a better or more moral person	• activist outlook	• open to higher purpose for the human species
Religion and spirituality	• systematic rejection	• God as parent • prayer, charitable acts, safeguarding personal purity • values tradition	• life-force/ energy • methods for altered states • rejection of group-based religion	• rejects practices • rejects institutions • ambiguity over divinity and beliefs
Emotions and experiences	• inspired by paradox, mystery, music, art, poetry • content	• lack of negative impulses • stable	• values personal, nourishing experiences	• experiences of spirits, demons or saints • fear of death
Social orientation	• closest with those with the same outlook • positively engaged by other people's religions	• open to tradition • world's religious traditions point to a common truth	• individualistic • inclined to embrace elements from various traditions	• not closest with the same outlook • reluctant to reveal one's convictions • inclined to embrace elements from various traditions
Outlook stability	• stable	• longs for a deeper faith • more religious or spiritual at times of crisis • one-pointed	• has undergone a change in one's faith	• has undergone a change in one's faith • vague and shifting outlook • more religious or spiritual at times of crisis

Combining the Qualitative FQS and Quantitative Survey Results

As I got older, I realised how, like, repressive religion can be. So I, like, just moved away from it because I would ask questions about science, and they wouldn't answer me.

(American student, YUSTP052)

What are the profiles of non-religious young adults around the globe? Do socio-demographics and upbringing play a role in shaping their worldviews and how do they differ by culture? The mixed-methods exploratory analysis combines YARG qualitative FQS findings with the quantitative survey data to explore the following hypotheses.

Hypotheses

Non-religious outlook is associated with non-religious behaviour:

- The large differences are expected between the Secular Humanist – Prototype 1 and the Religion-Approving Humanist – Prototype 2.
- Students scoring high on Prototype 1 are most likely to exhibit non-religious behaviour.
- Students scoring high on Prototype 2 are most likely to exhibit religious behaviour.

Non-religious socialisation during childhood is associated with secular outlook among young people:

- We expect those who were raised with no religion to demonstrate a secular outlook in young adulthood when compared with those who were raised with a religion.
- Thus, young adults raised with no religion are likely to score higher on Prototype 1 and lower on Prototype 2.

The twelve countries can be divided into religious countries, secular countries and middle-of-the-road countries. Each group has a unique pattern of non-religious prototypes:

- We expect consistencies whereby countries with high scores on Prototype 1 will score low on Prototype 2.
- In the case of Israel, Arabs and Jews will most likely occupy different clusters, reflecting their religiosity gaps. Jews are expected to be part of the secular cluster while Arabs part of the religious one.

Findings

The share of non-religious students in the overall YARG sample varies greatly by country. Sweden, Israeli Jews and Canada stand out as having the most secular students; 30–40 per cent of them self-identified as "not at all religious", or 0. Ghana stands out at the other end with very few non-religious students – less than 5 per cent. Among Israeli Arabs in the sample less than 10 per cent self-identified as "not at all religious". In China, Peru, Poland, Japan and India, students were almost as likely to opt for 2 as for 0.

Now we focus only on students who chose categories 0, 1 or 2, which we classified as non-religious. We examine the occurrence of the four prototypes in each country. Every respondent was scored on all four prototypes. The analyses presented in Figures 6–11 introduce the scores of YARG students for each of the four emerging non-religious prototypes: the Secular Humanist; the Religion-Approving Humanist; the Spiritual but not Religious; and the Vaguely Non-religious. The analyses demonstrate the associations between these scores and various characteristics: socio-demographics, culture and several religious indicators. The countries with most affinity with the Secular Humanist prototype are Sweden and Finland, with the highest scores on Prototype 1. They are trailed by three groupings: Canada, Israeli Jews, and Poland; India, Russia and China; Peru, Turkey and the USA.

Those scoring highest on Prototype 2, Religion-Approving Humanist, are Israeli Arabs and Ghana. They also have the lowest scores on

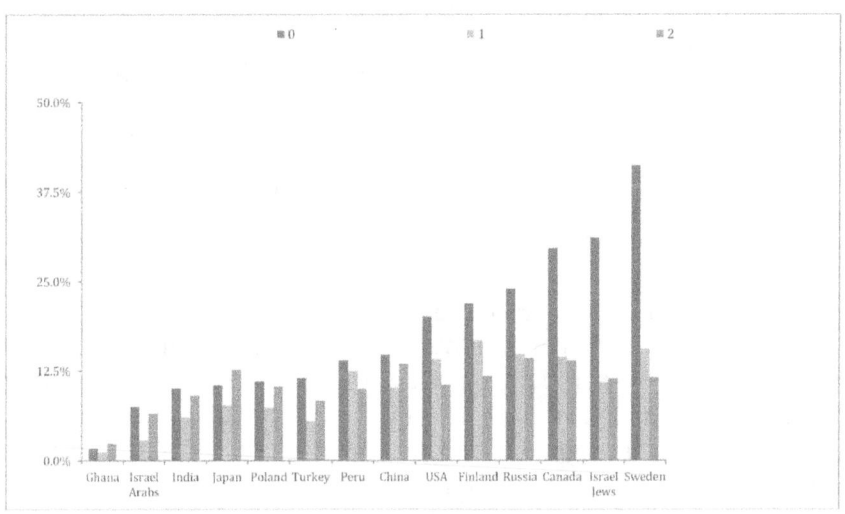

Figure 6. Non-religious as share of all YARG students.

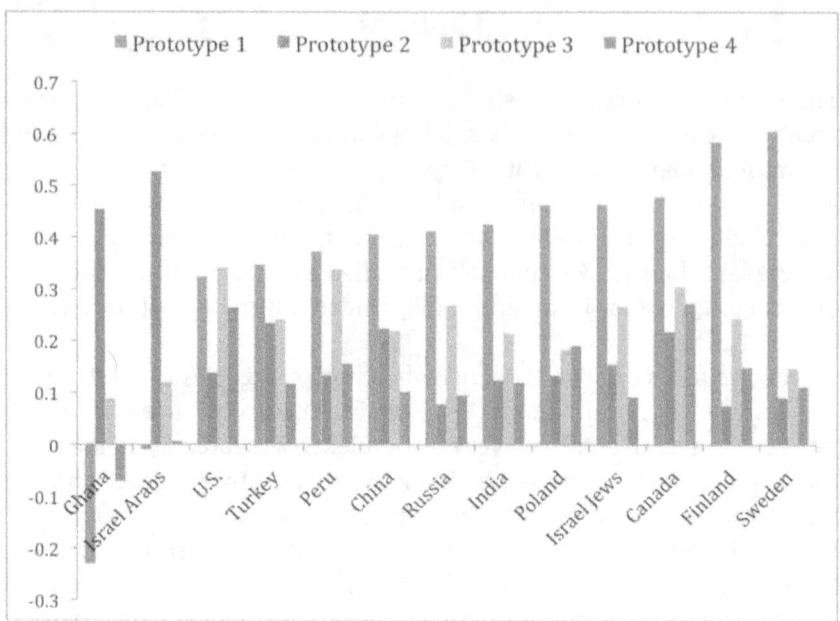

Figure 7. Prototype scoring per country.

Prototype 1. These findings confirm hypothesis 3. The spiritual cluster, Prototype 3, is led by the USA, followed by Peru and Canada. And for the Vaguely Non-religious, Prototype 4, the USA and Canada stand out with the highest scores while Israeli Arabs and Ghana with the lowest.

A Female Israeli Arab student explained:

> There are still red lines – red lines in everything, whether it was in staying out late, whether it was in meeting with certain people, or whether it was in trying things – certain things.
>
> (YILSK020)

Socio-demographics and Culture

Overall, there are small gender differences related to the four prototypes. Males scored higher on Prototype 1, the Secular Humanist, while females scored higher both on Prototype 2, the Religion-approving Humanist, and on Prototype 4, the Vaguely Non-religious. The gender gaps are statistically significant only on Prototype 4. The differences are not surprising, as males in general tend to be less religious than females. Somewhat surprisingly, however, YARG males and females scored the same on Prototype 3, the Spiritual but not Religious.

Religiosity

Raised Religious

Young adults who were raised with no religion tend to score higher on Prototype 1 and lower on Prototypes 2 and 4 compared with those who were raised with a religion, supporting hypothesis 2. The differences between religious vs. non-religious upbringings are most evident and indeed statistically significant with regard to Prototype 1. Interestingly, those with religious and non-religious upbringing have similar scores on Prototype 3. We exemplify the doubts the students describe having about religion in the words of a female Israeli Druze student:

> a couple of years ago, I was like, that is it, religion and religion, and like – I was [connected too much] to the thing, and afterwards, like, [suddenly] I started thinking – about that issue, I would say "Okay, like why? Like, why what they are telling us is correct?" I mean "Who said that it is – correct?"
> (YILSK276)

Current Religiosity

Comparing levels of non-religious self-identification, those who described themselves as "highly non-religious" (survey value 0) scored higher on Prototype 1 compared with those who described themselves as "somewhat non-religious" (survey value 2), scoring 0.47 and 0.3 respectively. At the same time, the "highly non-religious" scored the lowest

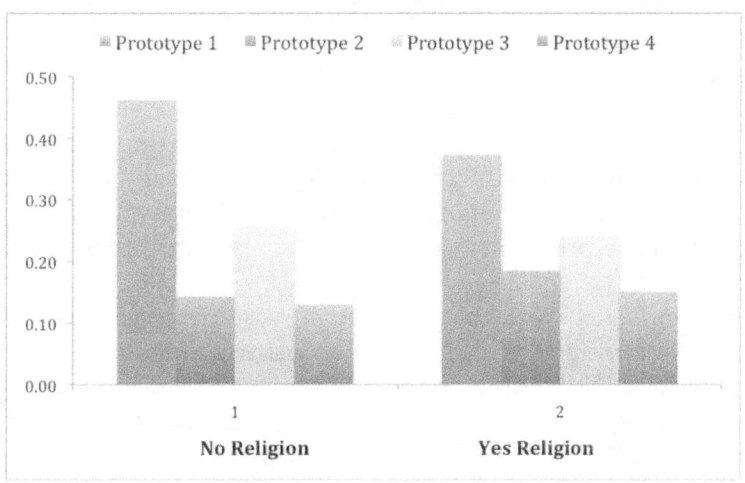

Figure 8. Religious upbringing and levels of non-religiosity.

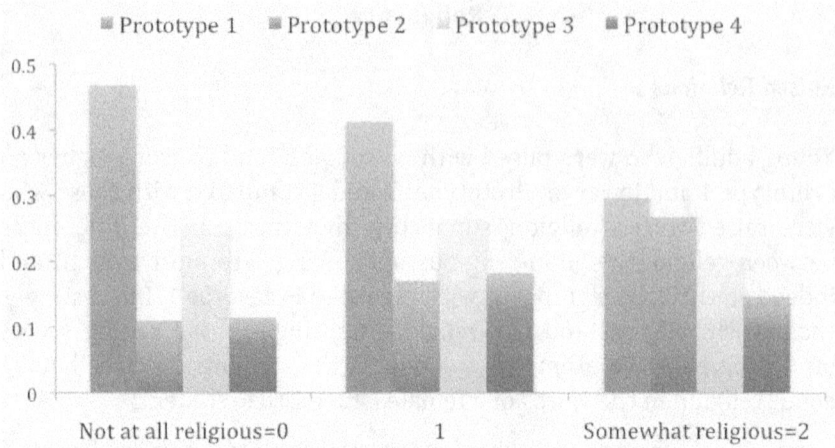

Figure 9. Prototype differences in levels of non-religiosity. The variations between the different levels of non-religiosity are statistically significant for Prototypes 1, 2 and 4 but not for Prototype 3.

on Prototype 2 (0.11 vs. 0.27). Prototypes 1 and 2 seem to be correlated linearly (although in a different direction) with level of non-religiosity of young people. However, Prototypes 3 and 4 do not seem correlated linearly with level of non-religiosity.

Attendance at Religious Services

Young adults who scored highly on Prototype 1 are most likely to never attend religious ceremonies or services. They are also more likely to never engage in private religious or spiritual practices, such as worship, prayer or meditation. In contrast, students who attend religious services regularly scored the highest on Prototype 2, supporting hypothesis 1. Differences in religious attendance are highly statistically significant for Prototypes 1 and 2 and marginally significant for Prototype 4. For private religious and spiritual practices, differences are statistically significant for prototypes 1, 2 and 3.

The conclusion from the religious practices is that the Religion-Approving Humanists are most keen on participating in religious services, whereas the Spiritual but not Religious are most likely to engage in private religious or spiritual practices. These distinctions are in line with the prototype descriptions, where the Spiritual but not Religious were found to have a more individualistic outlook, hence emphasis on *private* practices. The Religions-Approving Humanist, on the other hand,

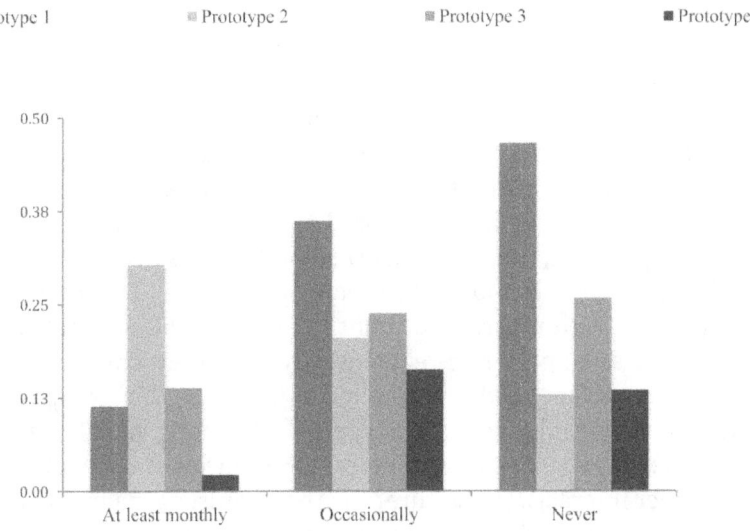

Figure 10. Prototype differences for levels of attendance at religious services.

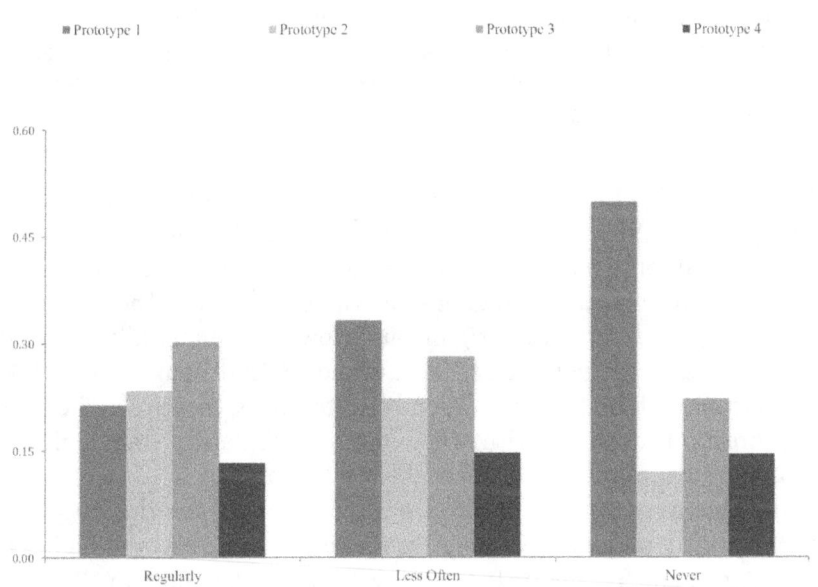

Figure 11. Prototype differences in levels of private religious or spiritual practices.

showed most openness towards tradition. It is conceivable that being favourable towards tradition translates into participation in religious services.

Do these differences in outlook among YARG participants persist once we control for gender? Indeed religion, gender, and prototypes seem to interact. Among YARG participants who were raised with no religion, gender gaps are evident: males scored higher on prototype 1 and lower on prototype 2. Yet, there are only small differences between males and females among those who were raised with a religion. The interaction is also apparent with regard to current religion. Females are reluctant to self-identify as "highly non-religious". Instead, they gravitate towards calling themselves "mildly non-religious". Among this group, females scored slightly higher on Prototype 1 (0.3 among females and 0.27 among males). Another intriguing research question we explore here: does gender interact with culture? In other words, do males and females subscribe to different worldviews in the various countries? And are the patterns consistent?

Large gender gaps exist in secular countries, e.g. Canada and Sweden, but also in religious ones, such as Israeli Arabs and India, Turkey and the United States, primarily with larger scores among males on Prototype 1. A male Israeli Muslim student explains:

> I go to the mosque maybe once or twice a year, when a death takes place, meaning, I do not pray – but when I enter the mosque, like, I go in, and I am obliged to perform ablution and pray with those who pray, so [really feel good] as they say. That is – I get relaxed completely, and – or specially when I listen to Quran.
>
> (YILSK064P)

Among Israeli Jews, and interestingly in Poland as well, females scored far higher than males on Prototype 2 and lower on Prototype 3. Finland is another example where gender gaps are apparent yet only on Prototype 4 are they noteworthy, with higher scores among females. These reported gender gaps are statistically significant. However, gender differences do not follow a consistent pattern. Peru stands out. Although Peru's YARG participants exhibit substantial gender differences, they are in the opposite direction compared with other countries: females scored higher on Prototype 1 while males scored higher on Prototype 2.

In China, a country in transition, YARG participants' worldviews divert from the general model. Usually, we found that males scored higher on Prototype 1 and females on Prototype 2. In contrast, in China YARG males and females scored the same on Prototype 1 and Prototype 4. In addition, unlike in other cultures, males scored significantly higher on Prototype

2 and females scored significantly higher on Prototype 3. Given China's sheer population size and its vast global effects, it is important to know whether young males and females in China will converge in the future. It is hard to predict. Will they follow the secular direction, like Canada and Sweden, or the religious one, like the USA? Follow-up research is needed to answer these questions.

Concluding Discussion

Initially we need to underline that these YARG analyses are not necessarily representative. The samples are based on a relatively small number of cases, especially in Ghana and India. Participants were not randomly selected. As college students, their level of education is high compared with counterparts in their cohort. Yet they cover a variety of societies and cultures around the globe, in the East and in the West. YARG includes a diverse group of participants who were raised as Christians, Muslim, Hindus, Jews, or with no religion. This exploratory global analysis of young people's identities and worldviews is constructive. Its contribution, even if limited, is important. These comparisons should be replicated and the prototypes framework ought to be tested further. Yet the innovative and sophisticated mixed-methods approach employed adds substantially to the novelty and relevance of the findings.

Regardless of the limitations addressed we can conclude that non-religious young adults are a diverse group. The most non-religious – those identifying themselves as "highly non-religious" (value 0 in survey question about current religiosity) is the largest sub-group in our sample. It consists of almost half of the non-religious respondents. The other two sub-groups, the moderately and mildly non-religious (categories 1 and 2) constitute each approximately 25 per cent of the respondents.

Each of the three non-religious identity groups has a distinct profile in terms of religious upbringing, demographics and culture, measured by the student's country of residence. Males and females are almost evenly distributed among "highly non-religious" students. However, females are the majority (67 per cent) among the moderately and mildly non-religious (categories of 1 and 2). The patterns indicated here connecting gender and religiosity are similar to results from several analyses of the entire YARG sample (see Kontala *et al.* 2022; Nynäs *et al.* 2022; Sjö *et al.* 2022).

Culture is another distinguishing characteristic. It creates a secular–religious spectrum among the non-religious. Students from Canada, Finland and Israel (Jews), and to some extent Sweden, construct the most secular cluster, with a majority of their students opting for the "highly non-religious" identity. Ghana and Israeli Arabs, on the other end, emerge as the least secular. Students from Peru, Poland, Russia, USA and China appear in the middle of the spectrum.

About half of the "highly non-religious" students (51 per cent) were raised in non-religious families. Moreover, 27 per cent of them were raised as "not at all religious", compared with only 9 per cent and 12 per cent of the non-religious groups 1 and 2 respectively. Again, similar patterns come into view among the entire YARG sample. These results indicate that many of the students who describe themselves as non-religious were actually raised in religious families. Being raised in a non-religious family, however, seems to contribute to holding a non-religious worldview in adulthood.

College is a powerful experience. Students are exposed to the campus environment, which is often liberal. These young adults separate from their families and embark on an independent life in college, away from home. Many of them distance themselves from the way of life they were raised in and rebel against their family tradition, as described by these Israeli Arab, American, Finnish and Swedish students:

> I was not going to be going against their habits and traditions in order for me to discover myself, so I preferred to get away.
>
> (YILSK020P)

> When I first made the transition to college, I found myself very divided in that when I was home I was very religious, and when I would come back here [...] I wouldn't be going to church at all. And then as I've gotten older, I've realised, even when I'm at home I'm not that religious, and when I'm here I'm the same.
>
> (YUSTP008)

> I maybe get this overdose somewhere from families [...] I know about my relatives, that some have kept the same stance and are very strict, so I see this religiousness like completely as a delusion, like what's this, you have to follow some specific diets, rules, restrictions like that. So I don't experience them at all.
>
> (YFIKD147T)

> one and the same people basically, with three different religions [...] when I later learned more and more about how it can simply go when people mix religion and politics and so on, and it has lately led to [...] that I don't want to have anything to do with religion.
>
> (YSEJK020)

Finally, many students express frustration, feeling inadequate because of what they perceived as a lack of knowledge about religion. This sentiment might explain our observed inconsistencies between the students' non-religious self-identification and their religious behaviour. A Female Israeli Druze student explains:

> the thing is that I do not know much about religion. I think any one of us, most of us, for example, do not know much about religion. That is, we know – the thing is more about society, we know about conventions of religion, like, how to behave.
>
> (YILSK276)

The contribution of this global research is its assessment of non-religious expressions among young adults. We, the researchers, relied on respondents' self-identification: regardless of whether they consider themselves as belonging or being close to a particular religious group, community or tradition, respondents were asked to evaluate how religious they are. On the premise of their self-definition, we discovered different types of non-religiosity: Secular Humanist, Spiritual but not Religious, the Vaguely Non-religious, and also the seemingly most religious ones, the Religion-Approving Humanist young adults. Most students fit the classic non-religious 3 B's – not belonging, not believing and not behaving religiously. However, there are students, in particular cultures, who engage in religious activities or believe in God despite calling themselves non-religious.

One Israeli Muslim who self-identified as non-religious described a family life that would seem highly religious in many societies. Speaking of his mother, he said:

> Uh – not very religious, it is true that she is wearing the hijab, prays regularly like me, I mean, it is not that her whole life is [related] to religion, that everything is about religion. No, she does her duties [...] and that is it [...] My father is the same – like me.
>
> (YILSK143P)

Why might a young adult self-identify as non-religious while exhibiting religious behaviour? Relying on the research on millennials we can infer that they are well known for rejecting religious authority, not necessarily for rejecting religion (Kosmin and Keysar 2009); for their political disdain of the religious right (Hout and Fischer 2002); and for preferring to be on the side of science and free inquiry (Sherkat 2014).

Casting the net wide and allowing people to name their own level of religiosity allowed us to capture people who might have been missed using the 3 B's model of belief, belonging and behaviour. Using the four prototypes, we documented how what is understood to be non-religious means different things in different countries. In secular nations such as Sweden, only the Secular Humanists regard themselves as non-religious, whereas in Ghana and among Israeli Muslims, people may classify themselves as non-religious even while praying at a mosque, wearing a head scarf, keeping dietary laws or believing in God.

The results of this study contribute to the study of non-religion in some important ways. First, many of the previous studies have focused on Western samples, or treated non-Western samples separately. Zuckerman, Galen and Pasquale are explicit about the former aspect in their attempt to summarise the academic research on the topic: "Most of the data summarized in this book pertain to the United States and Western Europe" (Zuckerman, Galen and Pasquale 2016, 36). Zuckerman's *Atheism and Secularity: Volume 2: Global Expressions* (2010) exemplifies the second aspect by introducing expressions of atheism, a sub-category of non-religion, by country. In this study, we have a sample of both Western and non-Western students. By their engagement with survey questions, FQS and regular interviews, they explicated what a non-religious identity means for them. The results point to the usefulness of cross-cultural comparisons. We have found both patterns that go beyond national borders, and clusters of countries with common patterns.

Second, by using a mixed-methods approach, we have explicated a variety of shared outlooks that can be tied to non-religious self-identifications. The conclusion is that when it comes to self-identification, people measure themselves not against some theoretical framework but against their peers and families. The main non-religious identity found in this study is "highly non-religious", and the major non-religious worldview prototype is the Secular Humanist prototype. These findings are not surprising. It is, however, interesting to see the notable deviations from this norm. We found a Religion-Approving Humanist prototype, a Spiritual but not Religious prototype, and the Vaguely Non-religious prototype. The latter three worldview prototypes are important in that they show that non-religious self-identification does not automatically entail a clear-cut secular outlook. In fact, 32 per cent of the defining respondents defined a prototype other than the Secular Humanist. These non-religious individuals constitute a visible minority. It is not difficult to understand why the Spiritual but not Religious and the Vaguely Non-religious would identify as non-religious, but it is somewhat surprising that the second-largest prototype was the Religion-Approving Humanist.

The differences between the prototypes allow us to further distinguish different social styles, which have a bearing on one's identity. The Secular Humanists like to associate with persons with a similar outlook. The Religion-Approving Humanists are open to tradition, and hence, participating in religious services. The Spiritual but not Religious are individualistic, and the Vaguely Non-religious do not feel closest with those with the same outlook. However, all prototypes share one feature, namely openness towards others' faiths. Pluralism is an issue of growing importance, and at least for our respondents, it is clear which way they want to go: whatever their personal outlook and identity, there is appreciation, interest and openness towards faiths other than their own.

If we found common ground in a basic humanistic orientation and pluralistic ingredients in social orientation, we should also point out that non-religion varies by national, ethnic and cultural context. We found respondents who clearly regarded themselves as non-religious, since they compared themselves to persons in their social circle whom they considered to hold a stronger religious orientation. It is important to keep in mind that such identifications depend on the context. If we were to create an absolute scale, only measuring official membership in religious communities, religious or spiritual practices and participation, or beliefs, we might conclude that some non-religious self-identifiers are quite religious.

Cross-cultural studies on non-religion are few, and studies that consider qualitatively different kinds of non-religion fewer still. We derived divergent patterns regarding both intensity and kind of non-religion based on locations. Prototope 1 was mostly male-dominated, and prototype 2 mostly female-dominated, which would be in line with the general observation that non-religion correlates positively with being male. This, however, is based on the idea that non-religion means a clear rejection of religiosity, and our study shows that people can self-identify as non-religious while being open to many aspects of religion.

Moreover, the above-mentioned pattern was fully reversed in Peru, and partially reversed in China. If the results from China were indicative of the Chinese population at large, and Peru for Latin America (admitting the speculative nature of both conjectures), this would have considerable implications for how non-religion correlates with gender globally. At this point, we can say that our research strategy with a cross-cultural sample and attention to the nuances internal to non-religion points to the usefulness of such considerations. The conclusion is that the scholars of non-religion need to be cautious about creating global generalisations about what a non-religious identity means, and to whom. Whether the "nones" form a category distinct from the religious is also a matter of local comparison.

Janne Kontala, PhD, has worked as a researcher in Turku, Finland, in the Department Study of Religions at Åbo Akademi University Centre of Excellence in Research: Young Adults and Religion in a Global Perspective Project (2015–19). He specialises in the field of studies of non-religion and is the author of *Emerging*

Non-religious Worldview Prototypes: A Faith Q-sort-Study on Finnish Group-Affiliates (Åbo Akademi University, 2016). He previously worked as a researcher in a project entitled "Viewpoints to the World: Prototypes of Worldview and their Relation to Motivational Values in Different Social Movements", funded by the Academy of Finland (2011–15).

Dr Ariela Keysar, a demographer, is a recipient of the 2021 Marshall Sklare Award, given by the Association for the Social Scientific Study of Jewry to "a senior scholar who has made a significant scholarly contribution to the social scientific study of Jewry". Keysar is Senior Fellow in public policy and law at Trinity College, Hartford, Connecticut. She is co-principal investigator, The Class of 1995/5755 Longitudinal Study of Young American and Canadian Jews, 1995–2019; and US principal investigator, Young Adults and Religion in a Global Perspective, YARG (2015–19). She was associate director of the Institute for the Study of Secularism in Society and Culture at Trinity College (2005–19). She is co-author of *Religion in a Free Market* and *The Next Generation: Jewish Children and Adolescents* (Paramount Market Pub, 2006). She has co-edited volumes on secularism in relation to women, science and secularity. She holds a PhD in demography from the Hebrew University of Jerusalem, Israel.

Sawsan Kheir, MA, is a double-degree doctoral candidate at the School of Psychological Sciences at the University of Haifa, Israel, and the Study of Religions at Åbo Akademi University, Finland. She served as research assistant for the Åbo Akademi University Centre of Excellence Young Adults and Religion in a Global Perspective Project (2015–19) in Israel. Her dissertation research focuses on contemporary negotiations of modernisation in the value profiles and religiosities among Muslim and Druze students in Israel. She has co-authored recent publications on religious socialisation processes and internet use among minority students in Israel. Currently, she acts as a co-principal investigator for the international research project "Meaning-making, Agency and Worldviews during the COVID-19 Pandemic: A Comparative Study", which is being conducted in Israel, Finland and Turkey.

References

af Burén, Ann. 2015. *Living Simultaneity: On Religion among Semi-secular Swedes.* Huddinge: Södertörn University.

Argyle, Michael. 2000. *Psychology and Religion: An Introduction.* London: Routledge.

Azarvan, Amir. 2013. "Are Highly Theistic Countries Dumber? Critiquing the Intelligence-Religiosity Nexus Theory". *The Catholic Social Science Review* 18: 151–68.

Bagg, Samuel, and David Voas. 2010. "The Triumph of Indifference: Irreligion in British Society". In *Atheism and Secularity*, vol 2: *Global Expressions*, ed. Phil Zuckerman, 91–111. Santa Barbara: Praeger

Bainbridge, William Sims. 2009. "Atheism". In *The Oxford Handbook of the Sociology of Religion*, ed. Peter Clarke, 319–35. New York: Oxford University Press.

Beit-Hallahmi, Benjamin. 2007. "Atheists: A Psychological Profile". In *The Cambridge Companion to Atheism*, ed. Michael Martin, 300–18. Cambridge: Cambridge University Press.

Beit-Hallahmi, Benjamin. 2014. *Psychological Perspectives on Religion and Religiosity*. New York: Routledge.

Braun, Claude. 2012. "Explaining Global Secularity: Existential Security or Education?" *Secularism and Nonreligion* 1/2012: 68–93.

Cotter, Christopher. 2011. "Toward a Typology of 'Nonreligion'". MA dissertation, School of Divinity, University of Edinburgh.

Cragun, Ryan T. 2014. "Who Are the 'New Atheists'?" In *Atheist Identities: Spaces and Social Contexts*, ed. Lori Beamon and Steven Tomlins, 195–211. New York: Springer.

Davie, Grace. 1994. *Religion in Britain since 1945: Believing without Celonging*. Oxford: Blackwell.

Day, Abby. 2011. *Believing in Belonging: Belief and Social Identity in the Modern World*. New York: Oxford University Press.

Feigelman, William, Bernard S. Gorman and Joseph A. Varacalli. 1992. "Americans Who Give up Religion". *Sociology and Social Research* 76(3): 138–44.

Hadaway, Christopher K., and Wade C. Roof. 1988. "Apostasy in American Churches: Evidence from National Survey Data". In *Falling from the Faith: Causes and Consequences of Religious Apostasy*, ed. David G. Bromley, 29–46. Beverly Hills, CA: Sage.

Hout, Michael, and Claude S. Fischer. 2002. "Why More Americans Have No Religious Preference: Politics and Generations". *American Sociological Review* 67: 165–90.

Keysar, Ariela. 2007. "Who Are America's Atheists and Agnostics?" In *Secularism and Secularity: Contemporary International Perspectives*, ed. Barry A. Kosmin and Ariela Keysar, 33–9. Hartford, CT: Institute for the Study of Secularism in Society and Culture, Trinity College.

Keysar, Ariela. 2014. "Shifts along the American Religious-Secular Spectrum". *Secularism and Nonreligion* 3: 1–16.

Keysar, Ariela. 2015. "The International Demography of Atheists". In *Yearbook of International Religious Demography*, ed. Brian J. Grim, Todd M. Johnson, Vegard Skirbekk and Gina A. Zurlo, 136–53. Leiden: Brill.

Keysar, Ariela. 2017. "Religious/Nonreligious Demography and Religion versus Science: A Global Perspective". In *The Oxford Handbook of Secularism*, ed. Phil Zuckerman and John R. Shook, 40–54. Oxford: Oxford University Press.

Keysar, Ariela, and Barry A. Kosmin. 2007. "The Freethinkers in a Free Market of Religion". In *Secularism and Secularity: Contemporary International Perspectives*, ed. Barry A. Kosmin and Ariela Keysar, 17–26. Hartford, CT: Institute for the Study of Secularism in Society and Culture, Trinity College.

Keysar, Ariela, and Barry A. Kosmin. 2008. *Worldviews and Opinions of Scientists, International Survey: India 2007-8, Summary Report*. Hartford, CT: Institute for the Study of Secularism in Society and Culture, Trinity College.

Keysar, Ariela, and Juhem Navarro-Rivera. 2013. "A World of Atheism: Global Demographics". In *The Oxford Handbook of Atheism*, ed. Stephen Bullivant and Michael Ruse, 553–86. Oxford: Oxford University Press.

Kontala, Janne. 2016. *Emerging Non-religious Worldview Prototypes. A Faith Q-sort-Study on Finnish Group-Affiliates*. Turku: Åbo Akademi University.

Kontala, Janne, Mika Lassander, Maria Klingenberg, Ariela Keysar and Martin Lagerström. 2022. "The Global Variation of Non-religious Worldviews". In *The Diversity of Worldviews among Young Adults: Contemporary (Non)Religiosity and Spirituality through the Lens of an International Mixed Method Study*, ed. Peter Nynäs, Ariela Keysar, Janne Kontala, Ben-Willie Kwaku Golo, Mika T. Lassander, Marat Shterin, Sofia Sjö and Paul Stenner, 153–74. Cham: Springer. https://doi.org/10.1007/978-3-030-94691-3_8

Kosmin, Barry A. 2007. "Contemporary Secularity and Secularism". In *Secularism and Secularity: Contemporary International Perspectives*. Institute for the Study of Secularism in Society and Culture, ed. Barry A. Kosmin and Ariela Keysar, 1–13. Hartford, CT: Trinity College.

Kosmin, Barry A., and Ariela Keysar. 2009. *American Nones: The Profile of the No Religion Population, A Report Based on the American Religious Identification Survey 2008*. Institute for the Study of Secularism in Society and Culture. Hartford, CT: Trinity College.

Kosmin, Barry A., Ariela Keysar, Ryan Cragun and Juhem Navarro-Rivera. 2009. "American Nones: The Profile of the No Religion Population, A Report Based on the American Religious Identification Survey 2008". Hartford, CT: Faculty Scholarship. Paper 14. Retrieved from http://digitalrepository.trincoll.edu/facpub/14

Lüchau, Peter. 2010. "Atheism and Secularity: The Scandinavian Paradox". In *Atheism and Secularity*, vol. 2: *Global Expressions*, ed. Phil Zuckerman, 177–96. Santa Barbara, CA: Praeger.

McAnulla, Stuart. 2012. "Radical Atheism and Religious Power. New Atheist Politics". *Approaching Religion* 2(1): 87–99. https://doi.org/10.30664/ar.67495

Mayrl, Damon, and Freeden Oeur. 2009. "Religion and Higher Education: Current Knowledge and Directions for Future Research". *Journal for the Scientific Study of Religion* 48(2): 260–75.

Naugle, David. 2002. *Worldview: The History of a Concept*. Grand Rapids, MI: Eerdmans Publishing.

Nilsson, Arthur. 2007. "Worldview: Personal Ideology, Values and Beliefs concerning Metaphysics, Epistemology, Human Nature and Morality". MA thesis, Lund University.

Nilsson, Arthur. 2013. *The Psychology of Worldviews: Toward a Non-Reductive Science of Personality*. Lund: Media-tryck, Lund University.

Nynäs, Peter, Ariela Keysar and Martin Lagerström. 2022. "Who are they and what do they value? The Five Global Worldviews of Young Adults". In *The Diversity of Worldviews among Young Adults: Contemporary (Non)Religiosity and Spirituality through the Lens of an International Mixed Method Study*, ed. Peter Nynäs, Ariela Keysar, Janne Kontala, Ben-Willie Kwaku Golo, Mika T. Lassander, Marat Shterin, Sofia Sjö and Paul Stenner, 47–71. Cham: Springer. https://doi.org/10.1007/978-3-030-94691-3_3

Pasquale, Frank L. 2010. "A Portrait of Secular Group Affiliates". In *Atheism and Secularity*, vol 1: *Issues, Concepts, and Definitions*, ed. Phil Zuckerman, 43–88. Santa Barbara, CA: Praeger.

Pew Research Center. 2012. "'Nones' on the Rise". Retrieved from www.pewforum.org/2012/10/09/nones-on-the-rise. Accessed 11 March 2021.

Pew Research Center. 2015. "The Future of World Religions: Population Growth Projections, 2010–2050". Retrieved from www.pewforum.org/2015/04/02/religious-projection-table. Accessed 11 March 2021.

Pew Research Center. 2018. "The Religious Typology: A New Way to Categorize Americans by Religion". Retrieved from www.pewforum.org/2018/08/29/the-religious-typology/. Accessed 14 October 2018.

Phillips, Bruce E. 2007. "Putting Secularity in Context". In *Secularism and Secularity: Contemporary International Perspectives*, ed. Barry A. Kosmin and Ariela Keysar, 27–31. Hartford: Institute for the Study of Secularism in Society and Culture.

Quack, Johannes. 2017a. "Conceptualizing Religious Indifferences in Relation to Religion and Nonreligion". In *Religious Indifference: New Perspectives from Studies on Secularization and Nonreligion*, ed. Johannes Quack and Cora Schuh, 1–23. Wiesbaden: Springer.

Quack, Johannes. 2017b. "Bio- and Ethnographic Approaches to Indifference, Detachment, and Disingagement in the Study of Religion". In *Religious Indifference: New Perspectives from Studies on Secularization and Nonreligion*, ed. Johannes Quack and Cora Schuh, 193–218. Wiesbaden: Springer.

Roemer, Michael. 2010. "Atheism and Secularity in Modern Japan". In *Atheism and Secularity*, vol. 2: *Global Expressions*, ed. Phil Zuckerman, 23–44. Santa Barbara, CA: Praeger.

Schnell, Tatjana, and William J. F. Keenan. 2011. "Meaning-Making in an Atheist World". *Archive for the Psychology of Religion* 33: 55–78.

Sherkat, Darren E. 2014 *Changing Faith: The Dynamics and Consequences of Americans' Shifting Religious Identities*. New York: New York University Press.

Sherkat, Darren, and Christopher G. Ellison. 1999. "Recent Developments and Current Controversies in the Sociology of Religion". *Annual Review of Sociology* 25: 363–94.

Silver, Christopher F., Thomas J. Coleman III, Ralph W. Hood Jr and Jenny M. Holcombe. 2014. "The Six Types of Non-belief: A Qualitative and Quantitative Study of Type and Narrative". *Mental Health*, Religion and Culture 17: 990–1001.

Sjö, Sofia, Maria Klingenberg, Ben-Willie Kwaku Golo and Clara Marlijn Meijer. 2022. "Gendered Views Among Young Adults in a Global Study: Male and Female Worldview Prototypes". In *The Diversity of Worldviews among Young Adults: Contemporary (Non)Religiosity and Spirituality through the Lens of an International Mixed Method Study*, ed. Peter Nynäs, Ariela Keysar, Janne Kontala, Ben-Willie Kwaku Golo, Mika T. Lassander, Marat Shterin, Sofia Sjö and Paul Stenner, 175–95. Cham: Springer. https://doi.org/10.1007/978-3-030-94691-3_9

World Values Survey. 2014. World Values Survey Wave 6: 2010–2014. Retrieved from www.worldvaluessurvey.org/WVSOnline.jsp

Wulff, David. 2019. "Prototypes of Faith: Findings with the Faith Q-Sort". *Journal for the Scientific Study of Religion* 58(3): 643–65

Zuckerman, Phil. 2007. "Atheism: Contemporary Numbers and Patterns". In *The Cambridge Companion to Atheism*, ed. Michael Martin, 300–18. Cambridge: Cambridge University Press.

Zuckerman, Phil, ed. 2010. *Atheism and Secularity*, vol. 2: *Global Expressions*. Santa Barbara: Praeger.

Zuckerman, Phil, Luke W. Galen and Frank L. Pasquale. 2016. *The Nonreligious: Understanding Secular People and Societies*. New York: Oxford University Press.

– 8 –

Multiple Identifications

Growing Diversity and Complexity in Religious and Secular Worldviews

RUTH ILLMAN, PETER NYNÄS AND
NURIT NOVIS-DEUTSCH

Many young adults today seem to express multiple religious identifications as part of their life-views. Yet it remains unclear how we should comprehend and conceptualise this phenomenon. Observations about multiple religious identifications offer an impetus to better capture the heterogeneity, complexity and fluidity with regard to how religion is currently reconfigured and structured owing, for example, to religious change and globalisation. It also implies a need to further investigate the diversification of secular and religious identities. The aim of this chapter is to explore forms of multiple identifications as part of a larger discussion on contemporary diversity and pluralism. We assess several recent contributions to understanding multiple identifications from a cross-disciplinary perspective, including how diversity as a social process of change has been contested in more general terms. Analyses of diverse mixed-methods data from thirteen countries contribute empirical observations regarding both overarching patterns of identifications and individual life narratives.

Introduction

Though I do not think there are gods I sometimes rely on them.

With these words, a young Japanese man describes his attitude to faith and religion in the YARG survey, thus putting his finger on what seems to be a timely feature of young people's religiosity all over the world: open-ended and personal perspectives seem to be preferred to assertive and tradition-bound ones. Unlike older generations, young adults today often cross the conventional boundaries between different cultures and religions as they shape their own life-views: a Christian identity may well be matched with the belief in reincarnation, a Muslim one with the reverence for ancient Middle Eastern deities (Klingenberg and Sjö 2019). Furthermore, as the quotation reveals, the divide between religious and secular approaches to life – which previous scholarship has often portrayed as a binary opposition, the quintessential inconsistency of logical thinking – seems to be fading and losing its definitive character. Even though this young man reports not really believing in gods, there are apparently moments in his life when he still chooses to appeal to higher powers, putting his life in the hands of the divine. For him, trusting while not believing is neither inconsistent nor confused. Quite the contrary: it seems to provide him with meaning and feelings of belonging and security.

Phenomena like these have often been explained as part of a complex process of religious change, specifically pointing to growing individualism: starting from Bellah's description of "Sheilaism" in the 1980s (Bellah 1985) to contemporary descriptions of a "trend of privatisation" and "sacralisation of subjectivities", feeding on the paramount importance of "self-authority" and freedom of choice (Keysar 2014; Partridge 2014; Nynäs, Illman and Martikainen 2015). As Catherine Cornille writes, the "heightened and widespread awareness of religious pluralism has presently left the religious person with the choice not only of *which* religion, but also *how many* religions she or he might belong to" (Cornille 2010, 1).

Yet, when closely examining the ethnographic data on individual narratives on multiple religious identifications gathered for the research project Young Adults and Religion in a Global Perspective (YARG) presented in this book (see Chapter 1, this volume), it turns out that the story is more complicated than that. The social and cultural logic of the overarching processes described above as well as the power relations and hierarchies that orchestrate them cannot be neglected. Social, ethnic, gendered and economic restraints form the context in which religious choices are made, and, hence, subjectivity and choice are easily attributed too decisive a role in processes of forming contemporary religious positions (Illman 2017). Within the wide research fields of the study of religions, similar discussions are under way, raising other kinds of critiques against simplified perceptions of pluralism from epistemological and ethical points of view. Current scholarly understandings of diversification as a social process of change have been critically assessed and challenged, on the one hand for being too vague, and, on the other hand, for not being radical enough. Here, we refer primarily to the critical assessments of approaches to the study of religions, resting on the World Religions Paradigm and on clear-cut division between religious and secular, official and vernacular, personal and political (see e.g. Balagangadhara 2014; af Burén 2015; Hedges 2017; Illman 2017).

Within the ethnographic study of religion, both the lived religion approach (McGuire 2008) and the analytical framework of vernacular religion underline the need to be sensitive to historical data and cultural context but also individual narratives and local nuances in mapping religion as part of daily life (Bowman and Valk 2012, 2022). This includes observing the interplay between social structures, history and institutional frameworks, on the one hand, and individual adaptation, change and complexity on the other (Illman and Czimbalmos 2020). From a psychological point of view, issues of multiple identifications and their correspondence to, or divergence from, concepts of pluralism and diversity are raised (Novis-Deutsch 2015; Nynäs 2018).

The current chapter adopts a cross-disciplinary approach, addressing recent conversations to form a critical approach to diversity, pluralism and multiple religious identifications. By further anchoring the discussion in the mixed-methods data from the YARG research project, the analysis sheds light on how a closer examination of contemporary religious subjectivities presents a challenging case for understanding religious identities. While multiple religious identifications were previously approached as a divided or confused identity formation or were perceived derogatively as a problematic concept, from the normative viewpoint of syncretism, we align more with recent scholarship, whose appreciative terminology focuses on multitude, abundance, creativity and richness (Cornille 2010; Kalsky and van der Braak 2017; Berghuijs et al. 2018). In this chapter, therefore, we focus on the dynamics of religious "identification" and "subjectivity" instead of the fixed states of "identity" or "belonging" and investigate how young adults around the world report such identifications: how they are formulated and expressed by the respondents themselves. We identify central patterns in these reports and account for the microcosm of individual life narratives of young adults in order to bring depth and richness to the understanding.

A Brief Methodological Note

The extensive mixed-methods data referred to were collected as part of the international research project Young Adults and Religion in Global Perspective (YARG) in Canada, China, Finland, France, Ghana, India, Israel, Peru, Poland, Russia, Sweden, Turkey and the United States. In this chapter we will draw on all parts of the mixed-methods design and consequently use survey data (*n* = 4964), data from a Q-methodological part and interview data. The Faith Q-Sort (FQS), designed by David Wulff (2019), is a novel method in the study of religions. It builds on Q-methodology and accounts for diversity in subjective construals of religiosity. It is specifically designed to discern shared but complex and varied patterns of religion and spirituality, including, for example, the growing influence of secular positions (Wulff 2019; Nynäs, Kontala and Lassander 2021). Our mixed-methods design and the YARG project are presented and discussed in depth in the Chapter 1, and we cannot account for all aspects here. Nevertheless, we emphasise that the study targeted young university students (aged 18–30) and thus our sample is not representative of the countries included. Our study was originally designed on the basis of an interest in "digital natives" as a window to better investigate current religiosity and religious change. We therefore turned to young adults enrolled in universities in all countries, since we expected this group to best match our interests. However, keep in mind that these young adults or digital natives are far from forming a homogeneous group (Klingenberg and Sjö 2019; Klingenberg, Sjö and Moberg 2022).

This chapter is based on analyses of a sub-sample from our survey that we selected based on how they responded to questions on religious adherence and identification. Specifically, we included all respondents from our survey that answered "yes" on two questions relevant to our current topic: "Do you consider yourself as belonging to one or more religious groups, communities, or traditions?" and the follow-up question "Whether or not you belong to any, are there religious, spiritual, or philosophical communities, traditions, or practices you feel close to or that reflect your views?" This subsample (*n* = 929) accounted for 18.7 per cent of all respondents.

Those who replied affirmatively to these questions were also asked to describe the religious groups to which they referred. In a strict sense responding affirmatively to both questions does not necessarily mean that the respondents display a form of multiple identification. Yet, with this sub-sample we were able to analyse the category of religious identity in explorative ways that were not narrowed down or limited in advance. By having two somewhat overlapping questions we gave the respondents more space and freedom to account for multiplicity, and by encouraging the respondents to describe or name the groups and traditions themselves, we allowed them to self-define their identifications. By adopting this strategy, we sought to avoid imposing pre-defined options such as Hindu, Christian, Muslim, etc., and then repeating this option as a means of claiming a "second identification". Such a strategy would not have yielded the sort of data needed to explore current diversity, or to help us better understand the complexity and fluidity that surface as relevant features in many studies of contemporary religiosity (Nynäs, Illman and Martikainen 2015).

This chapter does not provide a quantitative analysis of young adults displaying multiple identities in our study. Preliminary results, on the basis of a quantitative coding of the sample undertaken by Nurit Novis-Deutsch and her team (an analysis which will be presented in a separate article), indicate that a quantitative analysis of the data strengthens the observation that it is very hard to pin down exact criteria and categories of multiple identifications. Many survey answers seem to reflect a sense of disconnection from tradition without fully giving it up, and of spiritual seekership and hesitation. Thus, the overall frequency of respondents who directly state identification with formal adherence to several "world religions" simultaneously is small. Here, instead of investigating how many young adults belong to certain categories or how frequent some categories are, we explore the range of diversity regardless of numbers or frequency with the purpose of substantiating the claim that a kaleidoscopic variety of self-identifications is mirrored in our data. Rather, we first investigate the forms of self-defined multiple identifications young adults have reported in our survey. Second, we turn to other parts of our mixed-methods design that allow us to study individuals from this sample through other lenses. What can we learn in addition from these data about the multiple identifications that we identified in the survey?

A Critical Appraisal of Religious Identity

How can multiple identifications be understood? Are contemporary scholars of religion equipped with theoretical frameworks nuanced and sensitive enough to do justice to the truly varied ways of finding significant subjective positions in life? To clarify our understanding of the term "multiple identifications" we first need to take a step back and briefly discuss the term "identity". While we cannot account for all the main theories pertaining to understanding identity here, we wish to point to some general observations regarding the concept and to some relevant issues emerging in the study of religions today.

Commonly, the term "identity" refers to the way people define themselves or to the way they are defined by others based on collective categories. To cite a well-known definition, identities are the "ways in which individuals and collectivities are distinguished in their social relations with other individuals and collectivities" (Jenkins 1996, 4). The term has been central to many disciplines, where it has been applied and understood differently. Despite this vast academic interest in "identity", the concept remains somewhat enigmatic and hard to capture. Identities are neither isolated nor singular. They are related to different social circumstances, varying from context to context and situation to situation (Day *et al.* 2013). There are deep disparities in terms of how we acquire identities, and the extent to which we can create and express identities also involves diversity and differentiation as well as various symbolic aspects (Novis-Deutsch 2015). We can all be said to host multiple identities, foregrounding specific identities in given contexts formed by a host of external and internal factors. In fact, our everyday lives take place within a power-infused interactional web, which requires us to function as individuals with multiple identities, or at least context-specific identifications (Taylor *et al.* 2010; Richardson and Monro 2012).

Whereas the idea of multiple identities acknowledges how people combine and live in-between cultures or aspects of them, an additional form of complexity can be exemplified with the notion of intersectionality. Kimberlé Crenshaw (1989, 1991) coined the concept to make sense of discrimination on multiple grounds, but it has come to refer to the "mutually constitutive relations among social identities" (Shields 2008, 301). The term draws our attention to how social identities affect each other and why identities cannot be studied separately from each other (Romero 2018, 36). Banton (2011, 199) offers important insights about intersectionality:

> every human is assigned to, and identifies with, many social categories; each identification entails costs and benefits. The interrelation between categories presents a generalization of what is currently known as intersectionality. The relative importance of categories changes as individuals trade off advantages associated with one form of social alignment for that of another.

The relevance of these remarks is heightened from the perspective of everyday life. The publicly relevant aspects of identities are often deeply related to the more "mundane" and private aspects of a person's being. Everyday life and public social life are connected, but the implications of the messiness of everyday life are often forgotten. On the one hand it consists of subjectivities, experiences, emotions, bodies and desires that are lived out on individual and collective levels of spaces and politics, and on the other hand it is affected by the ways in which individuals as social actors both negotiate and challenge different practices and spaces (e.g. Miller 2008; Pink 2012). Identities as a social category cannot be separated from identities as a personal category. In order to address the relevance of the complex interplay and configurations at work in these processes, we need to bridge conceptually the "abstract level of politics and society and the deeply personal, inner landscapes of pluralism" (Illman *et al.* 2015, 215).

This requires a general shift towards attentiveness to identifications, i.e. the process of self-definition, how this is produced and reproduced in everyday life and contexts, and how it forms agencies. This corresponds with more recent ways of understanding identity in the study of religions that approach subjects as dialogical and multi-faceted (see Mitchell, 2009; Csordas 1994; Battaglia 1995; Jackson 1996; van Wolputte 2004). Here, the subject is viewed as constituted by being located "within and emerging through ongoing social process, and conceived as an unfolding condition of being" (Mitchell 2009, 54). This emphasis requires us to be attentive to nuances in how we perceive socially situated subjects as being parts of their environment and its symbolic qualities (Holm 2014).

The importance of focusing on identifications is particularly evident in the study of religions. Many researchers in the study of religions today emphasise how people mix ideas, practices and identities in ways that challenge given scholarly categories of religion and previous expectations (e.g. Luhrmann 2012; Bender and Taves 2012; Frisk and Åkerbäck 2013; Gilhus and Sutcliffe 2013; Day *et al.* 2013; Nynäs, Illman and Martikainen 2015). Ongoing processes of religious change have been described through a range of interrelated conceptual frameworks and with different emphases, such as desecularisation (Berger 1999), resacralisation (Davie 2010), re-enchantment (Partridge 2014), post-secularity (Habermas 2008; Nynäs, Lassander and Utriainen 2012), and de-Christianisation (Brown and Lynch 2012), to name a few. Some comprehend religious change against the background of a general "subjective or expressive turn" (Heelas and Woodhead 2005), while others describe an "Easternisation of the West" (Campbell 2007; Chapter 2, this volume). In varying ways, they all point to a condition where religion and religious subjectivities are being altered. Ulrich Beck (2010, 42) claims that in contrast to previous perceptions:

> we see the formation of a new, religiously determined, global sociality in which increased significance is attached to trans-national, religious imagined communities which complement, and enter into competition and conflict with the institutionalised forms of national societies and national institutions.

As a result of growing religious diversification, Beck argues, people are continuously engaged in internal and external negotiations. They are increasingly required to reflect on their own subjectivity in the light of religious "others", a process that gains enhanced significance both within and outside established religious institutions (Beck 2010). Research also shows that identity processes today are increasingly formed by negotiations of agency, authenticity and individualism, which strengthen their autonomy in relation to external religious influences (Hovi et al. 2015).

Current religious change may have a far-reaching influence and the categories that we impose on people do not necessarily correspond with how they live and experience their lives (Nynäs 2017). Here, the assumed distinction between the religious and the secular provides a good example. In research as well as in public debates, these notions have often been regarded as being at odds with each other. Central to many perspectives on secularisation was also the assumption of an inherent "incompatibility between some features of 'modernity' and religious belief" (Taylor 2007, 543). Still, when examining the wider public debates surrounding any given contested issue that involves both "religious" and "secular" parties, it is not always clear what constitutes a "religious" idea or argument as opposed to a "secular" one. Religious individuals today do not necessarily conceive of themselves as either religious *or* secular, and this requires us to question the dichotomous relation between the concepts. The religious and the secular are not necessarily mutually exclusive options: many people combine spiritual and religious positions with secular values into authentic and meaningful outlooks on life (Nynäs, Illman and Martikainen 2015; Chapter 7, this volume). For the study of religions, this implies the need to develop a research strategy that acknowledges the problems involved in studying religion based on dichotomies such as religious vs. secular or institutional structures vs. personal practice. At times, such dichotomies have implied the inferiority of personal practice, seeing it as "distorted" and "superficial" by nature (Bowman and Valk 2012; af Burén 2015). We argue that a non-binary approach is needed in order to study strategies of multiple identifications as a part of everyday life in a theoretically and methodologically rigorous way, to render ethnographic accounts such as those we are dealing with meaningful.

On the basis outlined above, we argue that there is a need to rethink the conceptual horizon of how we understand the notion of religious identity. Ann af Burén (2015) has addressed what she describes as "simultaneities of religious identities". The notion describes the "both/and" character of everyday religious identifications: how persons ascribe meaning to and interpret religiously significant events of everyday life and talk about themselves in relation to different religious and cultural designations. Simultaneities do not necessarily signal a lack of consistency or coherence; rather, they display a complex and situated dialogical interpretation of the boundaries of the subject and his or her surroundings, through which the individual is able to "relate to the many meanings of the concept of religion selectively" and "appreciate and appropriate religious aspects from a variety of contexts" (af Burén 2015, 212). Contemporary religious subjects often combine elements from various religious traditions in their personal outlooks on life, ranging from the self-conscious combination of two or more traditions to a perceived sense of lacking a belonging to any specific tradition. In addition, some people might "claim to embrace all religious traditions, rather than multiple individual religious traditions" (Kalsky and van der Braak 2017, 662).

Therefore, we find it important to broaden and nuance the perspective by abandoning both the notions of multiple *belonging* and multiple identities. The former implies formally adhering to the practices and beliefs of two or several religious institutions, which is too narrow a perspective. The latter implies a stability and clear-cut structure that is not supported in our data. Instead, we opt for the notion of *multiple religious identification* and will test its explanatory value in this chapter. In doing so, we hope to facilitate a more open-ended and qualitative understanding of multiple liaisons as they take form in the everyday lives of young adults today. The focus on fluid structures and everyday lived realities also shifts our focus from stable and monolithic entities of "identity" to the incomplete and continuously developing processes of identification. Multiple religious identifications, therefore, can be understood as a verb rather than a noun: something we "do" and "feel" and "shape" rather than "are". In making this claim, we build on a broad theoretical basis influenced by a cross-disciplinary engagement with issues of religion and processes of identity formation.

Multiple Religious Identifications in the Cross-disciplinary Study of Religions

As noted above, recent scholarship within the study of religions increasingly challenges the rigid and, at times, normative understanding of multiple religious identifications as a question of "syncretism". The term is often interpreted as derogatory, denoting a fusion of two or more historical religious institutions into a new tradition, implicitly understood to be artificial, inauthentic or merely shallow (Berghuijs 2017, 21). The term thus carries an "indelible political and social aspect" reminiscent of its origin in nineteenth-century evolutionary biology and its "notions of race and desire", Ruparell (2013, 118) contends. As a consequence, novel approaches to plurality in social and individual religious liaisons are today crafted on the foundation of a more nuanced understanding of religion in general and religious identification in particular (Cornille 2010; Hedges 2010; Kalsky and van der Braak 2017).

The scholarship of the theologians Reinhold Bernhardt and Perry Schmidt-Leukel (2008) has paved the way for such an approach among German-speaking scholars. They propose terms such as "religious creativity" or "religious flexibility" to capture the trends found not only within the vernacular practices of everyday religion, but also within the strands of theological scholarship that seek to uncover and describe current religiosity (Bernhardt and Schmidt-Leukel 2008, 5). Important steps towards a more nuanced understanding have also been taken by scholars such as Catherine Cornille (2010) and Paul Hedges (2010, 2017). As Hedges asserts, the discussion around multiple religious adherence in the West often rests on a problematic Western and Christian definition of "religion" where emphasis is placed on doctrinal structures, truth claims and institutional divisions, which is a limited way to approach religion in a global context. When regarded from a non-Western perspective, the "new" and "radical" elements of multiple religious identifications appear to be standard, even natural (Hedges 2010, 94). In a similar vein, syncretism has been reread from gender-sensitive and political perspectives, calling attention to the intersectional entanglements of cultural power, gender bias and political hegemony that has set the norms for scholarship on multiple religiosity (e.g. Egnell 2006; Grung 2015). Hence, Cornille concludes, a serious personal involvement with multiple religions can take many forms. While only a few might choose to pursue the possibility of formally belonging to several religious institutions simultaneously, many more may "pass through" several traditions in searching for their own spiritual path, perhaps remaining faithful to the symbols of one tradition while adopting the hermeneutical framework and ethical principles of another (Cornille 2010, 5–6).

Manuela Kalsky and André van der Braak (2017) point to the advances made within the study of lived religion in relation to understanding positions as the ones expressed in our data. They underline that current religious subjects form their religious identifications by combining elements not only from various religious traditions but also through different forms of multiple religious adherences. Empirically oriented research has substantiated many similar observations, calling the category of religion as such into question. These kinds of reflections follow from "the World Religions Paradigm", that is; the Western Protestant idea about religious traditions as mutually exclusive entities separated by borders (Balagangadhara 2014; Hedges 2017). Michal Pagis, for her part, stresses the methodological problems involved in applying this paradigm in research into religious subjects. In her view, it hinders us from accounting satisfactorily for religious self-constitution as interactional and relational in nature. This leads to a distorted view of subjects as autonomous objects that can be measured and comprehended in relation to a schematic understanding of religions as "processes that should be followed" (Pagis 2013, 96).

This also brings us back to the arguments related to the problematic dichotomy between secular and religious presented above. Not only has the binary differentiation between "world religions" started to crumble; so too have the sharp divisions into official against popular or personal and the idea of religious and secular as mutually exclusive categories (Berghuijs 2017). The diversified process through which human beings form religious knowledge and practice often includes elements from several different traditions as well as from secular sources such as popular culture. This development appears paradoxical only against the background of a narrow, theoretical apprehension of religion as a rigid intellectual search for plausible claims to truth (Bowman and Valk 2012). Today, we find increasing interest in how theologically unsystematic life-views are formed through everyday religious lives and practices – and how these relate to institutional religion in its dialectics with everyday practice and personal perspectives. To find a satisfactory way of describing contemporary religious identifications, therefore, we need to abandon dichotomous discourses on religion that rest on binary logics of either/or (af Burén 2015). In the discussion above, we have argued for the important insight that identities are never isolated and thus cannot be compartmentalised or detached from their context when trying to describe and understand contemporary religious identifications. Everyday life often requires multiple and context-specific identifications (Nynäs 2018). Conceptualising such identifications in terms of simultaneity or multiplicity therefore provides helpful tools and lenses onto a changing religious landscape. A compelling example of such identification processes at work is given by Nurit Novis-Deutsch (2015). By studying religious psychoanalytic therapists, she has shown that individuals committed to multiple identities that may seem conflicting – in this example a monistic religious identity as Orthodox Jews on the one hand and a monistic psychoanalytic professional identity on the other – can foster an empowering sense of what she calls "self-complexity". This recognition, in its turn, can be extended from the personal domain to the social, facilitating a positive attitude towards diversity, pluralism and so forth (Novis-Deutsch 2015, 497–8).

It might to some extent seem confusing that we do not make a clear distinction between concepts such as identity and self, or personhood, a concept that Pagis (2013) uses occasionally, but making such distinctions is not central to our arguments. Rather, we are interested in the implications they have for our comprehension of religious subjects, i.e. how they shift our focus towards interactional processes of reflexive identifications through which the self is objectified as a set of identities. Next, we will present an analysis of how the religious subjectivities formulated in the data are embedded in approaches to plurality that are positive and personal, sometimes even playful. They represent a more poignantly altered attitude towards hybridity than the derogatory assessments of syncretism, outlined above. Based on further observations from our data we will also stress the relevance of methodology to this matter in general.

Trends in the Research Material

As mentioned above, we focus this chapter on the subsample (n = 929) of respondents who answered affirmatively to both the following questions of the YARG survey (see Appendix 3):

B8. Do you consider yourself as belonging to one or more religious groups, communities, or traditions?

○ No
○ Yes, which?

B9. Whether or not you belong to any, are there religious, spiritual, or philosophical communities, traditions, or practices you feel close to or that reflect your views?

○ No
○ Yes, please, describe

We have investigated how people in our subsample responded to these two questions, analysing their comments and how they describe the patterns of identification most relevant to their own outlook on life, through thematic analysis (Schreier 2012). This represents an explorative approach, and it meets our ambition of bringing to the surface a diversity of identifications, as the thematic analysis does not centre on how prominent or representative such identifications are.

When assessing the answers, it is clear that multiple religious identifications come in a plethora of shapes and forms, combinations and expressions. To start with, we can conclude that the plurality of identifications uncovered by Kalsky and van der Braak (2017) in their study referenced above is visible also in the current data sample. Not all responses reflect multiple religious adherence as some who indicate a religious affiliation in the first question simply elaborated on aspects of the same religion in the second question, not broadening the scope to other traditions (e.g. first identifying as Muslim and then mentioning Islamic rituals and festivals). However, a number of respondents indicate not only an ecumenical identity, but a truly diverse pattern of identifications and belonging. To give an overview of the trends and tendencies in the data, we structure the responses into five different categories. The categories are not exhaustive or mutually exclusive but often overlap and blend. The idea is not to introduce a precise typology but rather to structure the presentation of a data set marked by deep diversity. Similarly, the examples chosen to elucidate each category are meant merely as illustrations of the argument; they are neither exclusive nor necessary conditions for the categories.

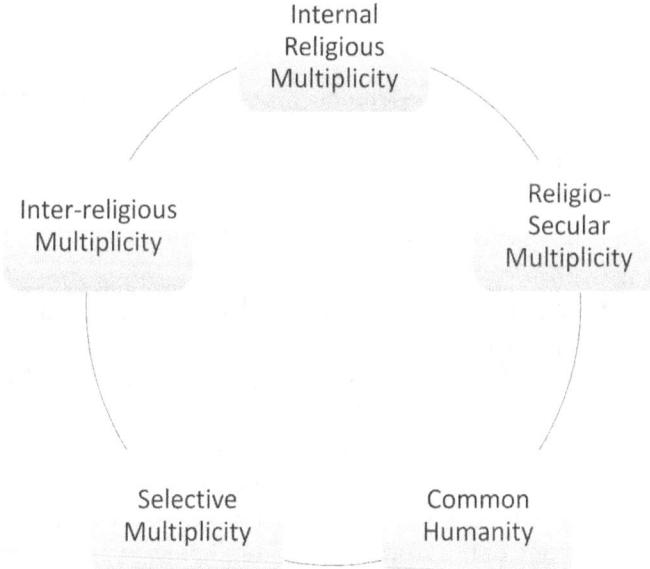

Figure 12. Forms of religious multiplicity.

Internal Religious Multiplicity

This category includes those who express an identification that could be described as traditionally ecumenical (formally belonging to or actively engaging in the communal life of e.g. two different Christian communities or branches of Islam). It also includes more personally hybrid attachments of intra-religious multiplicity, such as combining an Evangelical-Lutheran congregational identity with practices traditionally found in Orthodox Christianity, such as the use of incense and the veneration of saints. Double or multiple identifications of this kind are numerous in the research material and do not seem to pose any problems – moral, legal or social – for the majority of the respondents regardless of geographical location or life situation.

Table 12. Examples of internal religious multiplicity.

	Q B8	Q B9
Peru (male)	Catholic	Jesuits
Finland (female)	Lutheran Church	Pentecostalism
Canada (female)	Baptist	Jehovah's Witnesses
USA (female)	Muslim	Sufis
Turkey (female)	Kurdish Muslim	Alevism, Shiism, Yazidi

Inter-religious Multiplicity

This category consists of what could be called the "traditional" pattern of multiple religious adherence known to the scholarly literature, that is: narratives where two historical religious institutions are placed side by side (see e.g. Bernhardt and Schmidt-Leukel 2008). Sometimes, this is indicated briefly, even bluntly, by just stating a fact without giving any further details, such as a Peruvian male respondent noting that he is Catholic but also feels close to Buddhism. A common form would also be belonging to one of the so-called world religions while also identifying with or practising more local, traditional or ethnic forms of religion. Sometimes, a few words by way of explanation are also given, as in the case of the two Finnish respondents presented below.

Table 13. Examples of inter-religious multiplicity.

	Q B8	Q B9
Peru (male)	Catholic	Buddhism
Finland (female)	Lutheran Church	Asian religions that promote peace of mind, nature and drinking tea
Turkey (female)	Muslim	Shamanism
Ghana (male)	Christian	OK with Islamic ways too
Finland (male)	Western Esotericism and Buddhism	Paratheatre, Satanism, World-Mystics in general, Trans-humanism, Epicureanism, Anti-natalism

Religio-secular Multiplicity

This category of answers is indicative of the nuances we wish to highlight in the research data. Hence, double identifications are reported, which include a religious institution and a secular organisation, a school of philosophy or other kind of immanent worldview. Among these we find the example stated in the beginning of this chapter.

Table 14. Examples of religio-secular multiplicity.

	Q B8	Q B9
Finland (female)	Lutheran	Very interested in psychology and different philosophical traditions concerned with life after death and the meaning of life
Sweden (male)	Buddhist	AA (Alcoholics Anonymous)
Turkey (female)	Muslim	Atheism (not believing in anything)
Poland (female)	Christian	Neo-Platonic and Aristotelian philosophy
Israel (female)	Muslim	Religion is very compatible with science
Japan (male)	Buddhist and Agnostic	The philosophy of Horiemon, yin and yang philosophy and science which seems like religion
Japan (male)	Zen Buddhist	Shintoism. Though I do not think there are gods I sometimes rely on them

Selective Multiplicity

Among the respondents of our subsample, we find persons who report one main adherence but pick certain practices and ideas from other traditions in quite a functional way, integrating these rituals or beliefs into their personal religious repertoire.

Table 15. Examples of selective multiplicity.

	Q B8	Q B9
India (female)	Hindu	I like some traditions and rituals in Christianity
USA (female)	Christian	Christian, practise some Jewish holidays
Japan (male)	Presbyterian Christian	Muslim practice of charity
Turkey (female)	Muslim	I am interested in and respect the belief in Sky God that came with the Central Asian Turks
Ghana (female)	Christian	Islam upholds certain things that Christianity can adopt to be better based on personal experiences and views
USA (female)	Christian	Karma
Finland (female)	Lutheran Christian	The idea of reincarnation feels very close to me. I believe that the universe takes care that things happen in the way they are meant to happen.
Finland (female)	Lutheran Christian	I find teachings that fascinate and appeal to me in many religions, but I don't feel that I can follow any of them completely.

Common Humanity

Finally, our last category is labelled "Common humanity" (as an ethical statement, paraphrasing the moral philosopher Raimond Gaita 2002). This category includes respondents who identify with a certain religious institution but also acknowledge the common core values and ethical principles manifest in many traditions. Many of them lean towards what philosophers of religion might call *perennialism* (as an existential position, not an essentialist theoretical stance; see Martin 2017). Several of the respondents mention principles such as loving one's neighbour, doing good, practising forgiveness, telling the truth, showing humility and kindness, compassion, respect, generosity, which they see as common to all religions. Also, equality and generally a humanistic outlook on life are held in high regard.

Table 16. Examples of common humanity.

	Q B8	Q B9
Several respondents across nationalities		Loving one's neighbour, doing good, forgiveness, truth, humility, kindness, compassion, respect, generosity = a humanistic outlook on life.
India (female)	Muslim	I'm attracted by almost all religions as they work to protect humanity.
India (female)	Nepali, Buddhist, Hindu etc.	Each and every religion has the same value, that is humanity.
Japan (female)	Presbyterian	I sympathise with many religious thoughts that admit human weakness and require people to help each other.
Finland (female)	Varying, but most of the time I'm a tomboy	Indeed the core idea of pluralism is that people are different. I think that should be respected, everyone is an awesome human being, regardless of their beliefs, looks or style. People can't be placed in boxes.

As this short and schematic overview indicates, multiple religious identifications take form in many different ways and along numerous trajectories among the 900+ young adults who have indicated such a stance in our questionnaire. It is also clear that the categories sketched above are not to be understood as watertight compartments that mutually exclude one another, as mentioned above. Rather, they represent fluctuating and intertwining lines of narration that emerge from our research data, taking individual form and shape as different persons actualise them in their own everyday lives and in their own words. The respondents are young; perhaps, their views are merely forming at the time of research and thus may be subject to even wider-ranging changes than worldviews in general. There is also a nuance of light-heartedness and humour in many responses, which is very interesting. Either the young adults have chosen to approach the survey in a playful way, or perhaps their attitude towards matters of religious identification is indeed relaxed and spirited rather than troubled, or coloured by angst and agony? These questions cannot be answered on the basis of our data but would form a fascinating topic for further research.

We also emphasise that our data hide further forms of multiple identities, not accounted for above. For instance, among those who do not report a primary religious adherence we find similar patterns to those we have described above. Many who view themselves as secular might still feel close to some religious, spiritual or philosophical community or tradition. Some respondents from the Chinese sample might, for example, identify with folk tradition, Buddhism or Christianity while maintaining a national secular identity embedded in socialist ideologies. Another category not well enough accounted for above is people whose primary interest is a certain practice, reporting, for example, that they engage in a variety of meditation practices, while leaving religious traditions as such in the background.

Taken out of their context these comments may seem thin and disparate. Therefore, we will offer an in-depth example of the trends of multiple religious identifications as they take shape in a life-narrative obtained in one of the research interviews conducted within the framework of the research project. At the same time, this also highlights the methodological issue involved, namely, that in order to capture complex processes of identifications we need more sophisticated approaches to collecting data. Our use of a mixed-methods approach was an attempt to respond to this challenge.

The Jubu Example – Some Methodological Observations

The example used for the discussion adumbrated above is taken from the interview conducted with a respondent from the USA, whom we call Kim. In the survey, Kim reported: "Yes, I consider myself as belonging to the religious group 'cultural Jews'", but in addition claimed that "Buddhism reflects my views and I feel close also to this tradition". Thus, Kim was one of the persons who seemed to combine two religious traditions and met the criteria for the category of inter-religious multiplicity. Kim kindly accepted our invitation to participate in the other parts of the study, the FQS-sorting and the interview. This provided additional information about Kim's religious identifications and related processes. Kim's sorting of the 101 statements resulted in the following position, here summarised through statements that were given high priority:

Kim embraces the idea of freedom of choice and thinks that one can be deeply moral without being religious. Kim explicitly distances themself from claims that the meaning of religious texts and teachings are clear and true. In contrast, Kim sees themself as actively working towards making the world a better place to live and seeks to change societal structures and values. They do not at all approve of sexual normativity and cannot identify with the ideal that one should remain loyal to the religion of one's nation. Simultaneously there is a commitment to following a spiritual path that is in harmony with the environment and for Kim this gives a direction, or goal in life.

We can here see how more secular progressive viewpoints take precedence in combination with more spiritually inclined emphases. The interview finally tied all these parts together in a narrative. During the interview Kim talks about Jewish upbringing and tradition and how Buddhism came briefly into their life at a certain point. Buddhism had become important to a significant other in Kim's life and Kim then did some googling to find out more. We can ask if this indicates that we should dismiss the reported Buddhism. Clearly, Kim does not practise Buddhism, and does not convey extensive insights into or knowledge about Buddhism in the interview. We will have to leave this question open. The role allotted to this information depends on our analytic focus and our research questions. Nevertheless, we claim that the fact that Kim recognises Buddhism as a part of their life means that this should be seen as a potential source for future identifications and agencies, an implicit resource for future identity processes. However, the interview brings us back to the results of Kim's sorting of the FQS statements. In this context, societal activism surfaces as a (third) layer in terms of religious identifications. Kim emphasises a life-view predominantly shaped by commitment to animal rights and vegan ideology whereas the other identifications currently fall into the shadows.

Not only do different methods help us to identify layers of religious and secular identifications and, furthermore, how these come together in a narrative. Our mixed method also helped us comprehend how these layers could be weighed in relation to each other. Religious identifications are the result of both external and internal negotiations and they take place within the multiplicity of contexts where people's everyday lives unfold. Similar insights are aptly caught in Mira Niculescu's (2012) conclusion, based on her research on so-called Jubus, that is, Jews who double identify as Buddhists (see Katz 2013, 401–4).[1] While such

---

1. The term Jubu is spelled differently across research literature, spanning JewBu, JUBU, BuJu and many other variants. These terms all indicate some amalgamation of Judaism/Jewish and Buddhism/Buddhist. See Sigalow 2019, xi–xii.

"multi-religious labels" have become common in academia today, they often fail to represent the diversity of the phenomenon, she warns. The "lived realities" of the persons placed within these categories are much more complex than the labels reveal. Therefore, she concludes in parallel to our argument in this article: "In today's cultural context, it is more accurate to address this phenomenon in terms of an inner dialogue rather than of multi-religious belonging" (Niculescu 2012, 350).

Niculescu's point is relevant both in relation to the theoretical framework and to Kim's narrative, as an acknowledgement of the central role allotted to practice, embodiment and emotions as a complement to rational dimensions, institutional recognition and truth claims in forming new religious identifications. Multiple identifications are easily thought of in terms of openness to other traditions, cultures, communities, etc., but this view may be an over-simplification, and the identifications are not necessarily dependent on specific attitudes or values. Yet we may claim that the aspect of self-reflective recognition of diverse identifications is dependent on attentiveness and sensitivity to boundaries. From Niculescu (2012) we can also draw the conclusion that multiple identities primarily reflect lived social realities, and that the context is relevant. We may conclude by returning to the observations of af Burén (2015, 212) on simultaneities:

> [T]he local discourses on religion [...] are of crucial importance when it comes to establishing which "elements" of religion they consider interesting and of value, and what they perceive they are "allowed" to disclose in different settings and what not.

Concluding Discussion

As we hope to have shown in this chapter, there is a need to assess the ongoing discussion on multiple religious identifications critically in relation both to social structures and individual worldviews by anchoring the discussion in ethnographic data. In this chapter, we have drawn on current critical discussions within the study of religions, pertaining both to pluralism and diversity on a societal level and as individual outlooks on life, including recent contributions advocating a more open and positive approach to multiple religious adherence. Turning to the analysis of our research data, we suggested five interlinked categories of multiple identifications in our material: internal religious multiplicity, inter-religious multiplicity, religio-secular multiplicity, selective multiplicity and common humanity. To deepen the analysis, these broad-scale findings were placed within the context of a life-narrative emerging from the cross-reading of the survey and in-depth interview data obtained within the research project: Kim's story of engaging with both Judaism and Buddhism.

To facilitate a more flexible and fruitful description of current approbations of diversity and pluralism on individual and societal levels, we have suggested the notion of *multiple religious identifications* as an emergent contribution to the multi-disciplinary theoretical debate. This, we claim, better matches the multi-faceted forms of engaging with religious, spiritual and secular views and practices and the fact that this is something that unfolds as a process over time and in relation to a diversity of social contexts. Furthermore, in some cases, given categories, such as the religious and the spiritual, are not necessarily inclusive enough. In this chapter we needed to refer also to life-views and worldviews in order to adequately catch the complexities involved. As Nynäs, Keysar, Shterin and Sjö (2022, 309–10) claim, referring to Holm (1996), "there is a need for a broadening that explicitly recognises current diversity with regards to (non-)religious worldviews in a global perspective. Religious or not, all people have some kind of worldview that is essential to them in various ways".

"How we conceive of the 'religious' subject is a matter that cuts through epistemology, methodology, and theory, and easily causes implicit biases in our studies", Nynäs (2018, 344) contends. To this we can, by way of conclusion, also add the ethical perspective: how we apply our theoretical concepts and structure the world by means of our methodologies also carries ethical implications for those whose lives and worldviews we present to the scholarly community. As Nurit Novis-Deutsch concludes in her analysis of multiple identifications, principled complexity and principled pluralism as strategies for forming one's own identity may also influence the way one tends to think of others. Hence, she suggests: "encouraging thoughtful reflections on multiple personal identities and value conflicts may promote pluralism" (Novis-Deutsch 2015, 501). By raising the awareness of multiple identification processes to a conscious level, normalising them as conflicting but creative, the multiplicity described in this chapter can increasingly be regarded as a source of growth and maturity rather than confusion or a threat, she maintains:

> the more a religious person is involved with and committed to manifold worldviews, the more likely it is that something about his or her unambiguous world order will shift and a space will be made for a pluralistic outlook, which may enable the integration of religious commitment with openness to others. In sum, juxtaposing identity and pluralism from

individual and social perspectives highlights possible links between the two concepts and suggests that the personal and the social are two facets of the same human experience, and should be studied in tandem.
(Novis-Deutsch 2015, 501–2)

Finally, one may wonder whether multiple religious identifications among young adults in a global perspective, as discussed above, is something new, or just a more straightforward way of describing worldviews on a personal level. Or is it a matter of acknowledging, even accepting, that rather than being a grand narrative of truth claims, the question of finding meaning in life is largely a matter of practical limitations and the experiences of daily human life, which cannot be formalised into a strict compliance plan where neither doubt nor brokenness is allowed? Our mixed-methods approach suggests that there is value in continuously and critically evaluating our methodologies and allowing them to challenge and talk to each other. For researchers of religion, the challenge remains to develop and describe categories that are nuanced and broad enough to harbour the multiple religious identifications in the colourful complexity that we encounter in the field, while simultaneously creating analytic tools and terms precise and distinct enough to enable tenable scholarly comparison. As the analysis presented in this chapter has shown, the young Japanese man, with whom we began our journey, who revealed his willingness to rely on the gods but not believe in them, is not a singular case.

Dr Ruth Illman is the director of the Donner Institute for Research in Religion and Culture in Turku, Finland. She holds the title of docent in the study or religions at Åbo Akademi University (ÅAU) and in the history of religions at Uppsala University, as well as doctoral degrees in the study of religions (2004) and Jewish studies (2018). Her main research interests include cultural encounters and diversity, contemporary Judaism, religion and the arts (especially music) and ethnographic research, primarily by developing the analytical approach to vernacular religion. Illman acted as Co-PI for the Centre of Excellence Young Adults and Religion in a Global Perspective at ÅAU (2015–19). Currently, she leads the research project Boundaries of Jewish Identities in Contemporary Finland and acts as editor-in-chief of the open-access peer-review journal *Nordisk judaistik / Scandinavian Jewish Studies* with Svante Lundgren. Recent publications are found at https://research.abo.fi/en/persons/ruth-illman

Peter Nynäs, Dr Theol., is a professor of the Study of Religions at Åbo Akademi University (ÅAU), Finland, and dean of the Faculty of Arts, Psychology and Theology. He is the director and PI of the Åbo Akademi University Centre of Excellence in Research Young Adults and Religion in a Global Perspective Project (2015–19) and earlier the Centre of Excellence in Research Post-secular Culture and a Changing Religious Landscape in Finland Project (2010–14). Among the books he has edited are *On the Outskirts of "the Church": Diversities, Fluidities, and New Spaces of Religion in Finland* (with R. Illman and T. Martikainen; LIT-Verlag, 2015), *Religion, Gender, and Sexuality in Everyday Life* (with A. Yip; Ashgate, 2012), and *The Diversity of Worldviews among Young Adults: Contemporary (Non)Religiosity and Spirituality through the Lens of an International Mixed Method Study* (with A. Keysar, J. Kontala, B.-W. Kwaku Golo, M. Lassander, M. Shterin, S. Sjö and P. Stenner; Springer, 2021).

Dr Nurit Novis-Deutsch is a social psychologist, researching values and moral development in the Department of Learning and Instructional Sciences at the University of Haifa in Israel. Her research concerns the ways in which people create and manage contradictory frames of meaning and values and how they organise their identities and relate to others in social contexts. Other aspects of her research apply these topics to the field of education. Recent and current research projects include: pluralistic reasoning; outgroup dehumanisation; the challenges of ultra-religious college students; religious meaning-making during the COVID-19 crisis, prejudice and religiosity, religious subjectivities of young adults globally (the YARG project), interdisciplinary education, and Holocaust education and memory. Her research has been published in various psychological and educational journals and books.

References

af Burén, Ann. 2015. *Living Simultaneity: On Religion among Semi-secular Swedes.* Huddinge: Södertörn University.

Balagangadhara, S. N. 2014. "On the Dark Side of the 'Secular': Is the religious-secular distinction a binary?" *Numen* 61(1): 33–52.

Banton, Michael. 2011. "A Theory of Social Categories". *Sociology* 45(2): 187–201.

Battaglia, Debbora, ed. 1995. *Rhetorics of Self-Making.* Berkeley, CA: University of California Press.

Beck, Ulrich. 2010. *A God of One's Own: Religion's Capacity for Peace and Potential for Violence.* Cambridge: Polity Press.

Bellah, Robert N., Richard Madsen, William M. Sullivan, Ann Swidler and Steven M. Tipton. 1985. *Habits of the Heart: Individualism and Commitment in American Life.* Berkeley, CA: University of California Press.

Bender, Courtney, and Ann Taves, eds. 2012. *What Matters? Ethnographies of Value in a Not so Secular Age.* New York: Columbia University Press.

Berger, Peter, L., ed. 1999. *The Desecularization of the World: Resurgent Religion and World Politics.* Washington, DC: Ethics and Public Policy Center.

Berghuijs, Joantine. 2017. "Multiple Religious Belonging in the Netherlands: An Empirical Approach to Hybrid Religiosity". *Open Theology* 3 (1): 19–37. https://doi.org/10.1515/opth-2017-0003

Berghuijs, Joantine, Hans Schilderman, André van der Braak and Manuela Kalsky. 2018. "Exploring Single and Multiple Religious Belonging". *Journal of Empirical Theology* 31(1): 18–48. https://doi.org/10.1163/15709256-12341365

Bernhardt, Reinhold, and Perry Schmidt-Leukel, eds. 2008. *Multiple religiöse Identität: Aus verschiedenen religiösen Traditionen schöpfen.* Zürich: TVZ.

Bowman, Marion, and Ülo Valk, eds. 2012. *Vernacular Religion in Everyday Life: Expressions of Belief.* London: Equinox Publications.

Bowman, Marion, and Ülo Valk, eds. 2022. *Vernacular Knowledge: Contesting Authority, Expressing Beliefs.* London: Equinox Publications.

Brown, Callum, and Gordon Lynch. 2012. "Cultural Perspectives". In *Religion and Change in Modern Britain*, ed. Linda Woodhead and Rebecca Catto, 329–51. London: Routledge.

Campbell, Colin. 2007. *The Easternization of the West: A Thematic Account of Cultural Change in the Modern Era.* Boulder, CO: Paradigm.

Cornille, Catherine. 2010. *Many Mansions? Multiple Religious Belonging and Christian Identity.* Eugene, OR: Wipf & Stock Publishers.

Crenshaw, Kimberlé. 1989. "Demarginalizing the Intersection of Race and Sex: A Black Feminist Critique of Antidiscrimination Doctrine, Feminist Theory, and Antiracist Politics". *University of Chicago Legal Forum* 1: 139–67.

Crenshaw, Kimberlé. 1991. "Mapping the Margins: Intersectionality, Identity Politics, and Violence against Women of Color". *Stanford Law Review* 43(6): 1241–99.

Csordas, Thomas. 1994. *The Sacred Self: A Cultural Phenomenology of Charismatic Healing.* Berkeley, CA: University of California Press.

Davie, Grace. 2010. "Resacralisation". In *The New Blackwell Companion to the Sociology of Religion*, ed. Bryan S. Turner, 160–78. Chichester: Wiley-Blackwell.

Day, Abby, Giselle Vincett and Christopher Cotter, eds. 2013. *Social Identities Between the Sacred and the Secular.* Farnham: Ashgate.

Egnell, Helene. 2006. *Other Voices: A Study of Christian Feminist Approaches to Religious Plurality East and West.* Uppsala: Studia Missionalia Svecana C.

Frisk, Liselotte, and Peter Åkerbäck. 2013. *Den mediterande dalahästen: religion på nya arenor i samtidens Sverige.* Stockholm: Dialogos.

Gaita, Raimond. 2002. *Common Humanity: Thinking about Love and Truth and Justice.* London: Routledge.

Gilhus, Ingvild Saelid, and Steven J. Sutcliffe. 2013. "Conclusion: New Age Spiritualities – 'Good to Think' in the Study of Religion". In *New Age Spirituality: Rethinking Religion*, ed. Steven J. Sutcliffe and Ingvild Saelid Gilhus, 356–62. Durham: Acumen.

Grung, Anne Hege. 2015. *Gender Justice in Muslim-Christian Readings: Christian and Muslim Women in Norway Making Meaning of Texts from the Bible, the Koran and the Hadith*. Leiden: Brill.

Habermas, Jürgen. 2008. "Notes on Post-Secular Society". *New Perspectives Quarterly* 25(4): 17–29.

Hedges, Paul. 2010. *Controversies in Interreligious Dialogue and the Theology of Religions*. London: SCM Press.

Hedges, Paul. 2017. "Multiple Religious Belonging after Religion: Theorising Strategic Religious Participation in a Shared Religious Landscape as a Chinese Model". *Open Theology* 3: 48–72.

Heelas, Paul, and Linda Woodhead. 2005. *The Spiritual Revolution: Why Religion is Giving Way to Spirituality*. London: Wiley-Blackwell.

Holm, Nils G. 1996. "Introduction: The Study of World Views". In *World Views in Modern Society: Empirical Studies on the Relationship between World View, Culture, Personality, and Upbringing*, ed. Nils G. Holm and Kaj Björkqvist, 1–9. Turku: Åbo Akademi University.

Holm, Nils, G. 2014. *The Human Symbolic Construction of Reality: A Psycho-Phenomenological Study*. Zürich: LIT Verlag.

Hovi, Tuija, Ruth Illman and Peik Ingman. 2015. "Interlacing Identities, Agencies and Resources". In *On the Outskirts of "the Church": Diversities, Fluidities and New Spaces of Religion in Finland*, ed. Peter Nynäs, Ruth Illman and Tuomas Martikainen, 89–109. Zürich: LIT Verlag.

Illman, Ruth. 2017. "'Retaining the Tradition – but with an Open Mind': Change and Choice in Jewish Musical Practices". *Temenos: Nordic Journal of Comparative Religion* 53(2): 207–29. https://doi.org/10.33356/temenos.60982

Illman, Ruth, and Mercédesz Czimbalmos. 2020. "Knowing, Being, and Doing Religion: Introducing an Analytical Model for Researching Vernacular Religion". *Temenos. Nordic Journal of Comparative Religion* 56(2): 171–99. https://doi.org/10.33356/temenos.97275.

Illman, Ruth, Tuija Hovi, Tuomas Martikainen, Peter Nynäs, Sofia Sjö and Laura Wickström. 2015. "Reframing Pluralism". In *On the Outskirts of "the Church". Diversities, Fluidities and New Spaces of Religion in Finland*, ed. Peter Nynäs, Ruth Illman and Tuomas Martikainen, 197–216. Zürich: LIT Verlag.

Jackson, Michael, ed. 1996. *Things as They Are: New Directions in Phenomenological Anthropology*. Bloomington, IN: Indiana University Press.

Jenkins, Richard. 1996. *Social Identity*. London: Routledge.

Kalsky, Manuela, and André van der Braak. 2017. "Introduction to the Topical Issue 'Multiple Religious Belonging'". *Open Theology* 3: 662–4.

Katz, Nathan. 2013. "Buddhist-Jewish Relations". In *Wiley-Blackwell Companion to Inter-religious Dialogue*, ed. Catherine Cornille, 394–409. Malden, MA: Wiley-Blackwell.

Keysar, Ariela. 2014. "From Jerusalem to New York: Researching Jewish Erosion and Resilience". *Contemporary Jewry* 34(2): 147–62.

Klingenberg, Maria, and Sofia Sjö. 2019. "Theorizing Religious Sozialisation: A Critical Assessment". *Religion* 49(2): 163–78.

Klingenberg, Maria, Sofia Sjö and Marcus Moberg. 2022. "Young Adults as a Social Category: Findings from an International Study in Light of Developmental and Cohort Perspectives". In *The Diversity of Worldviews among Young Adults: Contemporary (Non)Religiosity and Spirituality through the Lens of an International Mixed Method Study*, ed. Peter Nynäs, Ariela Keysar, Janne Kontala, Ben-Willie Kwaku Golo, Mika Lassander, Marat Shterin, Sofia Sjö and Paul Stenner, 23–46. Cham: Springer. https://doi.org/10.1007/978-3-030-94691-3_2

Luhrmann, Tanya, M. 2012. *When God Talks Back: Understanding the American Evangelical Relationship with God*. New York: Alfred A. Knopf.

McGuire, Meredith B. 2008. *Lived Religion: Faith and Practice in Everyday Life*. Oxford:Oxford University Press.

Martin, Craig. 2017. "'Yes, ... but ...': The Neo-Perennialists". *Method and Theory in the Study of Religion* 29(4–5): 313–26. https://doi.org/10.1163/15700682-12341396

Miller, Daniel. 2008. *The Comfort of Things*. Cambridge: Polity Press.

Mitchell, Jon. 2009. "Ritual Transformation and the Existential Grounds of Selfhood". *Journal of Ritual Studies* 23(2): 53–66.

Niculescu, Mira. 2012. "I the Jew, I the Buddhist. Multi-Religious Belonging as Inner Dialogue". *Cross Currents* 62(3): 350–9.

Novis-Deutsch, Nurit. 2015. "Identity Conflicts and Value Pluralism – What Can We Learn from Religious Psychoanalytic Therapists?" *Journal of the Theory of Social Behaviour* 45(4): 484–505. https://doi.org/10.1111/jtsb.12079

Nynäs, Peter. 2017. "Making Space for a Dialogical Notion of Religious Subjects: A Critical Discussion from the Perspective of Postsecularity and Religious Change in the West". *Journal of Constructivist Psychology* 31: 54–71.

Nynäs, Peter. 2018. "Some Critical Remarks on Religious Identity". In *The Routledge Handbook of Postsecularity*, ed. Justin Beamount, 336–48. New York: Routledge.

Nynäs, Peter, Ruth Illman and Tuomas Martikainen. 2015. "Rethinking the Place of Religion in Finland". In *On the Outskirts of "the Church": Diversities, Fluidities and New Spaces of Religion in Finland*, ed. Peter Nynäs, Ruth Illman and Tuomas Martikainen, 11–28. Zürich: LIT Verlag.

Nynäs, Peter, Ariela Keysar, Janne Kontala, Ben-Willie Kwaku Golo, Mika Lassander, Marat Shterin, Sofia Sjö and Paul Stenner, eds. 2022. *The Diversity of Worldviews among Young Adults: Contemporary (Non)Religiosity and Spirituality through the Lens of an International Mixed Method Study*. Cham: Springer.

Nynäs, Peter, Ariela Keysar, Marat Shterin and Sofia Sjö. 2022. "Beyond the Secular, the Religious and the Spiritual: Appreciating the Complexity of Contemporary Worldviews. In The Diversity of Worldviews among Young Adults: Contemporary (Non)Religiosity and Spirituality through the Lens of an International Mixed Method Study, ed. Peter Nynäs, Ariela Keysar, Janne Kontala, Ben-Willie Kwaku Golo, Mika Lassander, Marat Shterin, Sofia Sjö and Paul Stenner, 303–17. Cham: Springer.

Nynäs, Peter, Ariela Keysar, Marat Shterin and Sofia Sjö. 2022. "Beyond the Secular, the Religious and the Spiritual: Appreciating the Complexity of Contemporary Worldviews. In *The Diversity of Worldviews among Young Adults: Contemporary (Non)Religiosity and Spirituality through the Lens of an International Mixed Method Study*, ed. Peter Nynäs, Ariela Keysar, Janne Kontala, Ben-Willie Kwaku Golo, Mika Lassander, Marat Shterin, Sofia Sjö and Paul Stenner, 303–17. Cham: Springer.

Nynäs, Peter, Janne Kontala and Mika Lassander. 2021. "The Faith Q-Sort: In-Depth Assessment of Diverse Spirituality and Religiosity in 12 Countries". In *Assessing Spirituality in a Diverse World*, ed. Amy L. Ai, Paul Wink, Raymond F. Paloutzian and Kevin A. Harris, 554–73. Cham: Springer.

Nynäs, Peter, Mika Lassander and Terhi Utriainen, eds. 2012. *Post-secular Society*. New Brunswick, NJ: Transaction Publishers.

Pagis, Michal. 2013. "Religious Self-Constitution: A Relational Perspective". In *Religion on the Edge: De-centering and Re-centering the Sociology of Religion*, ed. Courtney Bender, Wendy Cadge, Peggy Levitt and David Smilde, 92–114. Oxford: Oxford University Press.

Partridge, Christopher. 2014. *The Lyre of Orpheus: Popular Music, the Sacred, and the Profane*. Oxford: Oxford University Press.

Pink, Sarah. 2012. *Situating Everyday Life: Practices and Places*. London: Sage.

Richardson, Diane, and Surya Monro. 2012. *Sexuality, Equality and Diversity*. Basingstoke: Palgrave Macmillan.

Romero, Mary. 2018. *Introducing Intersectionality*. Cambridge: Polity Press.

Ruparell, Tinu. 2013. "Inter-religious Dialogue and Interstitial Theology". In *Wiley-Blackwell Companion to Inter-religious Dialogue*, ed. Catherine Cornille, 117–32. Malden, MA: Wiley-Blackwell.

Schreier, Margit. 2012. *Qualitative Content Analysis in Practice*. Thousand Oaks, CA: Sage.

Shields, Stephanie, A. 2008. "Gender: An Intersectionality Perspective". *Sex Roles* 59(5): 301–11.

Sigalow, Emily. "A Note on the Spelling of JewBu". American JewBu: Jews, Buddhists, and Religious Change, Princeton: Princeton University Press, 2019, pp. xi–xii.

Taylor, Charles. 2007. *A Secular Age*. Cambridge, MA: The Belknap Press of Harvard University Press.

Taylor, Yvette, Sally Hines and Mark Casey, eds. 2010. *Theorizing Intersectionality and Sexuality*. Basingstoke: Palgrave Macmillan.

van Wolputte, Steven. 2004. "Hang on to Your Self: Of Bodies, Embodiment, and Selves". *Annual Review of Anthropology* 33: 251–69.

Wulff, D. M. 2019. "Prototypes of Faith: Findings with the Faith Q-Sort". *Journal for the Scientific Study of Religion* 58(3): 643–65.

– 9 –

Towards a New Methodological Perspective

Concluding Reflections on Cross-cultural Research in the Study of Religions

PETER NYNÄS, RUTH ILLMAN AND
RAFAEL FERNÁNDEZ HART

This concluding chapter brings together the main findings, discussions and perspectives developed over the preceding chapters. From a variety of theoretical starting points, these chapters have addressed the worldviews of young adults around the globe, elucidating what diversity means in practice on the overarching societal level, on the locally embedded cultural level, and for the individual. The chapter also discusses questions of methodology and research ethics. How should we as researchers navigate conceptually in a global landscape of complex religious and secular worldviews? Furthermore, the goal of dismantling dichotomies and illuminating the multiple identifications and diversity prevalent on all levels of analysis in our research lies not only in the descriptions that have been presented, but also in what they suggest. Can we meet the challenge of taking other and alternative voices seriously?

From various vantage points, the different chapters of this volume have shed light on the worldviews of young adults around the globe, often mapping out and seeking to understand what diversity means in practice – on the overarching societal level, on the locally embedded cultural level, and for the individual. However, the volume does not try to be exhaustive either with regards to these topics of relevance to the project Young Adults and Religion in a Global Perspective (YARG) or in light of the extensive research data collected within this project. Rather, it continues and adds to a series of previous publications from the same project. The more important of these are the volume *The Diversity of Worldviews among Young Adults: Contemporary (Non)Religiosity and Spirituality through the Lens of an International Mixed Method Study* (Nynäs, Keysar, Kontala et al. 2022), a special issue on religion and socialisation (Klingenberg and Sjö 2019) and a volume on religion and media (Moberg and Sjö 2020).

More specifically, we aimed in this volume to explore current challenges pertinent to cross-cultural research in today's world and this is emphasised with the title *Researching Global Religious Landscapes: A Methodology between Universalism and Particularism*. Based on the findings of this volume, it is evident that a sensitive conceptual and methodological toolbox is important in an increasingly interconnected world of religious and secular worldviews. Naturally, this claim taps into many ongoing discussions about how to understand contemporary religion and spirituality, and many scholars also address the need for critical methodological reflection (e.g. Bowman and Valk 2012; Bruce and Voas 2007; Day 2011; Droogers and van Harskamp 2014; Gilhus and Sutcliffe 2013; McGuire 2008; Nynäs, Illman and Martikainen 2015; Woodhead 2012). The volume overall and many of the chapters individually bear witness to the fact that altogether, it has become difficult to think about religions in a way "which organizes them into a set of discrete traditions with a supposedly 'global' import" (Cotter and Robertson 2016, vii) and to uphold a "world religions paradigm". The need for a critical and broad perspective is also apparent from current research on religion and the secular as part of young people's identities (Shipley and Arweck 2019; Gareau *et al.* 2019).

How should we as researchers navigate conceptually in a global landscape of religious and secular worldviews? On the one hand, we become increasingly aware of how this landscape is continuously knitted together by international mobility, digital global media and trans-national cultural and political processes. On the other hand, we have through the same processes become more and more attentive to the relevance of diversity and differences. Beyer captures this well when he writes that "overlapping the kind of reflexive subjectivity manifested in the religious identities of the youth is the *glocal* context in which they are enacted, a context that enhances and likely enables the variety they display" (Beyer 2019, 280).

In contrast, however, religion has thus far often been perceived one-sidedly as a trans-historical essence, while religion as a concept has often in practice been provincially European or Western (e.g. Asad 1993, 2003; Balagangadhara 2005; Chakrabarty 2000; Masuzawa 2005; Winzeler 2008). In several respects the world religions paradigm seems to remain dominant worldwide even though it fails to represent the religious variety within given traditions and tends to remodel what is "outside" them according to liberal Western Protestant Christian values (Owen 2011). In this volume we therefore took our point of departure in the debate on universalism vs. particularism, which we identified as pivotal for the growing scholarly interest in religion in a global context (see de Roover 2014; Lambek 2014).

This critical inquiry was part of the YARG project from the beginning and central to the cross-cultural, comparative and mixed-methods approach that was implemented. Described at length in the introductory chapter, the research project was based on a methodologically innovative approach designed to capture the characteristics of the religious subjectivities and values among young adults globally, shaped by institutional, social, cultural and other influences. The mixed-methods approach sported this by combining both quantitative and qualitative research instruments: a survey, interviews and the Faith Q-Sort (FQS), originally introduced by David Wulff (Wulff 2019; Nynäs, Kontala and Lassander 2021). The value of the novel FQS method and the mixed methods as such is emphasised in many of the chapters alongside observations about the challenges associated with cross-cultural research.

The YARG study gave access to extensive and varied data on the diversity of worldviews among contemporary young adults in thirteen countries. North America, with the USA and Canada; South America, with Peru; Africa, with Ghana; Asia, with India, China, Israel, Japan and Turkey; Western Europe, with Finland and Sweden; and Eastern Europe, with Poland and Russia. Even if many of the young adults identify with major religions at some level – as Buddhists, Christians, Hindus, Jews, Muslims, and the growing cluster of those with no religion – one of the major contributions of this volume is the clarification of the intrinsic heterogeneity ingrained in these unique data, also a feature at the surface of many of the chapters.

With regards to this, we find it central to underline that the YARG study as a whole, including the contributions presented as chapters of this book, in different ways shed light on an emerging observation to be taken seriously in the study of religions, namely simultaneous or multiple identifications that are rooted in self-identification. While as researchers and in our daily encounters with other people we still tend to be accustomed to defining subjects and their identities in a rigid religious or cultural way, individuals tend to construct personal narratives that are characterised by fluidity. One could imagine that fluidity can be seen as a potential problem, especially when moving from the general level of cultural contexts and societal trends into the personal sphere and the realm of morality. Here, individuals need a margin of precision to organise their agency in the world. While moral philosophical dimensions have not figured prominently among the aims and perspectives included in the YARG project, it is nevertheless relevant to reflect on this question in relation to the data sample generated among young adults world-wide.

Both our methodological approach in YARG and our global scope have been essential to our ambition to find ways to navigate critically a landscape of cross-cultural research on religious and secular worldviews. How this has been made sense of in different chapters has further helped us to articulate some general observations of a more methodological and conceptual nature here in this concluding chapter. We will draw attention to three different but overlapping critical themes regarding how we map the cross-cultural research landscape, how we impose assumptions and finally the direction we need to take when we seek new approaches. Together these themes capture some central observations we have made with regards to developing cross-cultural research in the study of religions.

Mapping the International and the Cross-cultural

There is a growing need in cross-cultural research to set aside premature and biased assumptions of universality – for instance as manifest in simplified notions of religion. Simultaneously we need be aware of the opposite methodological and conceptual trap based on assumptions, for instance of "the totally different Western culture" or the "totally different Asian or African culture" or similar notions attributed to national and cultural geographies. This is well exemplified in Chapter 5, which focuses on the routinised division into "Eastern" and "Western" religions (see Campbell 2007). Such distinctions have often been used as generic labels in the study of religions and the tendency to map a research landscape in terms of these kinds of distinctions also demonstrates how the idea of a wholly different other might just as much be about the need to presuppose a "we" defined by similarity or unity. In fact, Chapter 5 showed little support for any difference between East and West in terms of religious and secular worldviews. By bringing out the diversity of values and worldviews ingrained in the data generated in Asian countries (China and India) – and by carefully mapping similarities and differences in relation to data sets from "Western" countries such as Sweden and the USA – a strong case was in contrast made against a simplified reliance on patterns and structures in the study of contemporary religion.

This requires us to take some steps back and reflect critically on how we design the map of the global, the international and the cross-cultural. Historians are usually well aware of how fluid maps are, how they change over time and how they do not necessarily represent geographical, cultural or political realities. When doing cross-cultural research, we need to become better at critically assessing our maps of the cross-cultural. Nynäs and Långstedt (2024) have made some critical observations with regard to this matter. Internationalisation of research has become more and more important as the need for cross-cultural research has grown. Still, we need to ask when and how a research endeavour becomes international. When and how is it adequate to define something as cross-cultural? There are of course no given answers to these questions, but they are often neglected or not well discussed. One should not overlook the fact that the idea of something being cross-cultural, global or international – or constituted by cultural or linguistic difference – is in itself an interpretative pattern we impose on the situation or the research, and that it has implications for further actions (Nynäs 2006).

There are some implications embedded in this observation. For instance, on what grounds and why do we define a research perspective as international? Chapter 7 on non-religious worldviews addresses a similar problem when referring to the book *The Nonreligious. Understanding Secular People and Societies* (Zuckerman *et al.* 2016). Despite the lack of any indication in the title of the limited perspective adopted, the authors stress that the data summarised in the book pertain to the West, whereby this is made into the norm. The fact that the empirical base is too narrow or skewed is often a risk embedded in research projects and publications claiming a global or international perspective. In contrast, the more purposeful and systematic ambition of the YARG project guaranteed – despite many limitations in this case too – a significant empirical contribution to the study of non-religion and in particular how we might comprehend something like "the global expressions of e.g. secularism". Needless to say, there are also political implications of how as researchers we represent what religious, secular or spiritual worldviews are assumed to entail and how we describe them.

Categories such as "international" and "cross-cultural" seem easy to define as things that reach beyond national or cultural boundaries, but in practice these prove to be somehow problematic categories that require critical reflexivity. Still, we know that this often implies an added value to our research, bringing in knowledge, for example, of religion from a broader variety of contexts and drawing our attention to relevant variations along different axes (Altinordu 2013). This may help in acquiring a validity, nuance or breadth in our results that eschews limited views on a matter. This has been evident in the YARG project, and here lies an additional implication that we would like to draw attention to, namely how we approach the cross-cultural or the global methodologically. It is not enough to be conscious of how we define and approach these; we also need to reflect on how things can surface through the data we collect and how we handle them. In Chapter 4, we could see that the way we investigated the association between heteronormativity and religion – a triangulation of quantitative results, results from a cluster analysis and a multi-variate CHAID analysis – was decisive for the results we were able to account for and how particular contextual differences were allowed to emerge. It was not only the different factors we brought onto the table for consideration in trying to understand the complexity that were important; the methods and analyses we applied also had different epistemological consequences in this respect.

In the case of quantitative analyses this aspect is somehow self-evident and often accounted for by sophisticated measures. Yet, when we turn to Chapter 2, we can see that the road to producing instruments for cross-cultural studies was in itself a valuable method for sensitising cross-cultural differences of linguistic, conceptual and cultural nature. The double and back-translation procedure used in the YARG project brought central incommensurabilities to the surface, and was in itself a salient method for assessing the validity of central concepts such as religion and spirituality, the connotations they have and how they can be used. Furthermore, the malleability of the FQS and the way it entails a great variety of different ways of thinking and talking about these concepts is also decisive in sensitising differences and nuances. With the FQS we do not need to resort to limited and predefined ways of assessing religious or secular worldviews, and it has a capacity to adjust to different cross-cultural contexts. Hence, we could not only identify and confirm the multi-dimensional nature of religious, spiritual and secular worldviews; we could also systematically put our finger on how this varies across cultures in detail and conclude that this variation can be understood through Wittgenstein's (1998) notion of family resemblance (Nynäs, Kontala, Lassander *et al.* 2022).

There is one more aspect of doing international or cross-cultural research that we need to address, namely the challenge of taking other and alternative voices seriously (see Spickard 2017; Nynäs, Kontala, Lassander *et al.* 2022). Also, how research is organised is a significant methodological aspect of knowledge production in cross-cultural research (Nynäs and Långstedt 2024). Breaking dominance and making space for diversity in a research project includes giving researchers from outside one's own circles the opportunity to contribute to and influence the research process. Inevitably, this also challenges the power relations and requires a conscious effort to build new kinds of trusting relationships, within the diverse research team and between researchers and the young adults encountered during the research process. This entails breaking institutional and cultural boundaries as well as hierarchies based on gender, ethnicity and academic influence. This volume, and the YARG project in general, were rooted in the idea that responsible and impactful research is a collective effort. YARG brought together researchers with varying expertise and disciplinary affiliations from thirteen countries around the globe. Thinking and talking together were major aspects of the research process, but also co-authoring articles and reports was encouraged to widen horizons and resulted in conclusions and analyses that no individual researcher could have reached on their own. On a methodological level, this means that the cross-cultural aspect also has to be brought into the analyses of the data. This will be a necessary trajectory for future research.

Dismantling Dichotomies

The YARG project in general, and this volume in particular, rests heavily on ethnographic data. As a conclusion, we want to emphasise the necessity of moving away from perceptions of religious traditions as monolithic entities separated by clear-cut borders. Such a static understanding of religions directs attention to knowledge and creed, treating religions as consistent and mutually exclusive theories of the world built primarily upon words and genealogy (Cotter and Robertson 2016). In response to such narrow approaches, several alternatives have taken shape, seeking to create more nuanced understandings of religion by increasing attentiveness to ethnography. Common to such "religion-as-lived" approaches (e.g. lived religion, vernacular religion, everyday religion), as Helena Kupari and Elina Vuola (2020) jointly describe them, is the aim of capturing religion as a complex, contextual and changing component of life. This means exploring the tangible life of human beings with emotions, bodies, thoughts and mundane worries. It also means relating this intimate perspective to the larger social, historical and institutional structures that set the conditions for and shape the personal religious trajectory, paying attention to power relations and physical milieu (Kupari and Vuola 2020). Often, such investigations are also supported by conceptual analyses of materiality, embodiment and sensory apprehensions of religion (Illman 2019; Whitehead 2013).

The "religion-as-lived" perspective has proved a fruitful analytical approach also for the YARG project. The chapters in this volume all rely on the shared data and the shared methodology developed exploratively in the project, which has also paved the way for constructing a fairly homogeneous language in approach and theoretical framework. Hence, the following formative statement, made in the introduction of this volume, is well endorsed throughout the chapters: "We need to be cautious with regard to essentialist, limited, generic understandings of religion which are based on theistic, doctrinal, institutionally based faith". Throughout the presentations, categories are applied with caution and consideration in order to balance between the scientific need for descriptive and generalisable conceptualisations, on the one hand, and the close attention to detail needed to do justice to the diversity of identifications we have sought to elucidate on the other. Thus, particularism and universalism are forced to cohabit the analytical spaces created in each chapter. As concluded in the volume presenting the main findings of the YARG research project, summing up its methodological and theoretical and analytical implications for the research field as a whole: "A range of aspects and dimensions are central to comprehending the evasive patterns and family resemblances that constitute religious, spiritual and secular worldviews" (Nynäs, Kontala, Lassander *et al.* 2022, 87).

The "evasive patterns" highlighted in this volume centre on the theme of diversity, addressing the dichotomy of universality vs. particularism in the study of religious diversity, spirituality and non-religion from various vantage points. A thread running through the chapters is the insight that universality and particularity need not be regarded as mutually exclusive options when personal worldviews and larger patterns of change in values and outlooks on life are researched. Indeed, as the articles show, new paths in the study of religions can be paved by explicitly dismantling the binary and taking the both-and character of the world around us seriously (see Novis-Deutsch 2018).

As already mentioned, methodological considerations pertaining to this theme were central to Chapter 2. This first offered a methodological reflection on how the challenge of working with multiple languages can be dealt with, when seeking to map and compare worldviews in various cultural and linguistic settings. In this paragraph we would like to underline how Chapter 2 also shifts our focus from the dichotomy of commensurability or incommensurability related to contextual or linguistic differences, to the production of comprehensibility through historical contact and interaction. Communication – such as interviews – risks many misunderstandings in a cross-cultural setting, but it can also involve a mix of terminologies and negotiations that enables understanding across cultural and linguistical boundaries, an observation that relates to the translingual approach we have relied on in this chapter.

Another persistent dichotomy in research on religion was considered critically in Chapter 6, namely the division between sacred and secular. By looking explicitly at how the young adults included in the data talk about the "sacred individual" and what kind of ethical notions, characteristics and attitudes are coupled with this image, the authors show that the narratives seldom adhere to the predefined templates of the discipline. When the categories of sacred, spiritual and secular are not presupposed and introduced into the discussion at the outset, they seem not to figure in a decisive role as interpretative templates. This process of dismantling was followed up in Chapter 7, where the internal diversity of the increasingly popular segment of non-religious identifications was explored. Being a "none" means a lot of different things to the young adults of the study, ranging from sharp rejections of and active resistance to all forms of institutional religion and references to dimensions beyond the here and now to benevolent and curious explorations of personal spiritual trajectories. Not only is the division into religion or no-religion sharp; the no-religion option itself contains a diversity of identifications.

Finally, a similar observation was presented in Chapter 8, dealing with the wealth of ways in which multiple religious identifications are expressed and experienced by young adults worldwide. In order to meaningfully reflect the multiplicity and depth of such identifications, the authors maintained, research into contemporary religion needs to develop conceptual and methodological tools that are sensitive enough to account for deep-reaching complexity. Thus, accounting for a "diversity" of identifications that matches predefined cultural and religious groups is not enough: we need to move forward and explore the intra-diversity of such groups to catch sight of the "multiplicity" that arises on individual and social levels of identification. Yet another step forward is the recognition of "complexity", a term that challenges the (internal as well as external) borders of identity categories as such and critically questions their legitimacy in research that strives to describe lived experiences. All three levels arise as relevant from several of the chapters in this book and will continue to carry importance for future research in the field.

A Moving Methodological Balance

Where has this volume taken us in light of our aim of critically scrutinising de Roover's claim that "the contemporary study of religion has a unique opportunity to settle the debate on the cultural universality of religion" (de Roover 2014, 7)? Thus far a critical reader may well claim that we have mainly emphasised the need to deconstruct our idea of a world defined by tangible differences that we can map and explore, and of a world, organised in a comprehensible way, of categories that we can compare. Can we strike a balance between universal claims that shape all humans, value profiles and worldviews into patterns structured by a singular interpretative model and the particular focus on local detail that risks ending up in a relativistic solipsism that effectively erases all possibilities of drawing meaningful conclusions? Following Paul Hedges, we think that while the dynamics that shape values and identifications are always particular, culturally and individually specific, a purely particular perspective inevitably ends up in a form of relativism where no general conclusions or comparative patterns are possible. This, in its turn, "leads us into misunderstanding rather than providing [...] insights into human cultural diversity" (Hedges 2021, 19).

Nevertheless, we do not see this as a methodological deadlock. Rather, we emphasise the possibility of a pragmatic third option beyond the dichotomous academic positions on universality vs. particularism in terms of what Lambek, from an anthropological perspective, calls a "moving balance among several distinct epistemological positions" (Lambek 2014, 147). By this he refers to a pluralist and more "ostensibly disorderly approach" including "the conjunction of the universal and the particular or the general and the singular" as a matter of "discovering each through the other" (Lambek 2014, 156).

This so-called third option has often been evident in how we have addressed many methodological or epistemological challenges. It taps into the need to reconsider how we conceptualise and map the research landscape, and maybe need to live with several maps. It taps into how we need to distance ourselves from dichotomies and distinctions, maybe "taking the both-and character of the world around us seriously". We have continuously addressed the need to move between and beyond positions, or simultaneously rest in different positions, both positions that are opposed and those that are complementary. Chapter 3 also provides a relevant example in this respect. It outlined how approaches stemming from the cognitive study of religion and lived religion can be placed in dialogue; two perspectives often posited as counterparts at either far end of a mutual research scale, tightly locked into clearly separated compartments of the methodological toolbox that a researcher of religion has at their disposal. It can be relevant here to be reminded of the emic–etic distinction. This is a debated issue that has been amplified over time through such notions as the insider–outsider distinction, often relevant in the study of religions. Yet we need to remember that both emic and etic analyses are in fact positions that we produce or take in our research as part of a projected dichotomy (Mostowlansky and Rota 2016).

In a similar vein to Lambek, Bender *et al.* (2013, 290) emphasise "movement and connections, circulation and change", and we believe that there is in general a need for similar methodological developments. Also, Urry (2010) underlines a similar point from a sociological perspective, stressing the shift to a mobile sociology and what he calls "creative marginality" in the periphery of normative disciplines, concepts and perspectives. He writes that "creative marginality results from complex, overlapping and disjunctive processes [...] which can occur across disciplinary and/or geographical and/or social borders" (Urry 2010, 363). Another way to exemplify this moving methodology on a pragmatic level of methods is found in Chapter 4. Here, triangulation was used to investigate data from different perspectives and in different lights; this can be seen as a systematic approach whereby methodological conjunctions gain added value for knowledge and comprehension. Triangulation can in this form also be decisive for quality when researching complex phenomena such as worldviews and cross-cultural studies, and is, of course, facilitated by the use of mixed-methods approaches. It also showed that each part of the analysis in itself presented a limited view and hence the approach fosters a greater level of critical reflexivity.

How to systematically develop this agenda is important to future research, in light of current cultural and societal transformations and variations. Not all studies need to apply a cross-cultural perspective, but studies focusing on a given context can also aim to broaden their horizons by incorporating and developing new methods and allowing for a multi-method approach that can contribute to significant diversification. This captures our attempt, developed in this volume, to navigate and balance between universalism and particularism in the study of religions and outline a novel methodology for global landscapes. Several chapters in this volume acknowledge the complexity present in a changing world and seek ways of comprehending this, including the inherent divisions, ambiguities and similarities that it incorporates. This goes beyond reiterating the common calls for interdisciplinary research and means seeking unsettling approaches that locate the researcher on the edge of dominant tendencies and perspectives (Bender *et al.* 2013).

As a consequence of the aim of being on "the edge of dominant tendencies and perspectives", the unique methodology developed for the YARG project has led many of the researchers contributing to this volume quite far away from the methods, materials and perspectives they usually work with. As mentioned in the paragraph above on mapping the cross-cultural, this is also a necessity that has become more urgent in international research, and it involves how we develop our networks. Methodological movement requires us to break boundaries in several respects. Evaluating the chapters of this volume as a whole, focusing on the significant and challenging conclusions they present, we think that there is still reason for optimism. While not always straightforward and easy to structure in neat categories adhering to academic convention, we envisage the data as lending themselves to a hermeneutic experience and the starting point of a journey towards deepened understanding of the contexts, contours and implications of the values and worldviews expressed by the young adults we have studied.

A Final Remark

We would like to end this concluding chapter with a note on ethics and responsibility. Naturally, the ethical considerations become particularly striking in view of the circumstance that among the research locations included in the study, there are countries where religions – or state-mandated atheism – have assumed a dominant role, setting the rules of the game in the respective societies in an authoritative way. Such institutions have generally held control not only over what is possible or impossible to do, but also over what has been considered socially, culturally and at times legally acceptable, or rewarded, identities. Hence, the interest in dismantling dichotomies and illuminating the multiple identifications and diversity prevalent on all levels of analysis in our research – the level of overarching institutional religion, the contextual cultural level, and the deeply subjective level of the individual – lies not only in the descriptions that have been presented, but also in what they suggest.

From the YARG project we know well that authoritarian institutions and actors may perceive this as a threat and act upon it. International research needs to account also for the implications the scope has for individuals that are involved, but there are no straightforward models or answers with regards to how to proceed with this. Nevertheless, as researchers in this field we also need to evaluate the different trajectories of our findings, whether we are moving in the direction of a further differentiation and diversity and how we contribute to this. Should scholars of religions and worldviews actively and publicly promote and work for pluralism? How do we view our role in society and culture when we view this from a global perspective?

Peter Nynäs Dr. Theol. is professor of study of religions at Åbo Akademi University (ÅAU), Finland and Dean of the Faculty of Arts, Psychology and Theology. He is director and PI of the Åbo Akademi University Centre of Excellence in Research Young Adults and Religion in a Global Perspective Project (2015–19) and earlier the Centre of Excellence in Research Post-secular Culture and a Changing Religious Landscape in Finland Project (2010–14). Among the books he has edited are *On the Outskirts of "the Church": Diversities, Fluidities, and New Spaces of Religion in Finland* (with R. Illman and T. Martikainen, LIT-Verlag, 2015), *Religion, Gender, and Sexuality in Everyday Life* (with A. Yip, Ashgate, 2012), and *The Diversity of Worldviews among Young Adults: Contemporary (Non)Religiosity and Spirituality through the Lens of an International Mixed Method Study* (with A. Keysar, J. Kontala, B.-W. Kwaku Golo, M. Lassander, M. Shterin, S. Sjö, and P. Stenner, Springer, 2021). See https://research.abo.fi/en/persons/peter-nynäs.

Dr Ruth Illman is the director of the Donner Institute for Research in Religion and Culture in Turku, Finland. She holds the title of docent in the study or religions at Åbo Akademi University (ÅAU) and in the history of religions at Uppsala University, as well as doctoral degrees in the study of religions (2004) and Jewish studies (2018). Her main research interests include cultural encounters and diversity, contemporary Judaism, religion and the arts (especially music) and ethnographic research, primarily by developing the analytical approach of vernacular religion. Illman acted as Co-PI for the Centre of Excellence Young Adults and Religion in a Global Perspective at ÅAU (2015–19). Currently, she leads the research project Boundaries of Jewish Identities in Contemporary Finland and acts as editor-in-chief of the open access peer-review journal *Nordisk judaistik / Scandinavian Jewish Studies* with Svante Lundgren. Recent publications are found at https://research.abo.fi/en/persons/ruth-illman

Rafael Fernández Hart, PhD, is professor and director of the Facultad de Filosofía, Educación y Ciencias Humanas, Universidad Antonio Ruiz de Montoya, Lima, Peru. His research focuses on issues related to the philosophy of religion with a special emphasis on the development of the sacred in contexts of secularisation and the links between philosophy, theology and spirituality. Fernández functioned as local investigator for the YARG project in Peru. Recent publications include "Revelación y religion en Levinas" in *Estudios de Filosofía* (vol. 57, 2018) and "The Internet, Social Media, and the Critical Interrogation of Traditional Religion among Young Adults in Peru" with Sidney Castillo Cardenas and Marcus Moberg, in M. Moberg and S. Sjö (eds), *Digital Media, Young Adults, and Religion: An International Perspective* (Routledge, 2020).

References

Altinordu, Ateş. 2013. "Toward a Comparative-Historical Sociology Religious Politics: The Case for Cross-religious and Cross-regional Comparisons". In *Religion on the Edge: De-centering and Re-centering the Sociology of Religion*, ed. Courtney Bender, Wendy Cadge, Peggy Levitt and David Smilde, 67–91. Oxford: Oxford University Press.

Asad, Talal. 1993. *Genealogies of Religion: Discipline and Reasons of Power in Christianity and Islam*. Baltimore, MD: Johns Hopkins University Press.

Asad, Talal. 2003. *Formations of the Secular: Christianity, Islam, Modernity*. Stanford, CA: Stanford University Press.

Balagangadhara, S. N. 2005. *The Heathen in his Blindness …: Asia, the West, and the Dynamics of Religion* (2nd edn). Delhi: Manohar Publishers.

Bender, Courtney, Wendy Cadge, Peggy Levitt and David Smilde. 2013. "Conclusion: Working the Edges". In *Religion on the Edge: De-centering and Re-centering the Sociology of Religion*, ed. Cortney Bender, Wendy Cadge, Peggy Levitt and David Smilde, 284–91. Oxford: Oxford University Press.

Beyer, Peter. 2019. "Conclusion: Youth, Religion, and Identity in a Globalizing Context: International Case Studies". In *Youth, Religion, and Identity in a Globalizing Context*, ed. Paul L. Gareau, Spencer C. Bullivant, and Peter Beyer, 278–84. Leiden: Brill.

Bowman, Marion, and Ülo Valk, eds. 2012. *Vernacular Religion in Everyday Life: Expressions of Belief*. London: Routledge.

Bruce, Steve, and David Voas. 2007. "Religious Toleration and Organizational Typologies". *Journal of Contemporary Religion* 22(1): 1–17.

Campbell, Colin. 2007. *The Easternization of the West: A Thematic Account of Cultural Change in the Modern Era*. Boulder, CO: Paradigm.

Chakrabarty, Dipesh. 2000. *Provincializing Europe: Postcolonial Thought and Historical Difference*. Princeton, NJ: Princeton University Press.

Cotter, Christopher R., and David G. Robertson. 2016. "Preface". In *After World Religions: Reconstructing Religious Studies*, ed. Christopher R. Cotter and David G. Robertson, vii–viii. London: Routledge.

Day, Abby. 2011. *Believing in Belonging: Belief and Social Identity in the Modern World*. Oxford: Oxford University Press.

de Roover, Jacob. 2014 "Incurably Religious? Consensus Gentium and the Cultural Universality of Religion". *Numen* 61 (1): 5–32.

Droogers, André, and Anton van Harskamp, eds. 2014. *Methods for the Study of Religious Change: From Religious Studies to Worldview Studies*. Sheffield: Equinox.

Gareau, Paul, Spencer Bullivant and P. Beyer. 2019. "Introduction: Youth, Religion and Identity in a Globalizing Context: Canadian, Australian, American, and German Case Studies". In *Youth, Religion, and Identity in a Globalizing Context*, ed. Paul L. Gareau, Spencer C. Bullivant, and Peter Beyer, 33–52. Leiden: Brill.

Gilhus, Ingvild S., and Steven J. Sutcliffe. 2013. "Conclusion: New Age Spiritualities – 'Good to Think' in the Study of Religion". In *New Age Spirituality: Rethinking Religion*, ed. Steven J. Sutcliffe and Ingvild S. Gilhus, 256–62. Durham, NC: Acumen.

Hedges, Paul. 2021. *Religious Hatred. Prejudice, Islamophobia, and Antisemitism in Global Perspective.* London: Bloomsbury.

Illman, Ruth. 2019. "Researching Vernacular Judaism. Reflections on Theory and Method". *Nordisk judaistik / Scandinavian Jewish Studies* 30(1): 91–108. https://doi.org/10.30752/nj.77287

Klingenberg, Maria, and Sofia Sjö. 2019. "Introduction: Theorizing Religious Socialization: A Critical Assessment". *Religion* 49(2): 163–78.

Kupari, Helena, and Elina Vuola (eds). 2020. *Orthodox Christianity and Gender. Dynamics of Tradition, Culture and Lived Practice.* New York: Routledge. https://doi.org/10.4324/9780203701188

Lambek, Michael. 2014. "Recognizing Religion: Disciplinary Traditions, Epistemology, and History". *Numen* 61(2–3): 145–65.

McGuire, Meredith. 2008. *Lived Religion: Faith and Practice in Everyday Life.* Oxford: Oxford University Press.

Masuzawa, Tomoko. 2005. *The Invention of World Religions: Or how European universalism was preserved in the language of pluralism.* Chicago, IL: University of Chicago Press.

Moberg, Marcus, and Sofia Sjö, eds. 2020. *Digital Media, Young Adults and Religion. An International Perspective.* New York: Routledge.

Mostowlansky, Till, and Andrea Rota. 2016. "A Matter of Perspective? Disentangling the Emic–Etic Debate in the Scientific Study of Religion\s". *Method and Theory in the Study of Religion* 28(4/5): 317–36.

Novis-Deutsch, Nurit S. 2018. "The One and the Many: Both/And Reasoning and the Embracement of Pluralism". *Theory and Psychology* 28(4): 429–50. https://doi.org/10.1177/0959354318758935.

Nynäs, Peter. 2006. "Interpretative Models of Estrangement and Identification". In *Bridges of Understanding*, ed. Øivind Dahl, Iben Jensen and Peter Nynäs, 25–39. Oslo: Oslo Academic Press.

Nynäs, Peter, Ruth Illman and Tuomas Martikainen. 2015. "Emerging Trajectories of Religious Change in Finland. In *On the Outskirts of "the Church":*

Diversities, Fluidities, and New Spaces of Religion in Finland, ed. Peter Nynäs, Ruth Illman and Tuomas Martikainen, 217–26. Zürich: LIT Verlag.

Nynäs, Peter, Ariela Keysar, Janne Kontala, Ben-Willie Kwaku Golo, Mika Lassander, Marat Shterin, Sofia Sjö and Paul Stenner, eds. 2022. *The Diversity of Worldviews among Young Adults: Contemporary (Non)Religiosity and Spirituality through the Lens of an International Mixed Method Study*. Cham: Springer.

Nynäs, Peter, Janne Kontala and Mika Lassander. 2021. "The Faith Q-Sort: In-Depth Assessment of Diverse Spirituality and Religiosity in 12 Countries". In *Assessing Spirituality in a Diverse World*, ed. Amy L. Ai, Paul Wink, Raymond F. Paloutzian and Kevin A. Harris, 554–73. Cham: Springer.

Nynäs, Peter, Janne Kontala, Mika Lassander, Nurit Novis-Deutsch, Sofia Sjö and Paul Stenner. 2022. "Family Resemblance in Variations of Contemporary Religiosity and Spirituality: Findings from a Cross-cultural Study". In *The Diversity of Worldviews among Young Adults: Contemporary (Non)Religiosity and Spirituality through the Lens of an International Mixed Method Study*, ed. Peter Nynäs, Ariela Keysar, Janne Kontala, Ben-Willie Kwaku Golo, Mika Lassander, Marat Shterin, Sofia Sjö and Paul Stenner, 73–92. Cham: Springer. https://doi.org/10.1007/978-3-030-94691-3_4

Nynäs, Peter and Johnny Långstedt. 2024. "Observations on the International Character of Research: A Reflective Approach to Management". In *Doing Multidisciplinary Research on Religion - Methodological, Conceptual and Theoretical Challenges*, ed. Anna-Sara Lind and Martha Middlemiss Lé Mon. Leiden: Brill.

Owen, Suzanne. 2011. "The World Religions Paradigm: Time for a Change". *Arts and Humanities in Higher Education* 10(3): 253–68.

Shipley, Heather, and Elisabeth Arweck. 2019. "Young People and the Diversity of (Non)Religious Identities in International Perspective". In *Young People and the Diversity of (Non)Religious Identities in International Perspective*, ed. Elisabeth Arweck and Heather Shipley, 1–12. Cham: Springer.

Spickard, James V. 2017. *Alternative Sociologies of Religion. Through Non-Western Eyes*. New York: New York University Press.

Urry, John. 2010. "Mobile Sociology". *The British Journal of Sociology* 61(1): 347–66.

Whitehead, Amy. 2013. *Religious Statues and Personhood: Testing the Role of Materiality*. London: Bloomsbury.

Winzeler, Robert L. 2008. *Anthropology and Religion: What we know, think, and question*. Lanham, MD: AltaMira Press.

Wittgenstein, Ludwig. 1998. *The Blue and Brown Books. Preliminary Studies for the "Philosophical Investigations"* (2nd edn). Oxford: Blackwell.

Woodhead, Linda. 2012. "Introduction". In *Religion and Change in Modern Britain*, ed. Linda Woodhead and Rebecca Catto, 1–33. London: Routledge.

Wulff, David. 2019. "Prototypes of Faith: Findings with the Faith Q-Sort". *Journal for the Scientific Study of Religion* 58(3): 643–65.

Zuckerman, Phil, Luke W. Galen and Frank L. Pasquale. 2016. *The Nonreligious. Understanding Secular People and Societies*. New York: Oxford University Press.

Index

age 151, 169–170, 200
agnostic 169, 176–177
Allport, Gordon 6
Asad, Talal 65, 67
atheism 169, 190, 236

belief 59–61
    religious *see* religious belief
    theistic 170
    traditional 68
Bengal, Bengali 26, 33–43
    Hindu 127, 130, 134
Beyer, Peter 10, 226
Boyer, Pascal 57–59, 62–65, 73
Broo, Måns 34–35, 41–44, 80, 120, 127, 131, 134–135
Buddhism 133–136, 214–215
Burén, Ann af 171, 204–205, 216

Campbell, Colin 113–114, 117–119, 228
Canada, Canadian 169, 181, 186–187
China, Chinese 115–125, 186–188
Christianity 15, 69
    Lutheran 142, 162
    Orthodox 152, 210
    Protestant 117–118 *see also* Protestantism
    values 146
cognition 60, 64
    religious 56–57, 72
cognitive science of religion 55–58, 61, 63–64
    vs. lived religion 55–61
collective representation 143
common humanity 212–213
conservative 82
cross-cultural research 226–230
cultural transmission 58, 66

Day, Abby 2, 168, 202
de Roover, Jakob 2, 234
death 127, 177, 186
    fear of 68, 179
    life after 168, 211
Dillon, Michele 90, 97
diversity 197, 216–217
    linguistic...index 115
Druze 174, 183, 189
Durkheim, Émile 143–147, 149

education 169–170
    liberal 146
Eliade, Mircea 65, 144
ethnicity 10, 26, 231
Evangelical Lutheran Church of Finland (ELCF) 142, 152
evolutionary psychology 65

Faith Q-Sort (FQS) 26, 200
    FQS prototypes 119, 126
Finland, Finnish 141, 151–152, 157
freedom of choice 121–122

gender 81–84, 105–106
    difference 91, 182, 186
    gap 90, 186
generation
    older 198
    younger 10, 147, 152
Ghana, Ghanaian 67–68, 70–71

Hedges, Paul 199, 206–207, 234
heteronormativity 82–87, 102, 104–106
Hindu 36–41, 46, 127
    Bengali 130, 134
    tradition 116

Hinduism 115–117
Holm, Nils G. 203, 217
homophobia 80–81
homosexuality 100, 102–104
humanism 173

identity/identifications 82, 201–202
   fluidity 197, 227
   gender 80
   multiple religious 198–199, 209–210
   non-religious 187, 190
   processes 204–205, 214
   religious 43, 200
   self- 208, 217
ideology 65
Illman, Ruth 198–199, 231
India, Indian 35, 116–119, 126–134
individualism 145–146
Inglehart, Ronald 10, 142
intersectionality 202, 206
interviews 5
   analysis 148, 151
   interpretation of 41, 161
Islam 42, 80, 131 *see also* Muslim
Israel, Israeli 87, 97, 180
   Arab 181, 188
   Druze 174, 189
   Jews 181, 186 *see also* Jews
   Muslim 186, 189–190

Japan, Japanese 68, 168–169, 197
Jesus 70, 158, 160
Jews 180, 215
   Orthodox 207
Judaism 217
   Jubu 214–215

Ken-Q Analysis 8
Keysar, Ariela 167–168, 198, 217, 226
Klingenberg, Maria 3, 198, 200, 226
Kontala, Janne 7, 9, 170–171, 200, 226–227, 232
Kwaku Golo, Ben-Willie 128

Lambek, Michael 3, 26, 227, 234–235
languages 11, 27, 30
   incommensurability of 28
   Indian 37, 115 *see also* India
Lassander, Mika 4, 7, 80, 200, 227, 230, 232
LGBTQI 80–81, 87, 99
lived religion 55, 58, 67, 231
   everyday religion 59, 71

majority/minority 18, 41, 47
media 10, 226
memory 62
method/methodology
   comparative 141
   interpretative 64, 234
   linguistic 26–28, 230
   mixed-methods 3–5, 199
   Q-Methodology 6, 33, 200
   triangulation 84, 87, 104–106
Moberg, Marcus 3, 200, 226
moral individualism 145–146
multi-religious 68
   belonging 216
Muslim
   LGBTQ 80–81
   minority 40, 68, 117
   tradition 122
   in India 35, 126
   Israeli *see* Israel

nationalism 15, 117
non-belief 171
non-religion 16, 167–170, 190–191
   behaviour 171, 180
   identity 187–188, 190
   nones 18, 167, 191
   prototype 180–181
Novis-Deutsch, Nurit 201–202, 207–208, 217–218, 232
Nynäs, Peter 3–4, 59, 80–81, 120, 187, 198–199

open-minded 105, 121
Orthodox *see* Orthodox Christianity; Orthodox Jews
Otto, Rudolf 64, 144

particularism 1–3, 234–235
Peru, Peruvian 67–68, 186
pluralism 67, 191, 197–199, 216–217
Poland, Polish 87, 95–97, 186
Protestantism 32, 68 *see also* Protestant Christianity

Q-methodology *see* method/methodology

religion 25–26
    definition of 28, 63
    Eastern 113–115, 117–119
    and evolution 55–58, 77
    linguistic perspective on 27
    lived *see* lived religion
religious
    affiliation 90, 113
    authority 81, 83, 102–103, 173
    behaviour 63
    belief 59–60, 66, 103–104,
    cognition *see* cognition
    communication 71
    conventionally 151–152, 161
    experience 71–72
    meaning-making 31
    membership 152, 173, 191
    metaphor 61
    pluralism 198
    practice 43–45, 68, 184
    prototypes 14
    representation 57, 61–62
    vs. secular 13, 204
    secular dichotomy 207
    social categories 202–203
    symbol 61, 66
    upbringing 183, 187
    worldviews 69, 72
ritual 46, 63, 65, 143
Russia, Russian 17, 141–142, 148–156

sacred
    individual 141–142, 146, 148–151
    vs. profane 143–144
    and secular 142, 144, 146, 233
    theory of 142–143
Sapir-Whorf hypothesis 28–30
Schwartz, Shalom 4, 93–94, 105
secular
    countries/nation/state 81, 117, 186
    humanist 12, 127, 173, 189–190
    identity 167, 214–215, 226
    worldviews 67, 197, 225–226
seeker/seekership 14, 152, 201
self
    -determination 145, 154
    -identification 170–171, 189–190, 227
    -realisation 125, 153–154
sexuality 79–80, 82–84, 103–104, 128
Shterin, Marat 217
Sjö, Sofia 3, 120, 198, 200, 217, 226
spirituality 14–15, 42–47, 121, 175
Sztajer, Sławomir 56
Stenner, Paul 6–9
Study of Religions 2, 25–26, 203–205
subaltern 115, 135
subjectivities 198–199
    religious 3, 15, 208
    sexual 106
supernatural being 39, 60–61, 69
superstition 32, 126
survey 4, 10
    bias 5, 33
    data 170, 200
    result 13, 67, 147, 180, 201
Sweden, Swedish 118–119, 169, 173–174

translation
    double and back process of 11, 33–34, 230
    issues of 36, 41
    practice of ... within YARG 26, 30, 33
    process 16, 34, 46–47

translingual practice 30
transmission of culture *see* cultural transmission
Turkey 87, 95–97

universalism 1–3, 232, 234–235
   versus tradition 13
university students 10, 125–128
USA 90, 118–119, 147

values
   liberal 13–14, 133
   traditional 94–97, 105
   universal 146

Weber, Max 113–114
well-being 4, 17, 154

Wittgenstein, Ludwig 15, 230
Woodhead, Linda 14, 203
World Values Survey (WVS) 10, 142, 168
worldview
   global 12, 87
   prototype 13, 35, 170–171, 190
   religious *see* religious worldviews
   secular *see* secular worldviews
   studies 6, 235
Wulff, David 4–7, 26, 170, 200, 227

young adults 67, 99, 141, 171
   contemporary 169, 198
   identification 197, 201, 205
   non-religious 167
   worldviews of 225

www.ingramcontent.com/pod-product-compliance
Lightning Source LLC
Chambersburg PA
CBHW062009220426
43662CB00010B/1281